*Philosophy and Argumentation
in Third-Century China*

Princeton Library of Asian Translations

Advisory Committee: *Cyril Birch, Eugene Eoyang, F. W. Mote, A. W. Plaks*

*Philosophy and Argumentation
in Third-Century China*

::

The Essays of Hsi K'ang

Translated, with
Introduction and Annotation, by
ROBERT G. HENRICKS

Princeton University Press
Princeton, New Jersey

Copyright © 1983 by Princeton University Press

Published by Princeton University Press, 41 William Street,
Princeton, New Jersey
In the United Kingdom: Princeton University Press,
Guildford, Surrey

All Rights Reserved
Library of Congress Cataloging in Publication Data will
be found on the last printed page of this book

This book has been composed in Monophoto Plantin Light by
Asco Trade Typesetting Ltd., Hong Kong

Clothbound editions of Princeton University Press books
are printed on acid-free paper, and binding materials
are chosen for strength and durability

Printed in the United States of America by
Princeton University Press, Princeton, New Jersey

In memory of my father
GUY RICHARD HENRICKS

Preface

∷

I was introduced to the essays of Hsi K'ang about ten years ago when David Knechtges had us read Hsi K'ang's "Essay on Nourishing Life" in a seminar on Six Dynasties literature. I went on to do my seminar paper on the "nourishing life" debate, and later wrote my doctoral dissertation on the life and thought of Hsi K'ang ("Hsi K'ang: His Life, Literature and Thought," Wisconsin, 1976).

Throughout all of my work on Hsi K'ang, his essays have been for me the attraction. They are extremely well written and well thought out; clear, eloquent, to the point; humorous at times, at other times philosophically subtle and psychologically perceptive. Moreover, since these essays are an important source for our knowledge of third-century Chinese thought, their translation will be of interest to the Sinologist. But they will appeal to the general reader as well. For though they were written many hundreds of years ago in a quite different culture, they deal with issues that still concern us as twentieth-century Westerners—immortality, the nature of morality, the relation of music to emotion—and they deal with them in ways we can all understand. I here translate all nine of Hsi K'ang's essays, plus the four essays of his opponents in various debates.

An earlier translation by the present author of two of these essays—Juan K'an's "Residence Is Devoid of Good and Bad Fortune: You Must Rather Preserve Your Life" and Hsi K'ang's "A Refutation of Juan K'an's Essay"—was published in the *Journal of Chinese Philosophy*, 8 (1981), pp. 169–221.

I wish to thank my two teachers, David Knechtges and Chow Tse-tsung, for helping me in my graduate student days to understand many things in the text. I am also indebted to my colleague at Dartmouth, Li Hua-yüan Mowry, for helping me with several difficult passages. I am grateful to Dartmouth College for grant-

Preface

ing me sabbatical leave in the winter of 1981 and a Faculty Fellowship in the spring to work on bringing this project to completion. Thanks also go to Betsy Alexander for a splendid job in typing the manuscript. And for listening patiently to anxious thoughts, and putting up with my being present but not really there, I thank my wife Patricia.

July 23, 1981   ROBERT G. HENRICKS
Norwich, Vermont

Contents

::

	Preface	vii
	Introduction	3
	Translator's Note	17
HSI K'ANG	An Essay on Nourishing Life	21
HSIANG HSIU	A Refutation of Hsi K'ang's Essay on Nourishing Life	31
HSI K'ANG	An Answer to Hsiang Hsiu's Refutation of My Essay on Nourishing Life	38
HSI K'ANG	Music Has in It Neither Grief nor Joy	71
HSI K'ANG	Dispelling Self-interest	107
HSI K'ANG	An Essay on Kuan and Ts'ai	120
HSI K'ANG	An Essay on Wisdom and Courage	126
CHANG MIAO	People Naturally Delight in Learning	135
HSI K'ANG	A Refutation of Chang Miao's Essay—People Naturally Delight in Learning	139
JUAN K'AN	Residence is Devoid of Good and Bad Fortune: You Must Rather Preserve Your Life	144
HSI K'ANG	A Refutation of Juan K'an's Essay—Residence is Devoid of Good and Bad Fortune: You Must Rather Preserve Your Life	155
JUAN K'AN	An Explanation to Hsi K'ang's Refutation of My Essay—Residence is Devoid of Good and Bad Fortune: You Must Rather Preserve Your Life	169

Contents

HSI K'ANG   An Answer to Juan K'an's Explanation to My Refutation of His Essay—Residence is Devoid of Good and Bad Fortune: You Must Rather Preserve Your Life   180

Selected Bibliography   201

Index   203

*Philosophy and Argumentation
in Third-Century China*

Introduction

::

The Setting. Hsi K'ang 嵇康 (style, Shu-yeh 叔夜) lived at a very difficult time in Chinese history. China was divided into the Three Kingdoms, with the Wei (220–265) ruling most of the north, the Wu (222–280) in the southeast, and the Shu (221–264) in the southwest. And China was to remain divided in one way or another for another three hundred years, until the Sui reunification in 589. These were years of nearly constant warfare without and factionalism and intrigue within. It mattered very much who one's friends were and what were one's family ties. Whether to serve as an official was a very serious question. And many young men, who because of their position in society would have been expected to fill a government role, chose instead to live retired from the beginning, or resigned their duties at some point while they still had their lives.

The philosophy of this period is given two labels by historians of Chinese thought—*ch'ing-t'an* 清談 ("pure talk" or "pure conversation") and *hsüan-hsüeh* 玄學 ("profound studies"). *Ch'ing-t'an* has several connotations. The root meaning is "a discussion by the pure," "the pure" being men who kept themselves undefiled by staying out of political affairs. But through extension and association, *ch'ing-t'an* comes to refer not only to these meetings themselves, but to all that went on there as well. Thus, since the philosophy of Lao-tzu and Chuang-tzu was often discussed at these meetings, *ch'ing-t'an* means for some the revived interest in the thought of Lao and Chuang that characterized the Wei. Others use *ch'ing-t'an* in reference to the playful banter between guests at these parties, and the exchange of witty remarks which delighted the men of these times.[1] Finally, since

---

[1] Such an exchange is recorded for Hsi K'ang and Chung Hui 鍾會. When Chung Hui once paid a visit to Hsi K'ang, Hsi K'ang refused to show him the proper welcoming respects and continued to work at his forge. Chung Hui,

Introduction

formal debate, with presentation of a thesis, refutation, and rebuttal, was often a feature of these gatherings, *ch'ing-t'an* also connotes this interest in rhetoric and argumentation.[2] In traditional Chinese historiography, *ch'ing-t'an* is a pejorative expression, for people who delighted in *ch'ing-t'an* had turned their backs on their responsibility to society.

By "profound studies" the Chinese intend matters that we would call metaphysical and spiritual. And "profound studies" primarily refers to the cosmological speculations of Wang Pi 王弼 (226–249) and others on the relation of *wu* 無 (usually "non-being") to *yu* 有 ("being"), and the dialogues between Taoists and Buddhists in the ensuing years discussing the natures of *wu* and *k'ung* 空 ("emptiness," *śunyata*). But the topics debated by Hsi K'ang and his friends were also quite "profound"—e.g. the existence of immortals, the relation of residence to good and bad fortune, and the relation of wisdom to courage.[3]

Two other things are characteristic of the thought of this period. There was at this time a good deal of mixing of Confucian and Taoist thought. Many considered that Confucius and Lao-

---

rightly offended, went to leave, at which point Hsi K'ang asked, "What did you hear that made you come, and what have you seen that makes you leave?" To which Chung Hui replied, "It's because of what I heard that I came and because of what I've seen that I'm leaving." The anecdote is recorded in *Shih-shuo hsin-yü* 世說新語 24:3. For the Chinese text see Yang Yung 楊勇, *Shih-shuo hsin-yü chiao-chien* 校箋 (Hong Kong: Ta-chung 大眾, 1969), p. 578. For an English translation see Richard Mather, tr., *Shih-shuo Hsin-yü: A New Account of Tales of the World* (Minneapolis: University of Minnesota Press, 1976), p. 393.

[2] Arthur Wright, in his review of A. A. Petrov's *Wang Pi (226–249): His Place in the History of Chinese Philosophy* (*Harvard Journal of Asiatic Studies*, 10[1957], p. 80) says of *ch'ing-t'an*: "*Ch'ing-t'an* at its best was a form of philosophical dialogue in which two or more participants clarified their ideas and quickened their perceptions in vigorous and spirited interchange of argument and rebuttal."

[3] Not all intellectual historians would include Hsi K'ang in the *hsüan-hsüeh* movement. T'ang Yung-t'ung 湯用彤, for example, defines *hsüan-hsüeh* in such a way—as a move to the *wu-yu* cosmology and abandonment of interest in Yin-Yang and the Five Elements—as to exclude thinkers like Hsi K'ang. See his *Wei Chin hsüan-hsüeh lun-kao* 魏晉玄學論稿 (Peking: Jen-min 人民, 1957), p. 49.

Introduction

tzu had known the same truth but had expressed it in different ways or had expressed different aspects of it (e.g., the inner and outer). They were well aware that Confucius had not said anything about the very things that interested them the most—the spiritual and metaphysical—but this could be understood in a way that maintained his position as the great sage. Thus, Wang Pi claimed that Confucius was actually superior to Lao-tzu because he *embodied* non-being instead of talking about it. In *Shih-shuo hsin-yü* 4:8 we read:[4]

When Wang Pi was barely twenty he went to visit P'ei Hui. Hui asked him, "Non-actuality" [or non-being—present author's note] (*wu*) is indeed that by which all things are sustained, yet the Sage (Confucius) was unwilling to vouchsafe any words on the subject. Lao-tzu, on the other hand, expatiated on it endlessly. Why?"

Wang Pi replied, "The Sage *embodied* Non-actuality. Furthermore, Non-actuality may not be the subject of instruction. Therefore of necessity his words applied to Actuality [= being] (*yu*). Lao-tzu and Chuang-tzu, not yet free of Actuality, were continually giving instruction about that in which they felt a deficiency."

Hsi K'ang has nothing nice to say about Confucius—even though the *Analects* is one of the works he cites or alludes to the most in his essays. But he does have the same attitude as Wang Pi: that the ancients, including Confucius, knew about spiritual things, but they had their reasons for keeping silent. At the opening of his refutation of Juan K'an's 阮侃 essay "Residence is Devoid of Good and Bad Fortune: You Must Rather Preserve Your Life" he says:

The spirits of Heaven and Earth are far away and distant, and good and bad fortune are difficult to understand. Even though men of mediocre abilities might exhaust their resources, none would understand the principles involved, and it is easy by this to become confused about the Way. Therefore the Master [Confucius] stopped answering when questioned about the end [i.e., death]: he was cautious about spirits and

---

[4] See Yang Yung, *Shih-shuo hsin-yü chiao-chien*, p. 152. Translation here is by Mather, *A New Account of Tales of the World*, p. 96.

Introduction

prodigies and about them did not speak. And this is why the ancients displayed their benevolence to others but kept how it works to themselves. They knew these things could not be shared with the masses. It is not that they intentionally concealed them; these are things they would not understand.

Finally, many men of these times are known for their wild, unrestrained, unseemly behavior, what the Chinese call *fan li-fa* 反禮法, "anti-ritual and law." Juan Chi 阮籍 (210–263) is probably the most famous for this, having the audacity to eat meat and drink wine while in mourning for his mother.[5] The opinion was commonly expressed that one could not be "natural" and follow the rituals, and naturalness was preferred.[6] Current scholarship tends to see this behavior as more symbolic than real—that is to say, since those in authority were the upholders of ritual and law and traditional moral values (benevolence and righteousness), anti-ritual behavior and words were a way of showing disdain for the powers that be.[7] But while there is evidence to support this conclusion,[8] we must not overlook the likelihood that some of this, at least, was genuine Taoist distaste for conformity and restraint.

The Life of Hsi K'ang. Hsi K'ang was born in 223.[9] He was from Chih county 銍縣 in the principality of Ch'iao 譙國 (in

---

[5] See anecdotes 23:2, 23:9, and 23:11, for example, in *Shih-shuo hsin-yü*. For Mather's translation of these see pp. 372, 374, and 375 in *A New Account of Tales of the World*.

[6] See Richard Mather's excellent article, "The Controversy over Conformity and Naturalness During the Six Dynasties," *History of Religions*, 9:2&3 (November, 1969/February, 1970), pp. 160–180.

[7] See, for example, Lu Hsün's 魯迅 article, "Wei Chin feng-tu chi wen-chang yü yao chi chiu chih kuan-hsi" 魏晉風度及文章與藥及酒之關係, in *Erh-i chi* 而已集, Vol. 17 in *Lu Hsun san-shih nien chi* 三十年集 (Hong Kong: Hsin-i 新藝, 1965).

[8] For example, it is reported in Juan Chi's biography (*Chin shu* 晉書 49: Vol. 5, p. 1360 in the Peking—Chung-hua shu-chü 中華書局 edition [1974]) that he once stayed drunk for sixty days just to avoid a marriage alliance with the Ssu-ma's.

[9] For a detailed life of Hsi K'ang see Donald Holzman, *La Vie et la Pensée de Hi K'ang* (Leiden: E. J. Brill, 1957), pp. 12–51. For even greater detail, see my dissertation, "Hsi K'ang: His Life, Literature, and Thought," pp. 38–217.

Introduction

present-day Anhui), which was located in the southeast corner of the Wei kingdom. His family was neither rich nor poor. His father had been a minor official under the founder of the Wei, Ts'ao Ts'ao 曹操. But his father had died when he was young, a fact which Hsi K'ang claimed was very influential in making him who he was. For he was raised by his mother and an older brother, and they apparently spoiled him and let him do whatever he wished. So he grew up loving freedom and independence and delighting in Lao and Chuang.

In a letter written late in life, breaking off relations with his friend Shan T'ao 山濤 (205–283) for recommending him to office, Hsi K'ang stated:[10]

... I lost my father when young, [and] was spoiled by my mother and elder brother and never took up the study of the classics. I was already wayward and lazy by nature, so that my muscles became weak and my flesh flabby. I would commonly go half a month without washing my face, and until the itching became a considerable annoyance, I would not wash my hair. When I had to urinate, if I could stand it I would wait until my bladder cramped inside before I got up.

Further, I was long left to my own devices, and my disposition became arrogant and careless, my bluntness diametrically opposed to etiquette, laziness and rudeness reinforcing one another....

Besides, my taste for independence was aggravated by my reading of Chuang Tzu and Lao Tzu; as a result any desire for fame or success grew daily weaker, and my commitment to freedom increasingly firmer.

Sometime in the 240's Hsi K'ang married a royal princess, a woman with the title Ch'ang-lo t'ing-chu 長樂亭主, who was either the granddaughter or the great-granddaughter of Ts'ao Ts'ao.[11] In normal times this would have paved his way to success. But in 249 Ssu-ma I 司馬懿 (178–251), the powerful

---

[10] Translated by J. R. Hightower in Cyril Birch, ed., *Anthology of Chinese Literature* (New York: Grove Press, 1965), p. 163.

[11] Our sources do not agree. Wang Yin's 王隱 *Chin shu*, cited by Li Shan 李善 in his commentary to Hsiang Hsiu's "Rhapsody on Thinking of Old Times" (*Wen hsüan* 文選 16.19a—SPPY ed.) says it was Ts'ao Ts'ao's granddaughter: but the *Hsi-shih p'u* 嵇氏譜, cited by P'ei Sung-chih 裴松之 in his commentary to *San-kuo chih* 三國志 20 (p. 583 in the Chung-hua shu-chü edition [Peking, 1959] says she was the granddaughter of Ts'ao Lin 林, one of Ts'ao Ts'ao's sons.

Introduction

general who had helped Ts'ao Ts'ao to found the Wei, seized control of the government, putting to death in the process ten members of the Ts'ao family faction. Though members of the Ts'ao clan continued to occupy the throne for another fifteen years, real power now belonged to the Ssu-ma's. Hsi K'ang resigned the minor commissions he held and lived in retirement the rest of his life.

Throughout the 250's there were repeated attempts by Ts'ao family supporters to recapture their lost power; all of these failed and were mercilessly put down. So far as we know Hsi K'ang was not involved in any of these revolts, save one, In 255 Kuan-ch'iu Chien 毋丘儉 and Wen Ch'in 文欽 rebelled in Shou-ch'un (in present-day Anhui), and Hsi K'ang considered raising troops to support them, but he was talked out of it by Shan T'ao.[12] Kuan-ch'iu Chien was killed and Wen Ch'in fled to Wu.

It was also in the 250's that Hsi K'ang met with a very famous group of men. He was one of the leaders of the "Seven Worthies of the Bamboo Grove" (*chu-lin ch'i-hsien* 竹林七賢), a group which met from time to time at his estate in Shan-yang 山陽 (in present-day Honan) to drink a little wine, play the lute, and discuss philosophical issues of common interest. In the group were Hsi K'ang, Juan Chi, Shan T'ao, Hsiang Hsiu 向秀, Wang Jung 王戎, Juan Hsien 阮咸, and Liu Ling 劉伶.

In 261 an event occurred that was to lead to Hsi K'ang's death. He was good friends with a man named Lü An 呂安. In 261, Lü An's older brother, Lü Sun 巽, seduced Lü An's wife. Needless to say, Lü An was not terribly pleased, and he went to Hsi K'ang for counsel. Hsi K'ang urged him to let the matter be, and, like a good younger brother, to smooth over relations. Lü Sun, in the meantime, fearing that news of the whole sordid affair would leak out, turned the tables on his brother and turned him in on the charge of "unfilial conduct"; he said that he had beaten their mother.

---

[12] Reported in the *Shih-yü* 世語, cited by P'ei Sung-chih in his commentary to Hsi K'ang's *San-kuo chih* biography; *San-kuo chih* 21, p. 607.

Introduction

Lü An was arrested, brought to trial, and sent into exile. On his way into exile he sent a letter back to Hsi K'ang, a letter which sounds seditious, and a letter which the Ssu-ma's intercepted.[13] Lü An and Hsi K'ang were both thrown into prison. And, to their great misfortune, the man in charge of criminal proceedings at the capital at this time, Chung Hui, was someone whom Hsi K'ang had earlier offended.[14] Thus, he slandered them at court, claiming them to be a noxious influence on society. In 262 they were both put to death.

It is tragic that such a talented man had to die so young (at the age of forty in Chinese count, thirty-nine in the West). But we must remember his ties to the Ts'ao clan, and his considered support for Kuan-ch'iu Chien's rebellion (which Chung Hui brought up in his accusation). Also relevant, I feel, is the fact that he simply could not keep from talking. He was, as he admitted in his letter to Shan T'ao, arrogant, self-righteous, and indignant, and he considered it a principle (as the reader will see in his "Dispelling Self-interest") to be open and frank about one's views. Naturally, he despised the Ssu-ma's.

Hsi K'ang was an important poet;[15] he was also a talented musician, one of China's masters on the lute.[16] He was also a very fine debater, one of the best of the age, if not one of the best in Chinese history. Of the thirteen essays that survive in his col-

---

[13] The letter is found in *Wen hsüan* 43 (pp. 9a–10b in SPPY), but it is presented as a letter written by Chao Chih 趙至 (style, Ching-chen 景真)—an acquaintance of Hsi K'ang's—to Hsi K'ang's nephew Hsi Fan 蕃 (style, Mao-ch'i 茂齊). However, Tai Ming-yang 戴明揚, in an article on the authorship of this letter included in his *Hsi K'ang chi chiao-chu* 稽康集校注 (Peking: Jen-min, 1962), pp. 435–445, argues convincingly for Lü An as the author. And the text does begin, "An says..."

[14] See note 1, above.

[15] Sixty poems (*shou*) survive. For two excellent studies, see Peter Rushton, "An Interpretation of Hsi K'ang's Eighteen Poems Presented to Hsi Hsi on His Entry Into the Army," *Journal of the American Oriental Society*, 99:2 (April–June, 1979), pp. 175–190, and Donald Holzman, "La poésie de Ji Kang," *Journal Asiatique*, part I, in CCLXVIII: 1&2 (1980), pp. 107–177; part II, in CCLXVIII: 3&4 (1980), pp. 323–378.

[16] His "Rhapsody on the Lute" (Ch'in fu 琴賦) is translated by Robert van Gulik, *Hsi K'ang and His Poetical Essay on the Lute* (Tokyo and Rutland, Vt.: Charles E. Tuttle, 1968).

Introduction

lected works—the essays here translated—all but one ("Dispelling Self-interest") were written in the context of debate.[17]

The Thought of Hsi K'ang. As a thinker Hsi K'ang is best known for his views on nourishing life. And his views on nourishing life are best understood in relation to those of Chuang-tzu,[18] on the one hand, and to those of popular Taoism, on the other.[19] We can see this very well if we distinguish between goal and means. In contrast to what we find in popular Taoism, where full immortality—to become a *hsien* 仙, an immortal—is the goal, Hsi K'ang argued that immortals are born, not made; those who possess the possibility of immortality differ from others by nature. Nourishing life for most can only lead to long life. But in contrast to Chuang-tzu, for whom long life seems to be the normal long life of seventy to a hundred years, Hsi K'ang meant by long life several hundred to a thousand years. All of this he makes clear at the beginning of his "Essay on Nourishing Life":

In this world there are those who say that immortality can be attained by study, and "no-death" brought about by effort. Others say that the extreme of old age is one hundred and twenty, and that in this past and

---

[17] For more on Hsi K'ang the debater and an analysis of his principles and techniques of argumentation, see my article "Hsi K'ang and Argumentation in the Wei," *Journal of Chinese Philosophy*, 8:2 (June, 1981), pp. 169-221.

[18] Who is the first to use the term "nourishing life" (*yang-sheng* 養生): "Yang-sheng chu" 主, "The Essentials of Nourishing Life" being the title of Chapter 3 of the *Chuang-tzu*.

[19] For a synthetic and systematic analysis of the thought of Hsi K'ang based on an overview of all of his essays, see Hou Wai-lu 侯外廬 et al., *Chung-kuo ssu-hsiang t'ung-shih* 中國思想通史 (Peking: Jen-min, 1957), Vol. 2, pp. 164-196. He discusses Hsi K'ang's "world-view," "epistemology," "view of government," "theory of culture," and "theory of human existence." Hsiao Teng-fu 蕭登福 (*Hsi K'ang yen-chiu* 嵇康研究 [Taipei: Kuo-li cheng-chih ta-hsüeh 國立政治大學, 1976], pp. 102-111) does much the same, noting his "theory of government," his "view of human existence," and his "theory of culture." Donald Holzman's excellent analysis of the thought of Hsi K'ang (*La vie et la pensée de Hi K'ang*, pp. 52-79), on the other hand, summarizes the main theses of each of the essays and attempts to account for the origins of Hsi K'ang's thought.

Introduction

present are the same—[claims] of going beyond this are all wild and absurd.

Both of these miss the mark. Let me attempt to roughly discuss it. Although immortals are not seen with the eyes, nonetheless, they are cited in books and records and [their lives] are narrated in the former histories. When we compare these and discuss it, their existence becomes certain. But it seems that they uniquely receive a special breath. They are endowed with it by nature; it is not something that can be brought about by accumulation of study. Turning to "guiding and nourishing" and getting the principle to exhaust the limits of one's nature and fate, at the utmost reaching more than a thousand years, or in the least living several hundred—this is possible. But people of the world are all unrefined; thus none is able to attain it.

Hsi K'ang saw nothing unnatural about living so long. To the contrary, to die before this was unnatural. Moreover, like Chuang-tzu, this was for him a matter of living out one's heaven-given years.[20] One might have a fated upper limit to his life, but the only way to realize that limit was to take care of one's life properly.

On the means to nourishing life, Chuang-tzu emphasizes what might be called things of the mind and spirit. He speaks of making oneself useless in the eyes of the world (since the useful get used); of avoiding a reputation for being either too good or too bad (in moral terms); and of following the natural pattern of things.[21] In popular Taoism, on the other hand, physical techniques are recommended: breathing exercises to guide pure breath through the body, making it as light as the air; dietary regulations—avoiding meat, wine, and grains which clog up and decay the body, and living instead on dew and air and certain

---

[20] For the "heaven-given years" in *Chuang-tzu* see, for example, the stories at the end of Chapter 4, concerning the large tree on the Hill of Shang, and Crippled Shu. These are translated by Burton Watson, *The Complete Works of Chuang Tzu* (New York: Columbia University Press, 1968), pp. 65–66.

[21] See Chapter 3 of the *Chuang-tzu* (Watson, *The Complete Works of Chuang Tzu*, pp. 50–53), and also the stories on the "usefulness of the useless"—the two cited above in note 20 and the two at the end of Chapter 1 (Watson, *The Complete Works*, pp. 34–35).

Introduction

drugs of long life; and alchemical pursuits in which the elixir of immortality was produced by refining cinnabar.[22]

Hsi K'ang combines the two approaches, arguing that body and soul must both be nourished, both inner and outer cared for. In his "Essay on Nourishing Life" and later in his "Answer" to Hsiang Hsiu's "Refutation" of the same, he emphasizes three things as the means to nourishing life: (1) dispassion, (2) avoidance of wealth and rank, and (3) the dietary techniques.

Hsi K'ang counselled dispassion on two accounts. To begin with, he recognized that the feelings are unreliable; they change. What we love at one time we hate at another. Thus we can never be sure that what seems important at any given time is in reality worthy of our concern.

But the real reason that feelings are to be avoided is that they are simply physically damaging. Strong emotions—love, hate, anger, fear, lust—through the energy that they consume physically waste away the body (a point with which modern medicine would presumably agree). To use Hsi K'ang's words, "When the spirit is disturbed on the inside, the form wastes away on the out, just as when the ruler is confused above, the state is chaotic below." And prolonged emotion is not the problem; every single instance of strong feeling in the end takes its toll. But people fail to see this:

And yet [people] of the world constantly say that a single fit of anger is not enough to attack your nature, and a single instance of grief is not enough to harm your health. They treat these lightly and let them go. ... [But] the Gentleman knows that the form relies on the spirit to stand and the spirit needs the form to exist: [he] understands that the principle of life is easily lost and that a single mistake can injure life. Therefore he cultivates his nature to protect his spirit and calms his mind to keep his body intact.

---

[22] For readers unfamiliar with popular Taoism, it should be noted that immortality there is purely physical. It is thought of primarily in terms of transubstantiation, in which one transforms a body of gross physical substance into one of materials that are light, refined, and subtle, and thus capable of lasting long. There is no immortal soul. The soul is more refined than the body, but still made of physical matter, and therefore it will eventually deteriorate and dissolve.

Introduction

That wealth and rank would be seen as problems by Hsi K'ang makes good sense, given his experience. Wealth and rank simply place one in a position in society where harm is more likely to occur. Moreover, the more one has in possessions and power, the more one has to worry about, and anxiety is physically harmful. The dangers involved with wealth and rank remind us once again of Chuang-tzu and his sense of the usefulness of the useless. Nonetheless, it is important to remember that throughout the preceding years of the Han it was precisely the royalty and the nobles, those with wealth and rank, who most avidly cultivated the techniques of lengthening life.[23]

On the dietary regulations, some of Hsi K'ang's most colorful language is used to describe the evils of meat, wine, and grains—how they destroy the body—and to marvel, on the other hand, at the benefits of the drugs of long life. He speaks of both in one especially graphic passage in his "Answer to Hsiang Hsiu's Refutation of My Essay on Nourishing Life." Speaking of the common people, he begins:[24]

For caring for their parents or presentation to those respected, only pepper and chrysanthemum [wines] and Indian rice and spiked millet will do. For their guest parties and lavish feasts, they must have elegant dishes and the finest wines. They do not know that these are all dissolving their muscles and fluids, facilitating their destruction and hastening their decay. Although at first they are tasty and fragrant, when they enter the body, they stink and rot. They exhaust and defile essence and spirit, stain and pollute the six bowels, rot and contaminate breath and vapor, and spontaneously give rise to the killing worms. It is these that support gluttony and debauchery, and on these rely the one hundred diseases. Those who taste them lose their sense of taste; those who eat them shorten their blessings.

How could these compare to [the water of] a flowing fountain or a sweet spring, the agate stamens and flowers of jade, the red sulphur and stone mushrooms, the purple fungus and yellow essence? In all of these

---

[23] See Yü Ying-shih, "Life and Immortality in the Mind of Han China," *Harvard Journal of Asiatic Studies*, 25 (1964–65), p. 93ff.

[24] The plants, drugs, body organs, etc. mentioned in this passage are all identified below with the translation of the entire essay.

Introduction

are a host of spiritual properties, and they contain many beautiful things. They issue forth by themselves and mysteriously grow; their pure fragrance dissipates only with difficulty; and they are filled to overflowing with harmonious vapors. They bathe and cleanse the five viscera, dredge out and enlighten. One who swallows them [feels] his body become light. Moreover, they soften your skeleton and ease your breath, make flexible your bones and pliable your muscles. They wash away all dirt and dispel all filth, and your will mounts up to the blue clouds. If one can go on from this, why would he nourish himself with the five grains?

Dispassion, avoidance of wealth and rank, and correct diet by no means exhaust the things that need to be done to nourish one's life properly, as the reader will soon see. Music is important; so too is building a fortunate house. In fact, for Hsi K'ang, anything that can possibly help ought to be pursued. The key is to be "comprehensive" (*chien* 兼), and failure results from being the opposite, "one-sided" (*p'ien* 偏). Hsi K'ang says this at the end of his "Answer to Hsiang Hsiu," but he brings it up again in his debate with Juan K'an on residence and good fortune. Having used the analogy of a skilled farmer who selects fertile fields and weeds and cultivates to illustrate the interrelationship of various factors in determining good and bad fortune, he then says:

But these days if people believe in signs and omens then they reject what is proper to the principles of man; and if they maintain divination and physiognomy, they renounce the good and bad fortune of Yin and Yang; if they support knowledge and strength, they forget what is preserved by the Way of Heaven. How does this differ from knowing that the seasonal rain produces things, and accordingly doing nothing and hoping for excellent crops? For this reason, doubtful and strange theories arise, and one-sided opinions abound. When what they rely on is not the same, how can they understand one another? If there were someone who combined (*chien*) all things and perfected them, would it not have to be that half [of his concern] would be with residence and grave?

One would like to know in the end how Hsi K'ang would have understood his own failure to live past forty. Did he too fail to be

Introduction

"comprehensive"? But this is, after all, rhetoric. Hsi K'ang was first and foremost a debater trying to make a point. And while we have no reason to doubt the genuineness of his interest in nourishing life, we cannot necessarily use what he says in his essays as a guide to what he did in his life.[25]

[25] Thus, despite what he says about wine in his nourishing life essays, Hsi K'ang has a reputation for being quite a drinker, and he does say near the end of his letter to Shan T'ao, "—a cup of unstrained wine, a song to the lute: this is the sum of my desires and ambitions." (Tr. by Hightower, in Birch, ed., *Anthology of Chinese Literature*, p. 166.)

Translator's Note

::

The translation is based on Tai Ming-yang's 戴明揚 *Hsi K'ang chi chiao-chu* 嵇康集校注 (Peking: Jen-min, 1962), which in turn uses as its base text Huang Hsing-tseng's 黃省曾 *Hsi Chung-san chi* 嵇中散集 (published in 1525). The Huang text is one of two main editions of the works of Hsi K'ang: the other is Wu K'uan's 吳寬 (hao, Pao-an 匏菴, 1435–1504) *Hsi K'ang chi*. The Wu text is superior to the Huang. But since Tai Ming-yang's critical edition notes not only all of the variant Wu readings, but all other variants as well, it is the only text to use for the present purpose. I have also consulted Lu Hsün's 魯迅 *Hsi K'ang chi* (which prints the Wu text), using the edition published by Hsin-i 新藝 of Hong Kong in 1967. The Wu manuscript has been corrected by two editors. Thus I sometimes note what the "original" (i.e. uncorrected) text says.

Tai Ming-yang's text is annotated. Thus almost all of the allusions, quotations, etc. noted in the translation have been identified by him. I wish to acknowledge this at the outset and not add it with every note. Tai Ming-yang sometimes goes too far with his annotation, but all in all he has done a splendid job.

I have consulted with benefit the translations of the three nourishing life essays by Richard Howard, in English (unpublished M. A. thesis, "Hsi K'ang's Essays on Nurturing Life," Columbia, 1948), and Donald Holzman, in French (*La Vie et la Pensée de Hi K'ang*, pp. 83–121); I have also used Jerry Swanson's translation of the "Essay on Nourishing Life" ("A Third Century Taoist Treatise on the Nourishment of Life: Hsi K'ang and His *Yang-sheng lun*," in *Studies in Philosophy and in the History of Science: Essays in Honor of Max Fisch* [Lawrence, Kansas, 1970], pp. 139–158), and Donald Holzman's translation of "Dispelling Self-interest" ("Se délivrer des sentiments personnels," in *La Vie et la Pensée de Hi K'ang*, pp. 122–130).

For the footnotes I have used the Harvard-Yenching Concordance texts for the following works: 1) *Chou-i* 周易 (*I ching*); 2) *Chuang-tzu* 莊子; 3) *Ch'un-ch'iu ching-chuan* 春秋經傳 (*Tso chuan*); 4) *Hsiao ching* 孝經; 5) *Hsün-tzu* 荀子; 6) *Lun-yü* 論語; 7) *Mao shih* 毛詩 (*Shih ching*); 8) *Meng-tzu* 孟子; and 9) *Mo-tzu* 墨子. *Ssu-pu pei-yao* editions are used for the following: 1) *Chan-kuo ts'e* 戰國策; 2) (Wang Fu's 王符) *Ch'ien-fu lu* 潛夫論; 3) (Tung Chung-shu 董仲舒) *Ch'un-ch'iu fan-lu* 春秋繁露; 4) (Yang Hsiung's 楊雄) *Fa-yen* 法言; 5) *Han-fei-tzu* 韓非子; 6) (Huan T'an's 桓譚) *Hsin lun* 新論; 7) *Huai-nan-tzu* 淮南子; 8) *Kuan-tzu* 管子; 9) *K'ung-tzu chia-yü* 孔子家語; 10) *Lao-tzu* 老子; 11) *Li chi* (*Li chi hsün-tsuan* 禮記訓纂); 12) *Lieh-tzu* 列子; 13) *Lü-shih ch'un-ch'iu* 呂氏春秋; 14) (Wang Ch'ung's 王充) *Lun-heng* 論衡; 15) (Ko Hung's 葛洪) *Pao-p'u-tzu* 抱朴子; 16) *Shang shu* (*Shang shu chin-ku-wen chu-shu* 尚書今古文注疏); 17) *Wen hsüan* (*Wen hsüan Li Shan chu* 文選李善注); 18) *Yen-shih chia-hsün* 顏氏家訓; and 19) *Yen-tzu ch'un-ch'iu* 晏子春秋. For the standard histories (*Shih chi* 史記, *Han shu* 漢書, *Hou Han shu* 後漢書, *San-kuo chih* 三國志, and *Chin shu* 晉書) the recent Chung-hua shu-chü 中華書局 editions (Peking, 1959, 1962, 1965, 1959, and 1974 respectively) have been used.

In making this translation I have tried to follow the original Chinese as closely as possible, in the meaning of the words, the grammer, word order, and rhythm, within the limits of good sounding English, and English which best captures the sense. I have assumed the writers to be "cultured" gentlemen, dignified in bearing, with their noses slightly in the air.

The Essays

HSI K'ANG

An Essay on Nourishing Life

(Yang-sheng lun)

∷

Translator's Comments on the Nourishing Life Debate. Hsi K'ang's opponent in this debate is Hsiang Hsiu (style, Tzu-ch'i 子期), a close friend and fellow member of the "Seven Worthies of the Bamboo Grove." We have no dates for Hsiang Hsiu. He was from Huai in Ho-nei (in present-day Honan), and though he did not serve while Hsi K'ang was alive, he did after he died, rising to the position of Huang-men shih-lang (Imperial Attendant). He wrote a commentary on the Chuang-tzu. *And it has been known for some time that Kuo Hsiang's 郭象 (d. 312) commentary on that work is at least in part from the hand of Hsiang Hsiu.*[1]

The expression chih-li 至理 *occurs three times in Hsi K'ang's "Answer to Hsiang Hsiu." And li as "Principle", the one absolute underlying all phenomena, becomes very important in Neo-Confucianism. Does* chih-li *mean that here? The answer is no.*[2] Chih-li *once means "Perfect Reason", in contrast to "common reason" (*ch'ang-li 常理*). Another time I translate it "the ultimate order of things," which is meant to contrast with Hsiang Hsiu's "natural order" (*t'ien-li 天理*). The third time I translate "highest truths"—i.e., the truths, or principles, of nourishing life and good and bad fortune, etc., things which can only be known by the mind,*

---

[1] See *Shih-shuo hsin-yü* 4:17 (p. 157 in Yang Yung's *Shih-shuo hsin-yü chiao-chien*; p. 100 in Mather, *A New Account of Tales of the World*). For a good study of the issue see Ho Ch'i-min 何啓民, *Chu-lin ch'i-hsien yen-chiu* 竹林七賢研究 (Taipei: Commercial Press, 1966), pp. 115–131.

[2] But also see Wing-tsit Chan, "The Evolution of the Neo-Confucian Concept *Li* 理 as Principle," *Tsing Hua Journal of Chinese Studies*, New Series, IV:2 (February, 1964), pp. 131–132 and the notes.

Nourishing Life

not by the eyes. In this sense chih-li means the same as the chih-wu 至物 *("highest things") mentioned by Hsi K'ang in his "Essay on Nourishing Life."*

Hsi K'ang's "Essay on Nourishing Life" was included by Hsiao T'ung 蕭統 *(501–531) in his* Wen hsüan *(chüan 53), which says something for its literary quality. Moreover, Wang Tao* 王導 *in the fourth century is said to have talked about only three things, "Music Has in it Neither Grief nor Joy," "Nourishing Life," and "Words Completely Express Meaning"*[3]—*the first two Hsi K'ang's essays and the third an essay by Ou-yang Chien* 歐陽堅 *(c. 265–300). So the "Essay on Nourishing Life"—and presumably the "Answer to Hsiang Hsiu" as well—was well known and respected.*

In this world[1] there are those who say that immortality can be attained by study and "no-death"[2] brought about by effort. Others say that the extreme of old age is one hundred and twenty, and that in this past and present are the same—[claims] of going beyond this are all wild and absurd.

Both of these miss the mark. Let me attempt to discuss it roughly. Although immortals are not seen with the eyes, nonetheless they are cited in books and records and [their lives] are narrated in the former histories. When we compare these and discuss it, their existence becomes certain. But it seems that they uniquely receive a special breath. They are endowed with it by nature; it is not something that can be brought about by ac-

---

[3] See *Shih-shuo hsin-yü* 4:21 (p. 162 in Yang Yung, 102 in Mather). There is a record, by the way, in the *Sui shu* Bibliography and in the *Yü-hai* 玉海, that Hsi K'ang wrote an essay "Words Do Not Completely Exhaust Meaning" (言不盡意論). This is no longer extant.

[1] The word is *shih* 世. One could also read "For *generations* now there have been those who say...." In the nourishing life essays Hsi K'ang tends to use *shih* in a pejorative way: "people of the world," those given to worldly delights.

[2] For the early (pre-Han) meaning of "no-death" (*pu-ssu* 不死) see Ying-shih Yü's article, "Life and Immortality in the Mind of Han China," *Harvard Journal of Asiatic Studies*, 25 (1964–1965), pp. 87–93.

Nourishing Life

cumulation of study. Turning to "guiding and nourishing"[3] and getting the principle, to exhaust the limits of one's nature and fate, at the utmost reaching more than a thousand years, or at the least living several hundred—this is possible. But people of the world are all unrefined; thus none is able to attain it.

What can I use to explain this? When we take drugs to make us sweat we sometimes do not succeed. But when feelings of shame build up inside, perspiration pours out in streams. When we have not eaten all morning long, we hungrily think of food. But Tseng-tzu was filled with grief, and felt no hunger for seven days.[4] When we sit up until midnight we become drowsy and think of rest; when inside beset with deep sorrow, we go until dawn without sleep.[5] A stiff brush will comb the temples; rich wine flushes the face. Only with these will you get those results. But with the anger of a brave knight—glowing red with rage he glares, his hair on end pushing into his cap.[6] Speaking on the basis of this, the relation of essence and spirit to form and body is

---

[3] *Tao-yang* 導養, "guiding and nourishing" might also be "stretching and nourishing." It refers to the Taoist practice of guiding pure breath through the body and in this way nourishing it. It is clearly related to *tao-yin* 引, the combined calisthenics and breathing exercise practiced by Taoists, and Maspero (in "Essai sur Le Taoïsme aux Premiers Siècles de l'Ère Chrétienne," in *Le Taoïsme et les religions chinoises* [Paris: Gallimard, 1971], p. 380) says that *tao-yin* means literally to "extend and contract the body." Pictures of *tao-yin* exercises have been found at Ma-wang-tui in south-central China (Changsha, Hunan): see *Ma-wang-tui Han mu po-shu tao-yin t'u* 馬王堆漢墓帛書導引圖 (Peking: Wen wu, 1979).

[4] In the *Li chi*, "T'an-kung" 檀弓, Part I, Tseng-tzu tells Tzu-ssu that he drank no liquid of any kind for several days when mourning for his parents. See *Li chi hsün-tsuan* 3.9a. The play on words here seems intended—literally, his "mouth was filled" (*hsien* 銜) with grief.

[5] Reading the Wu variant of 寐 for 瞑.

[6] Hsi K'ang probably has in mind the description of Kao Chien-li 高漸離 and Ching K'o 荊軻 as they set out on their attempted assassination of the King of Ch'in (the future Ch'in Shih-huang-ti). Yang Hsien-yi and Gladys Yang translate: "After this he [Ching K'o] sang a stirring, martial air, which made their eyes bulge with anger and their hair stand on end." (From *Selections from Records of the Historian by Szuma Chien* [Peking: Foreign Languages Press, 1979], p. 399.) For the text see *Shih-chi* 86 (Vol. 8, p. 2534).

Nourishing Life

like that of the ruler to the state. When the spirit is disturbed on the inside, the form wastes away on the out, just as when the ruler is confused above, the state is chaotic below.

In farming in the age of T'ang,[7] there was an effect when some things were favored with a single watering.[8] Although in the end [everything] was scorched and dry, the plants that were watered once were necessarily the last to wither. This being the case, the benefit of a single watering definitely cannot be denied. And yet [people] of the world constantly say that a single fit of anger is not enough to attack your nature, and a single instance of grief is not enough to harm your health. They treat these lightly and let them go. This is like knowing the benefit of a single watering, yet hoping for good grain from dried-up shoots. Therefore the Gentleman knows that the form relies on the spirit to stand and the spirit needs the form to exist: [he] understands that the principle of life is easily lost and that a single mistake can injure life. Therefore he cultivates his nature to protect his spirit and calms his mind to keep his body intact. Love and hate do not dwell in his feelings; anguish and delight do not stay in his thoughts. Quiet is he and unmoved, his body and breath harmonious and still. Moreover, he exhales the old and inhales the new and swallows the drugs to nourish his health, causing form and spirit to draw together and surface and interior to benefit alike.

Now those who sow crops call it a good field when they get "ten hu per mou."[9] This is a common saying in the world. They do not know that if you "plot-plant" you can get over a hundred hu [per mou].[10] The field and the seeds may be the same, but if

---

[7] T'ang 湯 is the legendary founder of the Shang dynasty. Traditional reign dates are 1766–1753 B.C.

[8] There is reported to have been a seven year drought in the time of T'ang.

[9] A *hu* 斛 is equal to ten *tou* 斗, and a *tou* is the Chinese peck. A *mou* is about one-seventh of an acre; 733.5 square yards.

[10] Li Shan 李善, in his commentary on Hsi K'ang's "Essay on Nourishing Life" (*Wen hsüan* 53.2a), cites Fan Sheng-chih's 氾勝之 *Book on Farming* (T'ien-nung shu 田農書) to explain "plot-planting" (*ch'ü-chung* 區種). This says that each *mou* is to be divided into 3700 "plots," each six inches (*ts'un* 寸) square and six inches deep, set seven inches apart. This will yield three *sheng* 升

Nourishing Life

the planting and cultivating are different, the resultant harvests will be far apart. To say that in marketing you cannot have ten times the value and in farming you cannot hope for one hundred hu—this is to hold on to the old ways and not change.

Moreover, beans make you heavy, and elm puts you to sleep;[11] mimosa removes anger, and the day lily makes you forget your cares.[12] This is known by wise and foolish alike. Strong-smelling foods [e.g., onions, leeks, hot peppers] hurt your eyes; and globefish provide no nourishment. This is known by the common people of the world. Lice become black from living on [people's] heads; musk deer are fragrant from eating cedar; people living in mountain passes develop tumors on their necks;[13] people living in Chin get yellow teeth.[14] To draw our inference from this: the essence of whatever we eat steams the nature and stains the body; there is nothing that does not affect something else. How can it be that though steaming makes things heavy, there is nothing that makes them light? Though

---

per plot (ten *sheng* = one *tou*), or one hundred *hu* per *mou*. This and other passages on "plot-planting" from Fan Sheng-chih's book are translated into English in Shih Sheng-han's 石聲漢 *On "Fan Sheng-chih Shu" An Agriculturist Book of China Written by Fan Sheng-chih in The First Century B.C.* (Peking: Science Press, 1974), pp. 31–41. Shih Sheng-han—who reads the *ch'ü* in *ch'ü-chung* as *ou*—understands *ch'ü-chung* to mean "cultivation in shallow pits."

[11] Reading the variant 眠 for 瞑. This probably means the bark of the elm. On both beans and elm see, for example, the *Po-wu chih* 博物志 (attributed to Hsi K'ang's contemporary, Chang Hua 張華), 2.2b. I quote: "If people eat beans for three years their bodies become heavy, and walking and stopping become difficult. If they eat elm, they fall asleep and do not want to wake up."

[12] According to Li Shan (*Wen hsüan*, 53.2b), Hsi K'ang is here quoting the *Shen Nung pen-ts'ao ching* 神農本草經. However, later on the same page he attributes this line to a *Yang-sheng ching* 經. I do not find the line in the present *Shen Nung pen-ts'ao ching* (SPPY ed.), but *ho-huan* 合歡 is listed (see p. 2.26a). For the identification of *ho-huan* as "mimosa" (Albizzia Julibrissin) see Bernard E. Read, *Chinese Medicinal Plants from the Pen Ts'ao Kang Mu* 本草綱目 *A.D. 1596* (Shanghai: 1936—here using a reprint—Taipei: Southern Materials Center, Inc., 1977), p. 110, item 370. On *hsüan-ts'ao* 萱草 as "day-lily" (Hemerocallis fulva), see Read, *Chinese Medicinal Plants*, p. 221, item 679.

[13] Chang Hua's *Po-wu chih* (2.2a) says these come from drinking spring water—water that does not flow.

[14] Apparently from eating the dates (or jujubes, *tsao* 棗) that grow there.

injury makes things stupid, there is nothing that makes them wise? Though smoking makes things yellow, there is nothing that makes them firm? Though sweet-smelling plants make things fragrant, there is nothing that lengthens their lives!

Therefore Shen Nung said: "The Superior Drugs nourish fate; The Middle Drugs nourish nature."[15] He truly understood the principles of nature and fate, and accordingly he assisted and nourished them to take them to completion. But people of the world do not study these; the "five grains"[16] alone they delight in,[17] and music and beauty they crave. Their eyes are dazzled by black and gold [beautiful colors], their ears straining to hear sounds lewd and perverse. Rich flavors fry their entrails; unstrained wine boils their bowels; fragrant, sweet smells rot their marrow; delight and anger upset their steady breath; thought and concern waste away essence and spirit; grief and joy destroy their purity and peace. It is such a tiny form, yet its attackers come from more than one direction; such an easily exhausted body, yet it suffers enemies outside and in. The body is not made of wood or stone. Can it last for long?

Those who indulge themselves to excess eat and drink without restraint, producing the one hundred diseases, and delight in lust without tiring, bringing on fatigue and exhaustion.[18] Injured by wind and cold, sickened by one hundred poisons, in the middle of their lives they die, cut down by a host of problems.

---

[15] Said at the beginnings of the first two sections of the *Shen Nung pen-ts'ao ching* (pp. 1.1a and 2.1a in SPPY), the early Chinese work on pharmacopoeia attributed to the legendary sage emperor Shen Nung (the Divine Farmer), whose traditional reign dates are 2737–2697 B.C. Drugs are here classified into three groups: the "Superior Drugs" (上藥) that nourish fate, the "Middle Drugs" (中藥) that nourish nature, and the "Lower Drugs" (下藥) that merely cure disease.

[16] The *wu-ku* 五穀. Various lists are given: one would be rice, panicled millet, wheat, glutinous millet, and pulse.

[17] Preferring the *T'ai-p'ing yü-lan* reading of *shih* 嗜, "delight in" or "crave" to *chien* 見, "see."

[18] *Fa-chüeh* 乏絕, "fatigue and exhaustion," is more commonly glossed as "deprivation and poverty."

Nourishing Life

Everyone in the world knows to laugh [at them] and lament,[19] saying they were unskilled at holding on to life.

Turning to [those who] in taking care of their bodies neglect the principle, they lose it in the unseen. When things unseen build up they turn into harm; accumulated harm becomes decline. From decline comes white hair; from white hair comes old age; from old age comes death. Unaware of what is going on, [they think] it has no cause. Those below middle intelligence say this is natural.

Even if there are some who are a little bit enlightened, they all sigh and lament at the first sign of trouble. They do not know to take precautions against the many dangers before the symptoms have appeared. This is like[20] Marquis Huan, who harbored a fatal disease and yet was angry with P'ien Ch'üeh's early detection, because he felt that the day one becomes aware of the pain is [the day] the disease begins.[21] Injury develops from the unseen, but they treat it when it manifests its signs; therefore, they have ineffective cures. They chase about in the realm of common men; therefore their long life is of the common sort. They look up and observe and down and examine [and claim] there are none who are not completely like this. Confirming themselves with the fact that this happens to the many, and consoling themselves with the assurance that this is the common [lot of mankind], they say that the principle of Heaven and Earth is nothing more than this. Even if they have heard of the business of nourishing life, limited to what they can see, they say it is not true.

---

[19] Following Li Shan's (*Wen-hsüan* 53.3a) interpretation of *hsiao-tao* 笑悼. But perhaps it is "laugh at their grief."

[20] Reading 由 in the sense of 猶.

[21] For this anecdote see *Han Fei-tzu*, "Yü-lao" 喻老 (7.2b–3a). The anecdote is translated in W. K. Liao's *The Complete Works of Han Fei Tzu* (London: Arthur Probsthain, 1959), pp. 214–215. Marquis Huan of Ts'ai 蔡 (according to the text; but others identify this as Duke Huan of Ch'i or Duke Huan of Chin), because he felt fine, three times refused to believe P'ien Ch'üeh's 扁鵲 diagnosis of disease. By the time the Marquis felt pain, P'ien Ch'üeh had fled, knowing it was too late for any cure.

Nourishing Life

Next are those who, although their doubts are few, never know where to begin.

Next are those who devote themselves to taking the drugs. But after half a year or a year, when they have worked hard but not yet seen any results, being fed up, their wills weaken, and in the midst of their efforts they stop.

Others add to it[22] by ditches and drains but let it leak out at Wei-lü,[23] desiring to [merely] sit by and hope for a glorious reward. Others repress their feelings and hold back their desires, cutting off and rejecting wishes for glory. But their cravings and delights are constantly in front of their eyes and ears, while what they long for is several tens of years away. Afraid they will lose both, they harbor doubts inside. Their minds divided on the inside and things tempting them on the out, distant and near topple each other, and in this way they suffer a double defeat. The highest things are subtle and unseen. They can be known with reason, but are difficult to discern with the eyes. They are like the silky spice-bush and the camphor, whose [differences] can be recognized only after they have grown for seven years.[24] In the present case, [these people] are traversing the path of silence and tranquillity with minds unsettled and divided. Their wish is to hurry, but these matters take time; they hope for something near, but the response is far away. Thus none is able to make it to the end.

The masses do not seek it [long life, immortality] since they

---

[22] Presumably their store of vitality—perhaps their "essence" (*ching* 精) or "breath" (*ch'i* 氣).

[23] The place where water leaks out of the ocean. See *Chuang-tzu*, Ch. 17 (p. 42, lines 7–8), translated by Burton Watson in *The Complete Works of Chuang Tzu* (New York: Columbia University Press, 1968), p. 176. *Wei-lü* 尾閭 is understood to be a huge rock against which the water is poured and turns into steam.

[24] For the explanation we must here resort to the *Cheng-i* 正義 commentary on Ssu-ma Hsiang-ju's 司馬相如 biography in *Shih chi* 117 (Vol. 9, p. 3008). This identifies the *yü* 豫 and *chang* 章 trees—which is literally what our text says—with "silky spice-bush" (*chen* 枕) and "camphor" (*chang* 樟) respectively, and says that only after they have grown seven years can they be distinguished. For "silky spice-bush" (L. sericea) and "camphor" (Cinnamomum Camphora) see Read, *Chinese Medicinal Plants*, pp. 157–158 (item 499) and pp. 154–155 (item 492).

Nourishing Life

have not yet seen any results; those who seek it defeat their own cause through lack of concentration; those who rely on one thing fail by not being comprehensive; those who pursue [mere] techniques lose themselves in the minor arts.[25] Everyone falls into one of these categories. Thus, of those who desire it, not one in ten thousand is able to succeed.

But one who is skilled at nourishing life is not like this. Pure, empty, tranquil, at peace, "he diminishes self-interest and lessens his desires."[26] He knows that fame and position injure virtue; therefore he disregards them and seeks them not. It is not that he desires them but forcefully forbids them. He knows that rich flavors harm the nature; therefore he rejects them and pays them no mind. It is not that he first longs for them and only then represses [his true feelings]. External things, because they ensnare the mind, he does not maintain.[27] Spirit and breath, because they are unsullied and pure, on these alone is his attention focussed. Open and unrestrained is he, free from worry and care, silent and still, devoid of thought and concern. Furthermore, he maintains this state with the one and nourishes it with harmony. Harmony and principle daily increase and he becomes one with the Great Accord.[28] After this he steams [himself] with magic fungus[29] and soaks in sweet water from a spring; dries [himself] off in the morning sun and soothes [himself] with the

---

[25] Surely reflecting Tzu-hsia's statement in *Analects* 19:2 (p. 39), which D. C. Lau (*Confucius: The Analects* [London & Baltimore: Penguin Books, 1979], p. 153) translates: "Tzu-hsia said, 'Even minor arts are sure to have their worthwhile aspects, but the gentleman does not take them up because the fear of a man who would go a long way is that he should be bogged down."

[26] Quoting the last two lines of Chapter 19 of the *Lao-tzu* (part I, p. 10b).

[27] This is to say, contact with, or thought of, external things he does not maintain.

[28] The "Great Accord" (*ta-shun* 大順) comes from the last line of Ch. 65 of the *Lao-tzu* (part II, p. 18a). Hsi K'ang seems to have four lines of the chapter in mind. Wing-tsit Chan (*The Way of Lao Tzu* [Indianapolis: Bobbs-Merrill, Inc., 1963], p. 216) translates: "Virtue becomes deep and far-reaching, and with it all things return to their original state. Then complete harmony [*ta-shun*] will be reached."

[29] *Ling-chih* 靈芝, "magic fungus," is identified as a lichen by Read in *Chinese Medicinal Plants* (p. 275, item 818). It has the alternate name of *shih-erh* 石耳, "stone ears."

Nourishing Life

five strings.[30] Without action and self-attained, his body ethereal and mind profound, he forgets happiness, and as a result his joy is complete; he leaves life behind, and as a result his person is preserved.[31] If he can go on from this, he can come close to comparing in old age with Hsien-men and matching his years with Prince Ch'iao.[32] How can it be that such people do not exist?

---

[30] Presumably referring to the five-stringed lute of antiquity. When Hsi K'ang here speaks of "steaming" (*cheng* 蒸), "soaking" (*jun* 潤), and "drying off" (*hsi* 晞), he probably speaks metaphorically—the fungus, the water, and the sun (or air purified by the sun) are all to be ingested. But if one did not know better it would seem that he is describing taking a sauna, followed by the usual dip in cold water and then drying off, and then enjoying some relaxing music.

[31] Tai Ming-yang (*Hsi K'ang chi chiao-chu*, p. 157) points out that Kuo Hsiang's commentary on the opening lines of *Chuang-tzu* Ch. 18 is: "He forgets happiness and, as a result, his joy is complete; his joy is complete, and as a result his body is preserved." (For the text see *Chiao-cheng Chuang-tzu chi-shih* 校正莊子集釋 [Taipei: Shih-chieh, 1971], Vol. II, p. 608.) The similarity to the words of Hsi K'ang is striking. One's initial impression would certainly be that Hsiang Hsiu, having refuted this essay, then took the words of Hsi K'ang in the essay and used them in his commentary on the *Chuang-tzu*. Of course Kuo Hsiang probably knew this essay as well.

[32] Hsien Men 羨門 and Prince Ch'iao (Wang-tzu Ch'iao 王子喬) are famous immortals of antiquity. Hsien Men is mentioned in the annals of Ch'in Shih-huang-ti (*Shih chi* 6: Vol. 1, p. 251). Ch'in Shih-huang-ti sent a man from Yen to search for the immortals Hsien Men and Kao Shih 高誓. Prince Ch'iao is supposed to have been Chin 晉, the eldest son of King Ling 靈 of the Chou (reigned 571–544 B.C.). His biography is recorded in the *Lieh-hsien chuan* 列仙傳: in the *Li-tai chen-hsien shih-chuan* 歷代真仙史傳 (Taipei: Tzu-yu, 1970) text, see *Lieh-hsien chuan*, p. 6a. This biography is translated in Max Kaltenmark, *Le Lie-sien Tchouan* 列仙傳 (*Biographies légendaires des Immortels taoïstes de l'antiquité*) (Peking: Publications de Centre d'études sinologiques de Pékin, 1953), pp. 109–114.

HSIANG HSIU

A Refutation of Hsi K'ang's Essay on Nourishing Life

(Nan Yang-sheng lun)

::

The Imperial Attendant Hsiang Tzu-ch'i[1] refutes this as follows:

Such things as restraining grief and joy, calming delight and anger, moderating food and drink, and tempering hot and cold—these were also practiced by the ancients.[2] But to turn to elimination of the five grains, rejection of rich flavors, lessening of emotions and desires, and repression of wealth and rank—these they never presumed to allow.

How can I explain it? Man receives form from the Creator and exists together with the ten thousand things. [But] he is the most intelligent of things that have life.[3] He is different from plants and trees. Plants and trees cannot escape wind and rain or avoid hatchet and axe. He [also] differs from birds and beasts. Birds and beasts cannot get away from traps and nets or flee from the heat and the cold. He has activity to make contact with things; he has intelligence to assist himself. This is the benefit of having a mind and the utility of having intelligence. If you shut it off and silence it [the mind, intelligence], you will be the same as [those

---

[1] Following the opening of the Wu manuscript. Other texts simply say "I refute this as follows," *nan yüeh* 難曰.

[2] Hsiang Hsiu might have specific texts in mind. For example the *Huai-nan-tzu*, "Ch'üan-yen hsün," 詮言訓, says: "Whoever controls his body and nourishes his nature, regulates sleep and rest, moderates food and drink, calms delight and anger, and is active and tranquil in appropriate degrees." (*Huai-nan-tzu* 14.7b)

[3] Said elsewhere as well. See for example the *Lieh-tzu*, "Yang Chu" 楊朱, 7.11a.

A Refutation

things] that lack intelligence. [Thus] what value is there in having intelligence?

If you have life then you have feelings,[4] and if you weigh your feelings you are being natural. If you cut them off and exclude them, it is the same as not being alive. [Thus] what value is there in being alive?

Moreover, craving and desire, love of glory and hatred of disgrace, love of ease and hatred of labor, all arise from nature. "The great virtue of Heaven and Earth is life; the great treasure of the sage is position."[5] "Of things lofty and exalted, none is greater than wealth and rank."[6] This being so,[7] wealth and rank are what everyone in the world wants.[8] If you have rank, then others will follow your lead and you can work for righteousness with those below; if you have wealth, then you can get what you want, and by means of riches bring people together.[9] These [wealth and rank] were both regarded as important by the former kings, and they founded[10] them as natural. We cannot put them aside.

They [the ancients] also said: "Wealth and rank are what men desire, but they must seek them in accord with morality and the right."[11] Those above suffer no harm because they do not be-

---

[4] One is reminded of the words of Hsün-tzu: "Beings that possess desires and those that do not belong to two different categories—the categories of the living and the dead." (Tr. by Burton Watson, *Hsün Tzu: Basic Writings* [New York: Columbia University Press, 1963], p. 150.) For the text see *Hsün-tzu*, Chapter 22 (p. 85, lines 56–57).

[5] Quoting from the *I ching*, *Hsi-tz'u* B.1 (p. 45).

[6] Also a quote from the *I*, here from *Hsi-tz'u*, A.11 (p. 44).

[7] Following the Wu manuscript in adding a 則 after the 然, but it does not need to be translated here.

[8] Or possibly something like "Wealth and rank are part of the natural makeup of Heaven and Earth." The phrase is *t'ien-ti chih ch'ing yeh* 天地之情也, which resembles *t'ien-ti chih li* 理. But Hsiang Hsiu is talking about desires and emotions.

[9] In the *I ching* (*Hsi-tz'u*, B.1: p. 45) we have the line: "How do you bring people together? With riches."

[10] Reading the Wu variant 開 in place of 闢.

[11] In part quoting, in part paraphrasing Confucius in *Analects* 4:5 (p. 6). D. C. Lau translates this: "Wealth and high station are what men desire but unless I got them in the right way I would not remain in them." (D. C. Lau, *Confucius: The Analects*, p. 72.)

A Refutation

come arrogant; they maintain things at their peak, but through reduction and frugality do not go to excess."[12] Since this is the case, how can it be that [wealth and rank] "injure virtue"?[13] Some see the excesses of wealth and rank, and accordingly fear and reject them. But that is like not eating the rest of your life, because you have seen someone choke on food.

Shen Nung introduced[14] the first [use of] grains and Hou Chi followed with the work of sowing seeds.[15] Birds and beasts by means of them [the grains] fly and run; living people by means of them see and breathe [live]; the [Duke of] Chou and Confucius by means of them exhausted the divine; Yen [Yüan] and Jan [Keng] by means of them established their virtue.[16] The worthies and sages treasured their cultivation and for hundreds of generations [this work] has not been abandoned. And now one morning you say the five grains are not suitable for the nourishing of life, and cooked meat and sweet wine are not things that benefit nature. Then [the sayings] "There is also this well-seasoned soup.... We will reach old age without limit" [and] "We make this spring wine to increase our years" are all empty words.[17] "Ample and large, plump and fat,[18] these are enjoyed

---

[12] This reflects the opening lines of Chapter 3 of the *Hsiao ching* (p. 2). James Legge, in F. Max Müller, ed., *The Sacred Books of the East* (Oxford: The Clarendon Press, 1879), Vol. III, p. 468, translates: "Above others, and yet free from pride, they dwell on high, without peril; adhering to economy, and carefully observant of the rules and laws, they are full, without overflowing."

[13] Referring back to Hsi K'ang's claim that one who is skilled at nourishing life "knows that fame and position injure virtue."

[14] Reading the variant 倡 in place of 唱.

[15] Shen Nung 神農 (the Divine Farmer) and Hou Chi 后稷 (Lord Millet) share the honor of being the father of agriculture in China. On the birth of the culture hero Hou Chi—who was regarded by the Chou as their first ancestor—and his discovery of agriculture, see poem 245 in the *Shih* (pp. 62–63).

[16] Yen Yüan 顏淵 (or Yen Hui 回) and Jan Po-niu 冉伯牛 (or Jan Keng 耕) were disciples of Confucius, the former his favorite and the best. They are both listed in the category of "virtuous conduct" (德行) in *Analects* 11:3 (p. 19).

[17] The first saying comes from poem 302 in the *Shih* (p. 81), and the second from poem 154 (*Shih*, p. 32). For Karlgren's translations, see Bernhard Karlgren, *The Book of Odes* (Stockholm: Museum of Far Eastern Antiquities, 1950), pp. 262 and 97–99 respectively.

[18] Referring to sacrificial offerings.

A Refutation

by God on High."[19] "It's only the millets that are fragrant; these bring down the spirits of Heaven and Earth."[20] If even the spirits of Heaven and Earth value them, how much the more should man?

When meat and grains are taken into the body, within ten days they will fatten you up. This is the proof that they are natural and the evidence that they are proper for life. Man is born embodying the five elements. His mouth thinks of the five flavors;[21] his eye thinks of the five colors;[22] when aroused he thinks of women;[23] when hungry he searches for food. These are principles of nature. They must simply be restrained with the rites. But now [you are saying] that although the five colors are displayed, the eye dare not look at them, and although the five flavors exist, the mouth cannot taste them. You might contest with me in words and win. [But] how can you look on the peony[24] as though it were sow-thistle or smartweed or see Hsi-shih as Mo-mu,[25] and disregard them and not want them? If the mind knows something is desirable but cannot pursue it, the nature and breath are distressed by being blocked, and the feelings and

---

[19] A fusion of lines from two sources. The first comes from the *Tso chuan*, Duke Huan the 6th year (p. 31). The second is from the "Yüeh ling" 月令 (Monthly Commands) section of the *Li chi*. See *Li chi hsün-tsuan*, 6.25b.

[20] This is also a fusion of lines. The first appears to be a deliberate corruption (unless Hsiang Hsiu has had a lapse of memory) of a passage in the *Tso chuan* (Duke Hsi, 5th year: p. 96) which says: "Offerings of millet are not fragrant; it is only virtue that is fragrant." (The "millets" are "glutinous millet" [*shu* 黍] and "panicled millet" [*chi* 稷].) The second appears not to be a direct quote, but mimics the form of similar lines on spirits descending for sacrifice in the *Shih*, the *Shu*, and the *Tso chuan*.

[21] That is, sour, salty, pungent, bitter, and sweet.

[22] That is, blue-green, red, yellow, white, and black.

[23] The word is *shih* 室, which simply means "house." But by extension it means the "women of the house" (wives, concubines), and Hsi K'ang and Hsiang Hsiu seem to use it in a general sense, "women."

[24] Reading 勾 as 芍. *Shao-yao* 芍藥, the Chinese peony, is highly regarded as the perfect blend of the five flavors. See note 151 to "Music Has in it Neither Grief nor Joy."

[25] The models in antiquity of beauty and ugliness respectively. Hsi-shih 西施 was presented as a gift to the King of Wu from the King of Yueh (Kou-chien, c. 490 B.C.) for the purpose of distracting him. Mo-mu 嫫母 was an ugly but virtuous concubine of the Yellow Emperor (traditional reign dates, 2697–2597 B.C.).

A Refutation

will are pent-up and cannot move. To say this is "nourishing it with harmony"[26]—of this I've never heard.

You also say that "by guiding and nourishing and getting the principle we can exhaust the limits of our nature and fate, at the utmost reaching more than a thousand years, or in the least several hundred." This is not totally correct.[27] If it truly could be this way, then there must be those who have done it. Where are these people? My eyes have never seen them. I am afraid these are nothing but rumors; they can be talked about, but they cannot be found. Even if, on occasion, there are those who live long and become very old, these people "uniquely receive a special breath,"[28] just as in trees there are the pine and the cypress. This is not accomplished by "guiding and nourishing."

If the length of one's life is related to being skilled or clumsy, then the sages, who "thoroughly understood the principles and exhausted their natures,"[29] ought to have enjoyed very long lives. But of Yao, Shun, Yü, T'ang, Wen, Wu, [the Duke of] Chou, and Confucius,[30] the oldest lived to one hundred[31] while

---

[26] Hsi K'ang had said, of the one who is good at nourishing life, "Furthermore he maintains this state with the one, and nourishes it with harmony."

[27] These words occur in *Analects* 3:25 (p. 5), where Confucius says of the *Wu* 武 music that "it was perfectly beautiful but *not perfectly good*" (未盡善也). (Tr. by D. C. Lau, *Confucius: The Analects*, p. 71.) Hsiang Hsiu is perhaps anticipating the fact that he is about to talk about Confucius.

[28] Mimicking Hsi K'ang's words in the opening of his essay concerning the attainment of full immortality. I agree with Tai Ming-yang (p. 166) that the — here should be read as 異.

[29] Quoting from the *I ching, Shuo-kua* 1 (p. 49).

[30] For non-Sinologists reading this text, Yao 堯 is one of the legendary emperors of antiquity; his traditional reign dates are 2356–2255 B.C. Shun 舜 is another of these emperors—reign dates 2255–2205. Yü 禹 is regarded as the founder of China's first dynasty, the Hsia 夏, and ruled from 2205–2197. T'ang 湯 founded the Shang 商 in 1766 and ruled to 1753. Wen 文 and Wu 武 were father and son, the first two kings of the Chou 周, which they founded in 1122 B.C. And the Duke of Chou 周公 was a brother of King Wu, who served as regent of the throne when Wu died. The Duke of Chou's role in events at the beginning of the Chou is discussed below in the "Essay on Kuan and Ts'ai."

[31] Shun, Yü, and T'ang are all said to have lived one hundred years. King Wen died at 97; King Wu at 93. The Duke of Chou was 99. But Yao must have been over 100. *Shih chi* 1 (Vol. 1, p. 30) says he *ruled* for ninety years and lived another twenty-eight after turning the throne over to Shun, and one assumes he did not rule from birth!

A Refutation

the youngest died at seventy.³² Could it be that they, to the contrary, neglected to "guide and nourish"? Thus, the appointment given by Heaven has a limit; it simply is not something things can increase.

Moreover, what makes life a thing of joy is the relating to others with kindness and affection. The natural order and the abiding ways of man [are such that] things pleasant and agreeable please the mind, and honor and glory delight the will. We eat the rich flavors to give vent to the five feelings,³³ enjoy music and beauty to satisfy our natures and moods. This is the natural order, nature, that which is appropriate for man, and that which the three kings³⁴ did not change.

Now you abandon the ways of the sages and rely on "plot-planting," take leave of the things you love and reject what you enjoy, restraining your self and belaboring your mind, hoping to build up dust and dew and turn them into mountains and oceans—I am afraid the achievement lies beyond the limits of your life; truly, it cannot be hoped for. Even if you diligently seek it, you will accomplish very little. Thus, to look at your shadow and sit like a corpse³⁵ with rocks and trees as your neighbors is [a case of] the so-called "cauterizing yourself without being sick,"³⁶ silencing yourself without being sad, eating coarse foods while not in mourning, and imprisoning

---

[32] That would be Confucius, who died at 73. His dates are traditionally given as 551–479 B.C.

[33] Delight, anger, grief, joy, and hate.

[34] Probably here referring to Yü, T'ang, and Wen, founders of the Hsia, Shang, and Chou dynasties.

[35] "Sitting like a corpse" (*shih-chü* 尸居) is attributed to Lao Tan by Tzu-kung in *Chuang-tzu* 14 (p. 39, line 63). Watson (*The Complete Works of Chuang Tzu*, p. 163) translates the line as follows: "Tzu-kung said, 'Then is it true that the Perfect Man can command *corpse-like stillness* [italics added by present author] and dragon vision, the voice of thunder and the silence of deep pools; that he breaks forth into movement like Heaven and earth?'"

[36] Said by Confucius about himself when he foolishly tried to instruct Robber Chih and received a sermon himself instead. See *Chuang-tzu*, Ch. 29 (p. 82, line 56). Watson translates this passage in *The Complete Works of Chuang Tzu*, p. 311.

A Refutation

yourself while having no crime. When you pursue the empty and pray for good luck, the results do not match your efforts. To nourish life in this way—I have never heard it was fitting.

Therefore [Ssu-ma] Hsiang-ju said: "If one must be like this[37] to live long and not die, even though one lived ten thousand generations, it would not be worth delighting in."[38] His meaning was that these things go against our feelings and neglect human nature and are not grounded in the natural order. If one is unhappy [in this way] even living long, how much more [unhappy] will he be doing this and living only a short time?

If you have some clear evidence, then we will discuss it further.

---

[37] Agreeing with Tai Ming-yang that the passage needs a 此 after the 若. The 此 is in Ssu-ma Hsiang-ju's original.

[38] From Ssu-ma Hsiang-ju's 司馬相如 "Ta-jen fu" 大人賦 (Rhapsody on the Big Man). See his biography in *Shih chi* 117 (Vol. 9, p. 3060). When Ssu-ma Hsiang-ju says "be like this" he has in mind the "Queen Mother of the West" (西王母), whom he has just described as someone with snow white hair who wears a crown and lives in a cave and is served by a three-legged bird. Hsiang Hsiu is obviously using the "to be like this" to refer to the things Hsi K'ang is advocating—tranquillity, lessening of desires, doing away with meat, grains, and wine.

HSI K'ANG

An Answer to Hsiang Hsiu's Refutation of My Essay on Nourishing Life

(Ta Nan Yang-sheng lun)

::

I respond as follows:

The reason why we value intelligence and esteem activity is that they can benefit life and enrich our persons. But when desires are active, regret and remorse arise, and when intelligence operates, foreknowledge is established. When foreknowledge is established, the mind[1] is opened and things are pursued. When regret and remorse arise, anxieties build up and the body is in danger. With these two [foreknowledge and regret] if you are not hiding something on the inside, you are tied up with something on the out. All these can do is harm your health; they are not things that enrich your life.

Now craving and desire, although they come from man, are not things that are proper to the Way. It is like the fact that trees have grubs;[2] although they are produced by the tree they are not appropriate to it. Therefore when grubs abound the wood decays, and when desires win out the body withers. This being so, desires and life cannot together endure, and fame and your body cannot both be maintained. This can generally be known. And yet the world has never understood it. They [people of the world] treat following their desires as attaining life. Although they wish

---

[1] Reading the Wu variant 心 instead of 志.
[2] The *ho* 蝎 or the *tu* 蠹, according to Bernard Read, is specifically the cerambycid larva. See Read, *Chinese Materia Medica: Insect Drugs; Dragon and Snake Drugs; Fish Drugs* (Taipei: Southern Materials Center Inc., 1977 reprint), pp. 108–109 for a description and discussion.

Answer to the Refutation

to enrich[3] their lives they do not know the principle for producing life. Therefore, in their activity they move toward death.[4]

Therefore the ancients, knowing that wine and meat[5] are sweet poisons, rejected them as things to be abandoned, and recognizing fame and position as sweet smelling baits, left them and did not look back. They made activity sufficient to benefit life but not to overflow into things, and knowledge to rectify their persons but not to concern itself with things outside. They turned their backs on what harmed them and went after the beneficial. This is the way of using intelligence to complete one's life, and nourishing the one without end.[6] Therefore, what makes intelligence a thing of beauty is that it benefits life and does not go beyond that; what makes life valuable is that it delights in harmony and does not become entangled.[7] How can we hate intelligence and neglect the body, highly regard our desires and lightly regard our lives?

Moreover, [in the sayings about] the "sage treasuring position" and "considering wealth and rank to be lofty and exalted"[8]—I take these to refer to the fact that the rank of the

---

[3] Reading the Wu variant 厚 for 後.

[4] Quoting the *Lao-tzu*, Ch. 50 (part II, p. 9a). The line is difficult in the *Lao-tzu* and remains so here. I have generally followed Wing-tsit Chan's interpretation (see Chan, *The Way of Lao Tzu*, p. 188). Hsi K'ang picks up the Chinese that follows this but transposes it to the lines that precede. That is to say, *Lao-tzu* reads (Chan's translation): "... three out of ten [people] in their lives lead from activity to death. And for what reason? Because of man's intense striving after life (以其生生之厚)." Hsi K'ang here also speaks of their "wish to enrich their lives" (厚生之情) as well as the "principle for producing life" (生生之理).

[5] Or according to the Wu variant "women" (*se* 色).

[6] The Wu manuscript has four additional characters after "complete one's life" (遂生)—養一示盍. Lu Hsün (*Hsi K'ang chi*, p. 55) suggests that 示盍 should be read as 不盡, giving "nourishing the one without end." Tai Ming-yang (p. 170), however, feels that 養一 is an error for 而: thus he would read "the way of using intelligence to complete one's life and not end." I have followed Lu Hsün.

[7] Mocking the words of Hsiang Hsiu, who had said, "What makes life a joy is the relating to others (相接) with kindness and affection." Here life (but I wonder if it should not be *tung* 動, "action") is of value because it does not get us entangled (不交).

[8] See Hsiang Hsiu's essay and footnotes 5 and 6 to it. The sayings referred to are in the *I ching*.

Answer to the Refutation

ruler of men is Son of Heaven, and his wealth is his possession of all within the four seas.⁹ The people cannot exist without a lord; the lord cannot hold his position without respect. Therefore, it is for the sake of the empire that he respects the position of ruler; it is not for himself alone that he values wealth and rank.

You also have the quote "Wealth and rank are what men desire."¹⁰ But I think [this was said] because it was the end of an age,¹¹ when people hate poverty and low station and love wealth and rank. They [the disciples of Confucius] were not yet able to put glory and honor aside and rest content in poverty and low station. Moreover, he had to force them to follow his way and not oppose him. He could not make them compete with their strength so he allowed them to struggle with their minds.¹² Men of the right temperament could not be found, so he put up with their being impetuous and overly scrupulous.¹³

But this is merely talking about the vulgar.¹⁴ He did not say

---

⁹ See *Mencius* 5A:1 (p. 34).

¹⁰ Quoting Confucius. See note 11 to Hsiang Hsiu's essay.

¹¹ The "end of an age" (*chi-shih* 季世) is more properly the last years of a dynasty. In this case, with Confucius speaking, that would mean the declining years of the Chou. Hsi K'ang's language reflects that of Confucius, who had said: "Wealth and high station are what men desire, but unless I got them in the right way I would not remain in them. Poverty and low station are what men dislike, but even if I did not get them in the right way I would not try to escape from them." (Tr. by D. C. Lau, *Confucius: The Analects*, p. 72.)

¹² Hsi K'ang probably has in mind the words of music master K'uang 師曠, who in the *Tso chuan* (Duke Hsiang, 26th year: p. 309) says to Duke P'ing of Chin: "I am afraid the duke's house will be reduced low. The ministers *do not contend together with their minds, but quarrel with their strength* [italics added]; they do not make virtue their object, but strive to be [thought] excellent. When such selfish desires are rampant, can it escape being reduced low?" (Tr. by James Legge, *The Chinese Classics*, Vol. V, *The Ch'un Ts'ew, with the Tso Chuen* [London: Henry Froude, 1872], Part II, p. 523.) Although Confucius' disciples "contend with their minds" (心競), they are probably like the ministers of Chin (in the eyes of Hsi K'ang) in merely striving to be thought excellent. Perhaps he means to say that they contend *only* with their minds and do not put their whole effort into it.

¹³ In *Analects* 13:21 (p. 26) Confucius says (quoting D. C. Lau's translation, *Confucius: The Analects*, p. 122): "Having failed to find moderate men for associates, one would, if there were no alternative, have to turn to the undisciplined and the over-scrupulous."

¹⁴ Preferring the Wu manuscript reading of 此俗之談耳. The "vulgar" office-seekers contrast with the Perfect Man of the next line.

Answer to the Refutation

that the *Perfect Man* would crave wealth and rank. The Perfect Man oversees the empire only when he has no choice,[15] taking the ten thousand things as his mind.[16] He leaves alone[17] the manifold things and guides himself with the Way. He is one with the whole nation in being self-attained. Meditative and still, he takes having no affairs[18] as his occupation; peaceful and calm, he considers the empire to be his duty.[19] Although he occupies the position of ruler and provides for the ten thousand states, he is peaceful and quiet, like an ordinary officer receiving guests. Though he sets out the dragon banner and wears the embroidered imperial robes, he pays them no attention, as though he had on the commoner's cotton clothes. Therefore ruler and ministers forget each other above, and the people are content with their families below. How could it be that he merely exhorts the common people to venerate him, cutting into [the wealth of] the empire to benefit himself, and considering wealth and rank to be lofty and exalted, desires them in his heart?

Moreover, Tzu-wen was three times promoted to office but showed no sign of pleasure;[20] Liu [-hsia] Hui was three times dismissed and his expression did not become sad.[21] Why?

---

[15] A paraphrase of a line in *Chuang-tzu*, Ch. 11 (p. 26, line 13). Watson translates: "If the gentleman finds he has no other choice than to direct and look after the world, then the best course for him is inaction." (Watson, *The Complete Works of Chuang Tzu*, p. 116.)

[16] Reflecting the language of *Lao-tzu*, Ch. 49 (part II, p. 8a): "The Sage has no fixed (personal) ideas. He regards the people's ideas as his own." (Tr. by Wing-tsit Chan, *The Way of Lao Tzu*, p. 186.)

[17] *Tsai-yu* 在宥, the title of Chapter 11 of the *Chuang-tzu*.

[18] *Wu-shih* 無事, as in *Lao-tzu* 63. Wing-tsit Chan (*The Way of Lao Tzu*, p. 212) translates: "Act without action, Do without ado" (為無為, 事無事).

[19] Hsi K'ang is probably alluding to the words of Confucius in the "Li yün" 禮運 chapter of the *Li chi* (*Li chi hsün-tsuan*, 9.1a). Legge translates, "When the Grand course was pursued, a public and common spirit ruled all under the sky [天下為公]. (See James Legge, *The Li Ki*, in F. Max Müller, ed., *The Sacred Books of the East* [Oxford: Clarendon Press, 1885], Vol. 27, p. 364.)

[20] See *Analects* 5:19 (p. 8). D. C. Lau (*Confucius: The Analects*, p. 79) translates: "Ling Yin Tzu-wen gave no appearance of pleasure when he was made prime minister three times." Tzu-wen 子文 was an officer in Ch'u in the mid-seventh century B.C.

[21] *Analects* 18:2 (p. 37) has: "Liu Hsia Hui was dismissed three times when he was judge." (Tr. by D. C. Lau, *Confucius: The Analects*, p. 149.) Liu-hsia Hui 柳下惠 was an official in Lu in the late seventh century B.C.

Answer to the Refutation

Because the honor of being prime minister is not like the honor of being virtuous and moral, and the disgrace of three dismissals does no harm to the beauty of harmony and purity. These two men, once having found wealth and rank in themselves, never let nobility conferred by men shackle their minds. Thus they looked on glory and disgrace as one. Speaking from this perspective, how can you say that desire for wealth and rank is the [natural] feeling of man?[22]

May I ask why you do not parade your brocaded tops and embroidered bottoms in rooms where you will not be seen?[23] Why must you care about what the masses [think] and act as though praise and slander meant happiness and grief? If you are like this, then when you want it you will worry about getting it, and having gotten it you will be afraid of losing it. "If you are worried about losing it, there are no lengths to which you will not go."[24] How will superiors not become arrogant, and maintain things at their peak without going to excess? How will those who seek it be able to avoid doing things improper?[25] Once you get it, how can you keep from losing it?

Moreover, "When the Gentleman speaks, if his words are

---

[22] Emending the text in accord with Tai Ming-yang's suggestion, making *chih ch'ing, jen chih ch'ing* 人之情. Hsiang Hsiu had said, "Wealth and rank are what everyone in the world wants" (富貴, 天地之情也).

[23] There seems to be a *ho* 何, "why," missing from this sentence, though I have translated as though it were there. My guess would be that it occurs at the end of the line and was mistakenly omitted by a copyist as duplication since the next line also begins with a *ho*.

[24] Quoting Confucius in *Analects* 17:13 (p. 36). The whole reads: "The Master said, 'Is it really possible to work side by side with a mean fellow in the service of a lord? Before he gets what he wants, he worries lest he should not get it. After he has got it, he worries lest he should lose it, and when that happens he will not stop at anything.'" (Tr. by D. C. Lau as 17:15 in *Confucius: The Analects*, p. 146.)

[25] All alluding to remarks by Hsiang Hsiu. He had said, himself alluding first to a passage in the *Analects* and then to the *Hsiao ching*, that "Wealth and rank are what men desire, but they must seek for them in accord with morality and the right. Those above suffer no harm because they do not become arrogant; they maintain things at their peak but through reduction and frugality do not go to excess." See his essay and notes 11 and 12.

Answer to the Refutation

good [people] will respond to them from beyond a thousand li."[26] How could he worry about going against the crowd[27] and desire to attain high rank? Maintaining the law and according with principle, he is unobstructed by worldly nets. He respects himself for being free of fault and considers not serving to be a life of ease. He lets his mind wander on virtue and morality, and rests himself in his humble abode. His peacefulness and contentment are undisturbed, and his spirit and breath flow even. How can it be that one is only noble if he first has glory and honor?

We plow and make food, cultivate silkworms and make clothes.[28] When we have clothes and food [sufficient] to take care of our lives, then we regard the riches of the world as surplus. It is like someone thirsty drinking from a river. He is content when his thirst is slaked; he does not greedily desire [to drink] the whole stream.[29] How can it be that one is only wealthy if he first gathers and accumulates [goods]?

The Gentleman is attentive in the following way. He sees fame and position as tumors and swellings,[30] goods and riches as dirt and filth. What use has he for wealth and rank? Thus the thing that is [truly] difficult to attain in this world is not riches, and it is not glory. It is simply to be concerned that your mind is not content. One whose mind is content, though he plough and till in

---

[26] A quote from the *I ching*, *Hsi-tz'u* A.6 (p. 41).

[27] Preferring the Wu reading, which is 豈患於多犯, to the Huang text 豈在於多.

[28] This is very similar to the words we find in the *Mo-tzu*, Ch. 49, "Lu wen" 魯問 (p. 90, line 49): "... the achievement of one who feeds the starving without plowing and clothes the cold without weaving is superior to the one who 'plows and feeds them' and 'weaves and clothes them.'" Angus Graham has shown that "to plow and eat and weave and have clothes" was a slogan of the *Nung-chia*, the "School of Tillers" in ancient China. See his "The *Nung-chia* 農家 'School of the Tillers' and the Origins of Peasant Utopianism in China," *Bulletin of the School of Oriental and African Studies*, XLII: 1 (1979), pp. 66–100.

[29] Hsi K'ang surely has in mind here the words of Chuang-tzu in Ch. 1 (p. 2, line 25). Watson (*The Complete Works of Chuang Tzu*, p. 32) translates: "When the mole drinks at the river, he takes no more than a bellyfull." These are the words of the recluse Hsü Yu 許由, by the way, declining the empire just offered to him by Yao.

[30] I.e., superfluous growths.

Answer to the Refutation

the fields, wear coarse clothes and eat cooked beans, how could he not be self-attained? But one who is not content, though he be nourished by everything in the whole world, and put in charge of the ten thousand things, he would still not be satisfied.

This being so, then one who is content needs nothing outside himself, and one who is not content has nothing outside himself that he does not need. Since there is nothing he does not need, there is no place he can go and not be lacking something; and since [in the other case] there is nothing he needs, there is no place he can go and not be content. He does not for glory and honor unleash his will; nor does he, because he is poor and unknown, go running after the vulgar. Blending in is he! Going forth together with the ten thousand things, he can be neither favored nor disgraced. This is to truly have wealth and rank. Therefore, those who neglect [true] nobility and desire [only] rank will end up in mean position; those who forget [true] wealth and desire [only] riches will end up impoverished. This is the way the principle works. If you sit in your glory and honor but are beset with anxieties, then even though you might grow old together with your glory and honor, they will also be the cause of great distress to the end of your days. Therefore Lao-tzu said: "There is no greater joy than being free from anxiety: there is no greater wealth than being content."[31] This is what he meant.

In your "Refutation" you say: "When a man is aroused he thinks of women; when hungry he searches for food. These are principles of nature." True indeed are these words! I would not have him not indulge in sexual relations and not eat. I simply wish to see sex and eating done in accord with reason. Desire [that arises] without calculating forethought is a movement[32] of

---

[31] Not exactly. At least these lines do not occur in the present text of *Lao-tzu*. He does say in Chapter 33, "He who is contented is rich." (Tr. by Wing-tsit Chan, *The Way of Lao Tzu*, p. 159.) He also says in Chapter 46, "There is no greater calamity than discontentment." (Translated by Chan, *The Way of Lao Tzu*, p. 181.)

[32] Reading the Wu variant 動 for 勛.

Answer to the Refutation

one's nature. But to become aware of something and then be moved is a function of the intelligence. With the movement of one's nature, [the desire] is equal to the thing encountered, and when it is satisfied there is nothing that remains. But with the functioning of the intelligence, one seeks [satisfaction] in accord with the [level] of arousal, and though exhausted he is unable to stop. Thus the problems of the world and the causes of disaster are always to be found in the functioning of intelligence, not in the stirrings of one's nature.

Now if you have a blind man meet a woman, he will feel the same if it is Hsi-shih or Mo-mu. And for someone with no sense of taste,[33] distillers' grains and polished rice will be equally delicious. Why must you recognize the distinctions of talented and stupid, beautiful and ugly, and throw the mind into confusion with love and hate?

The Gentleman knows that intelligence, because it is inconstant, harms life, and desires injure the nature because they pursue things. Thus if his intelligence [starts to] function, he pulls it back in with tranquillity, and if desires[34] stir he gathers them up with harmony. He causes intelligence to rest[35] in tranquillity and his nature to remain content with harmony. Then his spirit is purified by silence, and his body perfected by harmony. He gets rid of all ties and eliminates the harmful and "is born again with the other."[36] This is the so-called "not seeing the desirable keeps the heart from being disturbed."[37]

---

[33] The word is *k'uei* 瞶 which means someone who is deaf. But that cannot be Hsi K'ang's meaning.
[34] Following the Wu variant of 欲 for 性.
[35] Reading the variant 止 for 上.
[36] These words come from Chapter 19 of the *Chuang-tzu* (p. 48, line 5). Watson (*The Complete Works of Chuang Tzu*, p. 197) translates: "He who wants to avoid doing anything for his body had best abandon the world. By abandoning the world, he can be without entanglements. Being without entanglements, he can be upright and calm. Being upright and calm, he can be born again with others. Being born again, he can come close [to the Way]." The context here is that nourishing the body alone is not enough to preserve life.
[37] Quoting *Lao-tzu*, Chapter 3 (part I, p. 2b).

Answer to the Refutation

Even if rich flavors have already infected your mouth and if music and beauty have worked their way into your mind, you can still expel them with perfect reason and overcome them with much calculation. How can I explain it? One who wishes to become an official pays no mind to the position of ruler; one who longs for a woman does not consider relations and kin. Why? When we know[38] that something is impossible, we never give it a thought. Therefore, those who are given to drinking restrain themselves when it is poisoned wine, and gluttons put up with hunger when the meat is spoiled. They understand the principles of good and bad fortune, and therefore they refuse these things without hesitation and reject them without any doubt. How would they regret being deprived[39] of a tasty sip or a big bite?

Moreover, of the two concubines at the inn, the ugly one was given the position of honor because she knew that she was ugly, while the beautiful one had lowly rank because she saw herself as beautiful.[40] Beauty and ugliness can be seen with the eyes, but honor and baseness are not the same. [In this case] their feelings, right and wrong, were first made clear, and therefore their beauty and ugliness could not affect [this judgment]. If[41] reason is sufficient on the inside, and we make use of the one to deal with things outside, how can anything remain hidden? To speak from this perspective, when nature and breath are self-harmonized, there is nothing being "distressed by being blocked"; and when

---

[38] Preferring 知 to 止.
[39] Omitting the 向 along with the Wu manuscript.
[40] For this story see the end of Chapter 20 in the *Chuang-tzu* (p. 54, lines 68–70). Watson (*The Complete Works of Chuang Tzu*, p. 220) translates: "Yang Tzu, on his way to Sung, stopped for the night at an inn. The innkeeper had two concubines, one beautiful, the other ugly. But the ugly one was treated as a lady of rank, while the beautiful one was treated as a menial. When Yang Tzu asked the reason, a young boy of the inn replied, 'The beautiful one is only too aware of her beauty, and so we do not think of her as beautiful. The ugly one is only too aware of her ugliness, and so we do not think of her as ugly.'"
[41] *Yün* 云, "to say" follows "If" in the text. The sentence reads better without it.

Answer to the Refutation

feelings and will are self-calmed, they are not "pent-up and unable to move."[42]

The many entanglements of the world come from simply not seeing things clearly. To come to[43] the feelings of common people, with regard to things that are distant, there are none who do not disregard them even if they are great, and with what is close by, there are none who do not maintain them even if they are small [in significance]. What is the reason for this? Truly it is because what is near and what is far are mutually exclusive, and people have different feelings about what they [only] know and what they [actually] see. To not have sexual relations with wife or concubine during the three-year period of mourning is a prohibition of the Rites. No one ever goes against this. But wine and women are the enemies of the body, yet none is able to reject them. To speak from this perspective, prohibitions of the Rites are near at hand, and even though insignificant they are not opposed; but the enemies of the body are far away, so even though great they are not rejected.[44] But if someone could with his left hand take possession of a map of the world[45] [only if] he subsequently had to harm himself with his right, even a fool would not do it, which clearly shows that the world is less important than one's life.[46] That wine and women are less important than the world can also be understood. But people of the world sacrifice their lives for them and die without regret. This is to use [up] what is important while treating the insignificant as essential.[47] Can there be any other reason [for this] than

---

[42] Both quotes refer back to the words of Hsiang Hsiu.

[43] Reading the 及 of the Wu text in place of 又.

[44] The "near" (chiao 交) and "distant" (she 賒) in these lines are added in the Wu text.

[45] And thereby, I suppose, take possession of the world itself.

[46] An illustration and argument used earlier in the Huai-nan-tzu. See the chapter "Ching-shen hsün" 精神訓, 7.10a.

[47] Borrowing the language used in Chuang-tzu, Ch. 28 (p. 77, line 30). Watson translates: "The accomplishments of emperors and kings are superfluous affairs as far as the sage is concerned, not the means by which to keep the body whole and to care for life. Yet now many gentlemen of the vulgar world today endanger

Answer to the Refutation

that they turn their backs on the far away and chase after the near at hand?

But one who is wise is not like this. He acts only after careful examination of what is important and what is not; he weighs gain and loss in order to take his stand. The principles controlling near and far are the same. Therefore, he prepares for the distant as though it were close by. He takes precautions against the unseen as though it were manifest. Alone he walks through "the gate of manifold mysteries."[48] Therefore from beginning to end he has no fear. What a difference there is between this man and the one who indulges his desires and pleases his mind!

In your "Refutation" you say that "[since] the sages thoroughly understood the principles and exhausted their natures, they ought to have enjoyed very long lives. But from Yao to Confucius, the oldest lived to one hundred while the youngest died at seventy. Could it be that they, to the contrary, neglected to guide and nourish?" According to my view, Yao and Confucius [etc.] had destinies that were limited.[49] Therefore they guided and nourished to exhaust their years. This, then, was brought about by their thorough understanding of the principles—it is not that they [only] lived for a hundred years because they did not nourish their lives.

Moreover, Confucius thoroughly understood the principles and exhausted the limits of his nature in order to live to seventy, while among farmers, who because of the "six faults"[50] are

---

themselves and throw away their lives in the pursuit of mere things." Then "Now suppose there were a man here who took the priceless pearl of the Marquis of Sui and used it as a pellet to shoot a sparrow a thousand yards up in the air—the world would certainly laugh at him. Why? Because that which he is using is of such great value, and that which he is trying to acquire is so trifling." (Watson, *The Complete Works of Chuang Tzu*, p. 313.)

[48] *Chung-miao chih men* 眾妙之門, from *Lao-tzu*, Chapter 1 (part I, 1b).

[49] Or perhaps "Even though it was Yao and Confucius their destinies were limited." The Chinese is awkward.

[50] The "six faults" (*liu-pi* 六弊) are defined by Confucius in *Analects* 17:7 (pp. 35–36). In D. C. Lau's translation (*Confucius: The Analects*, 17:8, pp. 144–145) these come out as foolishness, deviation from the right path, harmful behavior, intolerance, insubordination, and indiscipline.

Answer to the Refutation

stupid and dumb, there are those who live to one hundred and twenty. If the perfect excellence of Confucius can rely on the perfect stupidity of the farmer, then why is the notion of living a thousand years [so] strange?

Moreover, among the sages there were those who injured themselves for the sake of the world. They showed off their actions and made known their achievements, making the whole world long to be with them, and [though] they moved three times, [each time their residence] turned into a city.[51] Others ate coarse fare and wore out their bodies managing the four quarters. Their minds were wearied and their forms fatigued, but they hastened on losing all sense of decorum.[52] Others developed surprise tactics and hidden schemes[53] which eventually led to armed conflict. With awesome might they slaughtered and punished, struggling for profit and glory.[54] Others "cultivated themselves to enlighten the impure" and "showed off their wisdom to astound the ignorant."[55] On the basis of their fame they stood above the entire age and were taken as the standard by the world. And they were diligent in teaching and skilled in leading, and assembled three thousand disciples. Their mouths were exhausted by discussion and debate; their bodies fatigued, bent over like musical stones [from polite bowing]. Their appearance

---

[51] Referring to Shun. See *Chuang-tzu*, Chapter 24 (p. 68, lines 92–95). Watson (*The Complete Works of Chuang Tzu*, p. 276) translates: "What I call the bent-with-burdens are those like Shun.... Shun must have done rank deeds for the hundred clans to have delighted in him so. Therefore, though he changed his residence three times, each place he lived in turned into a city.... When Shun was raised up from the barren plains, he was already well along in years and his hearing and eyesight were failing, and yet he was not able to go home and rest."

[52] All of this refers to Yü. That he ate "coarse fare" (*fei* 菲) is said by Confucius in *Analects* 8:21 (p. 15). That he was always in a hurry in doing his work of setting out the courses for China's rivers is well known. For example, Mencius (in III.A.4: p. 20) points out that "During this time [when he was clearing out the courses for the rivers] Yü spent eight years abroad and passed the door of his own house three times without entering." (Tr. by D. C. Lau, *Mencius* [London and Baltimore: Penguin Books, 1970], p. 102.)

[53] Reading the Wu variant 遘 in place of 稱, and then reading it as 構.

[54] All referring to the respective founders of the Shang and Chou dynasties—T'ang, and Wen and Wu.

[55] Quotes from the *Chuang-tzu* (Chapter 20: p. 52, line 32) on Confucius. The following all refers to Confucius.

Answer to the Refutation

was of someone trying to save the youth, but "in their eyes it is as though they were planning to run the whole land."[56] Their spirits chased about between the extremes of profit and harm; their minds galloped down the road of glory and disgrace. In the time it takes to look up and look down they had already twice made the rounds beyond the boundaries of space.[57]

If we compare these [the things done by these sages] with the inner examination and introspective listening,[58] with being stingy with one's breath and grudging with one's essence, with "clear understanding of all that there is"[59] which yet does not grasp and not act, with leaving the world behind and sitting in forgetfulness[60] so as to treasure one's nature and keep intact the real—I cannot see these as the same.

Now I am not saying that the cypress and the pine are not different from the willow and the elm. But in the growing of a cypress or pine, each must be planted well to realize the full possibilities of its nature. If you raise a pine in rich fertile soil, it will wither and fall in the middle of its years. But if you plant it [up high] on a multi-layered cliff, it will flourish and thrive and be each day renewed. This is one aspect of nurturing the form.

---

[56] Again something said explicitly about Confucius in the *Chuang-tzu*. In Chapter 26 (p. 74, lines 18–20) of the *Chuang-tzu* we find: "A disciple of Lao Lai-tzu was out gathering firewood when he happened to meet Confucius. He returned and reported, 'There's a man over there with a long body and short legs, his back a little humped and his ears set way back, who looks as though he were trying to attend to everything within the four seas. I don't know who it can be.'" (Tr. by Watson, *The Complete Works of Chuang Tzu*, p. 297.)

[57] Also reflecting a passage in *Chuang-tzu*. In Chapter 11 (p. 26, line 18), Lao Tan says of the mind: "Its swiftness [is] such that, in the time it takes to lift and lower the head, it has twice swept over the four seas and beyond." (Tr. by Watson, *The Complete Works of Chuang Tzu*, p. 116.)

[58] Explained as the kind of seeing and hearing you would do—getting to know yourself—if you were blind and deaf.

[59] *Ming-pai ssu-ta* 明白四達, from Chapter 10 of the *Lao-tzu* (part I, p. 5b).

[60] *Tso-wang* 坐忘, familiar to us from *Chuang-tzu*, Chapter 6 (p. 19, lines 92–93). Watson (*The Complete Works of Chuang Tzu*, p. 90) translates: "Yen Hui said, 'I smash up my limbs and body, drive out perception and intellect, cast off form, do away with understanding, and make myself identical with the Great Thoroughfare. This is what I mean by sitting down and forgetting everything.'"

Answer to the Refutation

Tou Kung ate none of the drugs but lived to one hundred and eighty. Was it not because he played the lute and pacified his mind?[61] This is also a piece of evidence[62] on nourishing the spirit.

If you heat silkworms they will [mature] in eighteen days; if you keep them cool they will take over thirty.[63] When the destiny that [you say] cannot be exceeded is nourished, things can flourish over twice as long. Things that are warm and fat come to an early end; those that are cool and thin retard their demise. This can definitely be known.

Stabled horses that are cared for but not ridden can all be used for sixty years.[64] Those whose bodies are exhausted fade quickly; those who keep themselves in good health are difficult to wear out.[65] This can also be known.

Wealth and rank mean much injury; the things that attack you are many. Rustics enjoy great age; the things that can harm them are few. This can also be seen.

When you can make your eyes see what the blind man sees and your mouth taste what the man without taste tastes, and keep at a distance the things that harm life while controlling the things that benefit your nature—then we can begin to talk together about the business of nourishing life.

Your "Refutation" says "Shen Nung introduced the first use of grains, and birds and beasts by means of them fly and run,

---

[61] On Tou Kung 竇公 see Huan T'an's 桓譚 *Hsin lun* 新論 11b. He was a musician in the court of Wen-ti of the Han (r. 179–156 B.C.) and was one hundred and eighty years old at the time. Wen-ti found that a bit odd and asked him what he had eaten (in the way of Taoist life-prolonging drugs) to live so long. But Tou Kung attributed his long life to playing the lute from the age of thirteen.

[62] Reading the Wu variant 徵 instead of 徼.

[63] Tai Ming-yang (p. 180) explains that silkworms are warmed so they will mature quicker—i.e., start spinning their cocoons—and eat less.

[64] Possibly alluding to a story in Huan T'an's *Hsin lun* (p. 26a) concerning ten horses that were to accompany Queen Yüan of Wei to the grave. They were well cared for and not ridden and lived to sixty.

[65] Reading the Wu variant 弊 for 斃. Otherwise it reads "difficult to kill" or "die only with difficulty."

Answer to the Refutation

while living people by means of them see and breathe." Now I am not saying that the five grains are not what Shen Nung introduced. The reason why, having discussed the Superior Drugs, he also introduced the five grains, is that the Superior Drugs are rare and few, and they are difficult to obtain even working hard, while the five grains are easy to plant, and by being cultivated they can last a long time. They benefit the common people and carry on the work of Heaven,[66] and therefore he [Shen Nung] maintained them along with [the Superior Drugs]. But only the worthy set their minds on the great; the unworthy simply go after the small.[67] Both of these [the five grains and the various kinds of drugs] come from one man. [And yet] when it comes to angelica,[68] which stops pain, you would use it without end. And ploughing to open up new lands—this you would continue and not stop. Why, when you come to[69] [the things that] "nourish destiny" [the Superior Drugs] do you disregard them and not discuss them?[70] This, I am afraid, is simply to enjoy that with which you are already familiar while regarding as strange what you do not yet understand.

Moreover, in plains and fields we find such things as dates and chestnuts; in ponds and swamps there are water chestnuts and chicken's heads.[71] Although they are not Superior Drugs, they

---

[66] Following the Wu reading of 繼天 for 繼天閒.

[67] A take-off on the words of Tzu-kung in *Analects* 19:22 (p. 40). D. C. Lau (*Confucius: The Analects*, p. 156) translates: "There is no man who does not have something of the way of Wen and Wu in him. Superior men have got hold of what is of major significance while inferior men have got hold of what is of minor significance."

[68] *Tang-kuei* 當歸, for which Read (*Chinese Medicinal Plants*, p. 54, item 210) has *A. sinensis* (Chinese angelica). The roots are used for medicine. *Tang-kuei* is classed in the *Shen Nung pen-ts'ao ching* (2.1a) as a "Middle Drug," one that "nourishes one's nature."

[69] Following the Wu text which adds a 至 at this point.

[70] Remember that the first section of the *Shen Nung pen-ts'ao ching* is devoted to the "Superior Drugs," which are said to "nourish destiny." (See p. 1a in the *Shen Nung pen-ts'ao ching*.)

[71] "Chicken's head" is *ch'ien* 芡, also called "foxnut"—Euryale ferox—according to Read (*Chinese Medicinal Plants*, p. 173, item 541). It resembles the water lily, and its seeds are used for food and medicine.

Answer to the Refutation

are still more deeply respected than the various varieties of millet.[72] As the means for supporting life, how could it be that he [Shen Nung] only established the five grains?[73]

You also say "It's only the millets that are fragrant: these bring down the spirits of Heaven and Earth." Pepperwort,[74] beech wormwood,[75] and mare's tail[76] are no match for sumptuous dishes; and pond water and rain water from the roadsides are no competition for the rich, twice-fermented wine. But when they were presented in the ancestral temple they moved the spirits to send down blessings.[77] From this we know that what the spirits enjoy is virtue and sincerity;[78] they do not need food-offerings to live. It is just like when the [leaders of] the nine divisions of the empire appeared at court to report on the performance of their duties, each presented goods from his region simply to verify his sincerity.

You also say, "When meats and grain are taken into the body, within ten days they will fatten you up, which testifies that they are things proper for life." In point of fact, these are things that

---

[72] The sentence is corrupt. It reads 猶於黍稷之篤恭也. Some texts mark a lacuna after the *yu* 猶, a lacuna for which several variants exist including 愈 and 勝. My feeling is that there is a character missing after the *chih* 之, a character corresponding to the "such things as" (*shu* 屬, and *lei* 類) in the two parallel phrases that precede.

[73] Following the syntactical arrangement of the Wu text.

[74] *P'in* 蘋 is commonly translated "duckweed." Read (*Chinese Medicinal Plants*, p. 273, item 807) identifies it as pepperwort.

[75] For *fan* 蘩 see Read, *Chinese Medicinal Plants*, p. 2, item 8. This is also known as "white artemisia" (*pai-hao* 白蒿), and is "white southernwood" in note 77 below.

[76] *Wen-tsao* 蕰藻 (also 薀藻) is an aquatic plant fed to goldfish; Legge makes it "pond-weed" in the note that follows.

[77] Hsi K'ang comes back to Hsiang Hsiu's allusion to the *Tso chuan* with an allusion of his own to that work. In the *Tso chuan*, (Duke Yin, 3rd year: p. 7) we find: "Where there are intelligence and sincerity, what is grown by streams in the valleys, by ponds, and in pools, the gatherings of duck-weed, white southernwood, and pond-weed, in baskets round and square, and cooked in pans and pots with the water from standing pools and road hollows, may be presented to the spirits, and set before kings and dukes." (Tr. by Legge, *The Chinese Classics*, Vol. V, Part I, p. 13.)

[78] Hsi K'ang here underscores Hsiang Hsiu's faulty allusion. See note 20 to Hsiang Hsiu's "Refutation."

Answer to the Refutation

encumber the body. Now I am not saying that meats and grains are of no benefit when it comes to fattening up the body; I simply mean that in terms of lengthening your life, they are no match for the Superior Drugs. Let me avail myself [of your argument] and use it to refute you. Everyone knows that wheat is better than pulse and rice superior to millet. We know it because of the effects. If there were a land which did not have rice and millet, [its inhabitants] would certainly regard wheat and pulse as delicious and nourishing and say that nothing could be better.[79] Thus, that the people of the world do not know that the Superior Drugs are better than rice and millet is like their maintaining that pulse and wheat are superior to garden daisies[80] and insisting that the world is devoid of rice and millet. If you can count on the drugs to make you eternal, then the lowly status of rice and millet can easily be known. The Gentleman knows it is like this. Therefore he makes his standard that which accords with the principle of his nature and relies on the profound things to nourish his body. He plants his mysterious roots in Beginning Nine,[81] and inhales the pink clouds of morning[82] to aid his spirit.

If you feel that spring wine leads to old age, [I must object that] I have never heard of any yellow-haired old men in Kao-yang.[83] If you feel it is good to be stuffed and contented, [I must object that] I have never heard of any one hundred year old guests

---

[79] The argument is a bit awkward. From what precedes one would expect him to say that this land lacks rice and wheat and treasures pulse and millet.

[80] *P'eng-hao* 蓬蒿 is Chrysanthemum coronarium, or garden daisy, according to Read (*Chinese Medicinal Plants*, p. 6, item 23).

[81] "Beginning Nine" (*ch'u-chiu* 初九) means a strong, Yang line (whose number is nine) in the first position of an *I ching* hexagram. "Beginning Nine" is here another way of saying Yang.

[82] Also filled with Yang.

[83] Following the Wu text in reading 春酒, "spring wine" in place of 肴酒, "meat and wine." This apparently alludes to Li I-ch'i's 酈食其 remarks in *Shih chi* 97 (Vol. 8, p. 2704), to the effect that he was an "alcoholic from Kao-yang" (高陽酒徒). Kao-yang was a county seat in Ch'en-liu 陳留 (in present-day Honan, east of Loyang).

Answer to the Refutation

among those who eat from cauldrons [the nobles]. Moreover, Mr. Jan was ill as a child, and Master Yen was cut-off short.[84] In years of plenty there is much disease; in years of famine few are ill. Therefore when the Ti barbarians eat rice they develop blotchy skin;[85] when people with wounds[86] eat grains their blood starts to flow; when horses feed on millet their hooves become heavy; and when wild geese nibble grains [of rice, millet, etc.] they become unable to fly.[87] To speak in accord with this, birds and beasts do not sufficiently [show] that we are "rewarded" with the five grains, and living people do not sufficiently [prove] that we receive "blessings" from the fields.[88] And yet people exhaust their strength managing them and kill themselves fighting over them. For caring for their parents or presentation to those respected, only[89] pepper and chrysanthemum [wines?], Indian rice and spiked millet will do.[90] For their guest parties and lavish feasts, they must have[91] elegant dishes and the finest wines. They do not know these are all

---

[84] Referring to the two disciples of Confucius, Jan Keng 冉耕 and Yen Hui 顏回. On Jan Keng (also known as Po-niu 伯牛) see *Analects* 6:10 (p. 10). Confucius, visiting Po-niu, who was ill, said "We are going to lose him. It must be Destiny. Why else should such a man be stricken with such a disease?" (Tr. by D. C. Lau, *Confucius: The Analects*, p. 82) Yen Hui was, of course, the favorite of Confucius, and did indeed die young. See, for example, *Analects* 6:3 (p. 10) where Confucius says, "There was one Yen Hui who was eager to learn.... Unfortunately his allotted span was a short one and he died." (Tr. by D. C. Lau, *Confucius: The Analects*, p. 81.)

[85] *Lai* 癩, possibly leprosy, but also scabs or ringworm.

[86] Reading the Wu variant 創 in place of 瘡, "ulcers."

[87] On horses and geese we find the following remarks in the *Po-wu chih* 博物志: "When horses eat grains their hooves become heavy and they can't run; when wild geese nibble grains their wings become heavy and they can't fly." (*Po-wu chih*, p. 2.2a.)

[88] Remember that Hsiang Hsiu had said: "Birds and beasts by means of them [the grains] fly and run; living people by means of them see and breathe [live]."

[89] Following the Wu text in adding the 唯. But the meaning is much the same without it.

[90] Following the reading in the Wen-chin 文津 text: 椒菊苽粱. For the identification of 苽 as "Indian rice," see Read, *Chinese Medicinal Plants*, p. 258, item 766—*ku* 苽.

[91] Again following the Wu text in adding the 唯.

Answer to the Refutation

dissolving their muscles and fluids,[92] facilitating their destruction and hastening their decay. Although at first they are tasty and fragrant, when they enter the body, they stink and rot.[93] They exhaust and defile essence and spirit, stain and pollute the six bowels,[94] rot and contaminate breath and vapor, and spontaneously give rise to the killing worms.[95] It is these that support gluttony and debauchery, and on these rely the one hundred diseases. Those who taste them lose their sense of taste; those who eat them shorten their blessings.

How could these compare to [the waters of] a flowing fountain or a sweet spring, the agate stamens and flowers of jade,[96] the red

---

[92] The Wu character is *yeh* 液, "vital fluids." The Huang text has 腋, "armpits."

[93] Preferring the variant 宿 to 處.

[94] Stomach, gall bladder, large and small intestines, and the *san-chiao* 三瞧 — the esophagus, interior section of the stomach, and urethra.

[95] Probably referring to the "Three Worms" (*san-ch'ung* 三蟲—but here the word is *tu* 蠱) which inhabit the three vital centers of the body—the "Three Fields of Cinnabar" (*tan-t'ien* 丹田), in the abdomen, the chest, and the head. If these worms do their work, one dies, and they unfortunately thrive on the five grains. On the "Three Worms" see Henri Maspero, "Essai sur le Taoïsme aux premiers siècles de l'ère Chrétienne," in *Le Taoïsme et les Religions Chinoises*, pp. 366–367. In English see Holmes Welch, *Taoism: The Parting of the Way* (Boston: Beacon Press, 1957), p. 108.

[96] "Agate" (*ch'iung* 瓊) and "jade" (*yü* 玉) are the foods of the poet Ch'ü Yüan on his travels, especially when he goes to K'un-lun 崑崙, the mountains of paradise in the West. They also figure in various recipes for the elixir of immortality. Tai Ming-yang (p. 184) notes that "agate stamens" (*ch'iung-jui* 蕊) are mentioned in a line of the "Li Sao" 離騷 (Encountering Sorrow) in the *Ch'u Tz'u*—"I piled up agate stamens to use as my provisions." I do not find this line in the present "Li Sao," and assume it does not occur there, unless I have made an oversight. The closest thing I find are the lines that Hawkes (David Hawkes, *Ch'u Tz'u: The Songs of the South* [Boston: Beacon Press, 1959], p. 33) translates: "I broke a branch of jasper [agate] to take for my meat, And ground fine jasper meal for my journey's provisions." (For the text see *Ch'u Tz'u chu pa-chung* 楚辭注八種 [Taipei: Shih-chieh, 1965], p. 24). "Flowers of Jade" (*yü-ying* 英) are mentioned in a line in "She chiang" 涉江 (Crossing the River) in the "Chiu chang" 九章 of *Ch'u Tz'u* (see *Ch'u Tz'u chu pa-chung*, p. 75.) Hawkes (*Ch'u Tz'u*, p. 63) translates: "[I] Climbed up K'un-lun and ate the flowers of jade, And won long life, lasting as heaven and earth."

Answer to the Refutation

sulphur[97] and stone mushrooms,[98] the purple fungus,[99] and yellow essence?[100] In all of these are a host of spiritual properties, and they contain many beautiful things. They issue forth by themselves[101] and mysteriously grow; their pure fragrance dissipates only with difficulty; and they are filled to overflowing with harmonious vapors. They bathe and cleanse the five viscera,[102] dredge out and enlighten. One who swallows them [feels] his body become light. Moreover, they soften your skeleton and ease your breath, make flexible your bones and pliable your muscles. They wash away all dirt and dispel[103] all filth, and your will mounts up to the blue clouds. If one can go on from this, why would he nourish himself with the five grains?

Moreover, "When the boll-worm has its young, the solitary

---

[97] Following the Wu text, which has *liu-tan* 留丹, though the *chin tan* (gold and cinnabar, or gold elixir) of other editions makes good sense as well. If we read 留丹 as 流丹—or 硫丹—we can find it mentioned in the *Pao-p'u-tzu* 抱朴子 ("Hsien yao" 仙藥 chapter; in "nei p'ien" 内篇, 11.3a) as "shih-liu tan" 石流丹, a variety of sulphur (*shih-liu huang* 黃). Read (*Chinese Materia Medica: Turtle and Shellfish Drugs; Avian Drugs; A Compendium of Minerals and Stones* [Taipei: Southern Materials Center, Inc., 1977, reprint]) does not list *shih-liu tan*, but he does have (p. 71) a *shih-liu ch'ih* 赤 ("red sulphur") which is used to make cinnabar.

[98] For "stone mushrooms" (*shih chün* 石菌), Tai Ming-yang (p. 184) cites the note of Hsüeh Tsung 薛綜 to Chang Heng's 張衡 "Rhapsody on the Western Capital" (*Hsi-ching fu*), where "stone mushrooms" are mentioned together with the aforementioned "magic fungus" (靈芝): "Stone mushrooms and magic fungus are both found on the isles of the divine in the middle of the ocean. They are divine plants; things the immortals eat."

[99] "Purple fungus" (*tzu-chih* 紫芝) is identified as Ganoderma in Shiu-ying Hu's *An Enumeration of Chinese Materia Medica* (Hong Kong: The Chinese University Press, 1980), p. 151. The *Shen Nung pen-ts'ao ching* (1.23a) has the following to say about it: "It protects the body, benefits essence and breath, strengthens muscles and bones, and improves your complexion. If you eat it for a long time, your body becomes light, you do not age, and it lengthens your years."

[100] *Huang-ching* 黃精 ("yellow essence") is identified by Read (*Chinese Medicinal Plants*, p. 223, item 687) as "deer bamboo" (Polygonatum falcatum).

[101] I.e. need not be cultivated to grow.

[102] Heart, liver, spleen, lungs, and kidneys.

[103] Reading 澤 as 釋.

Answer to the Refutation

wasp carries them off"[104]—this is a change in nature. "When the tangerine crosses the [Huai] river it becomes the thorny limebush;"[105] it changes with the shift in land—this is an alteration in form. How can it not be possible that, being affected by the essence of what you eat, you can reverse your substance and alter your nature?

Thus Ch'ih Fu developed red hair from [eating] refined cinnabar;[106] Master Chüan lived a long time by eating the essence of mountain thistle;[107] Wo Ch'üan got square eyes from eating the fruit of the pine [pine cones?];[108] Ch'ih-sung [tzu] could ride smoke from drinking liquid jade;[109] Wu Kuang

---

[104] Quoting the *Shih ching*, poem 196 (p. 46, stanza 3). It was commonly understood in ancient China that the solitary wasp (*kuo-luo* 蜾蠃) had no eggs of its own but adopted those of the boll-worm (*ming-ling* 螟蛉), which then turned into wasps. It seems rather that the solitary wasp lays its eggs in boll-worm cocoons. On all of this see Bernard Read, *Chinese Materia Medica: Insect Drugs*, pp. 32–34 (item 10).

[105] Very much the same is said in Chang Hua's *Po-wu chih* (p. 3.3a). *Chü* 橘 and *chih* 枳 are the names, respectively, of the two trees. See Read, *Chinese Medicinal Plants*, pp. 103 and 104 (itsems 347 and 349). The tangerine grows south of the Huai and the thorny limebush to the north.

[106] For Ch'ih fu 赤斧 see the *Lieh-hsien chuan* (p. 13a in the *Li-tai chen-hsien shih-chuan* text). For Kaltenmark's translation see *Le Lie-sien Tchouan*, pp. 171–172. He was a Jung 戎 barbarian from Pa 巴. After thirty years of refining cinnabar he developed the countenance of a child.

[107] Chüan-tzu 涓子 is also recorded in the *Lieh-hsien chuan*. See *Li-tai chen-hsien shih-chuan*, p. 3a. For Kaltenmark's translation, *Le Lie-sien Tchouan*, pp. 68–69. He was from Ch'i 齊 and lived for three hundred years. *Chu* 朮, "mountain thistle," is identified as Atractylis by Stuart (see G. A. Stuart, *Chinese Materia Medica: Vegetable Kingdom* [Shanghai: American Presbyterian Mission Press, 1911], pp. 57–58. He notes that "The structure is very open, and some of the interstices are filled with an orange-colored resinous substance, which dissolves in strong spirit, making a yellow tincture" (p. 58). And he notes that the drug is used in various long life elixirs.

[108] For Wo Ch'üan 偓佺 see the *Lieh-hsien chuan* (*Li-tai chen-hsien shih chuan*, p. 2a: Kaltenmark, *Le Lie-sien Tchouan*, pp. 53–55). Wo Ch'üan lived on Mt. Huai 槐, and not only did his eyes become square from eating the fruit of the pine, but his body grew hair and lengthened by several inches.

[109] For Ch'ih-sung tzu 赤松子 (Master Red Pine) see the *Lieh-hsien chuan* (*Li-tai chen-hsien shih-chuan*, p. 1a) and Kaltenmark's translation, *Le Lie-sien Tchouan*, pp. 35–37. "Liquid Jade" (*shui-yü* 水玉) is also identified as quartz (see Read, *Chinese Materia Medica: Minerals and Stones*, p. 23, item 37). But the *Pao-p'u-tzu* ("nei-p'ien," "Hsien yao" chapter, p. 11.7a) speaks of Ch'ih-sung tzu mixing jade with other things as a liquid and drinking it. (Kaltenmark, p. 36,

Answer to the Refutation

lengthened his ears from eating sweet flag and leek [roots];[110] Ch'iung Shu from stalactite was able to halt his years;[111] Fang Hui by eating mica was able to transform;[112] and Ch'ang Jung from eating bramble [roots] altered her appearance.[113] Examples of this kind cannot be cited in full. Who says the five grains are the best and the Superior Drugs without benefit?

You also object that [as for there being people] who have lived now for a thousand years, you have never seen them with your eyes, which means they do not exist. Now I must ask this speaker, if you saw someone who was a thousand, how would you distinguish him? If you wish to compare him by means of his form, he is no different from anyone else. And if you wish to prove it by means of his years—"the morning mushroom has no

---

note 2, also notices this.) Ch'ih-sung tzu was supposedly the Rain Master at the time of Shen Nung.

[110] The text has *p'u-chiu* 蒲韭. But Kaltenmark (*Le Lie-sien Tchouan*, p. 78), following a variant found in *Shih-shuo hsin-yü*, has *ch'ang-p'u chiu ken* 菖蒲韭根, "sweet flag (or calamus) and leek roots." For Wu Kuang 務光, see *Lieh-hsien chuan—Li-tai chen-hsien shih-chuan*, text, pp. 3b–4a. He was a man of Hsia dynasty times (traditionally 2305–1766 B.C.) who was also seen five hundred years earlier at the time of Wu-ting 武丁 of the Shang. The commentary on the *Lieh-hsien chuan* in *Li-tai chen-hsien shih-chuan* says that it "suspects that *p'u-chiu* is actually *ch'ang-p'u*," and that "its roots have nine divisions and its leaves resemble the leek."

[111] For Ch'iung Shu 邛疏 see *Lieh-hsien chuan* (p. 4a in *Li-tai chen-hsien shih-chuan*); also Kaltenmark, *Le Lie-sien Tchouan*, pp. 84–85. Ch'iung Shu lived in the Chou, and having lived for several hundred years he entered Mt. T'ai-shih 太室. Read (*Chinese Materia Medica: Minerals and Stones*, p. 42, item 68) calls *shih-sui* 石髓 the "stone of immortality," but glosses it as a "kind of stalactite."

[112] For Fang Hui 方回, see *Lieh-hsien chuan* (*Li-tai chen-hsien shih-chuan* text, pp. 2ab); Kaltenmark, *Le Lie-sien Tchouan*, pp. 58–60. He was a recluse living at the time of Yao. At the end of the rule of Ch'i 啟 of the Hsia (reigned 2197–2188 B.C.) he was attacked by a man who wanted to know his secrets but escaped by transforming himself (into something else). For the Taoist art of "metamorphosis" (*pien-hua* 變化) see Isabelle Robinet, "Metamorphosis and Deliverance from the Corpse in Taoism," *History of Religions*, 19:1 (August, 1979), pp. 37–70.

[113] For Ch'ang Jung 昌容, see *Lieh-hsien chuan* (*Li-tai chen-hsien shih-chuan* text, pp. 10b–11a); Kaltenmark, *Le Lie-sien Tchouan*, pp. 152–153. Ch'ang Jung lived on Mt. Heng 恒. "She" (according to Kaltenmark) was over two hundred years old, but everyone who saw her thought she was in her twenties.

Answer to the Refutation

way of knowing evening and dawn,"[114] and the mayfly has no way to recognize the sacred tortoise.[115] This being so, then even if someone who was a thousand was seen in a public place, he most definitely would not be discerned by one of few years.

P'eng-tsu was seven hundred and An Ch'i a thousand;[116] those of narrow views say the records are wrong. Liu Ken slept long periods without eating;[117] but some say he was [simply] able by chance to endure hunger.[118] Chung-tu went naked in the winter but his body stayed warm, wore furs in the summer and yet remained cool;[119] but Huan T'an said it was only by chance that he was able to resist heat and cold.[120] Li Shao-chün recognized Duke Huan's royal[121] bowl, but Mr. Juan says he knew by [simply] hitting upon it in divination.[122] Yao offered

---

[114] Paraphrasing *Chuang-tzu*, Ch. 1 (p. 1, line 10).

[115] The *Huai-nan-tzu* ("Ch'üan-yen hsün" 詮言訓, p. 14.13a) points out that the tortoise lives for three thousand years while the mayfly lives only three days.

[116] P'eng-tsu 彭祖 and An Ch'i 安期 are both mentioned in the *Lieh-hsien chuan*. See the *Li-tai chen-hsien shih-chuan* text, pp. 4a and 6b respectively; in Kaltenmark (*Le Lie-sien Tchouan*) see pp. 82-84 and 115-118. P'eng-tsu is reported to have been an official in the Yin (Shang), and his biography says he lived over eight hundred years. An Ch'i (full name Mr. [先生] An Ch'i) sold drugs on the coast of the Eastern Sea and was known as "the old man of a thousand years" (千歲翁). He had an interview with Ch'in Shih-huang-ti.

[117] For Liu Ken 劉根 one must consult the *Shen-hsien chuan* 神仙傳; in the *Li-tai chen-hsien shih-chuan* text see 3.10a-11b. He lived during the Han (fl. 7 B.C.) and left the world to study the Tao, living in a cave on Mt. Sung-kao 嵩高.

[118] Chang Hua's *Po-wu chih* (7.2b) cites Ts'ao P'i's 曹丕 *Tien-lun* 典論 as saying: "Liu Ken was unaware of hunger or thirst. Some say he was able to endure being full or being empty."

[119] Wang Chung-tu 王仲都 also lived in the Han and is also recorded in the *Shen-hsien chuan* (*Li-tai chen-hsien shih-chuan* text, p. 10.41a), a text which says he was protected against heat and cold.

[120] Huan T'an discusses Wang Chung-tu and his behavior in *Hsin lun* 12a. Chang Hua's *Po-wu chih* (7.2b) cites Ts'ao P'i's *Tien-lun* as saying: "Huan Shan-chün [Huan T'an; it should be Chün-shan] felt that his [Wang Chung-tu's] nature was such that he could resist heat and cold. Huan [Chün-]shan felt there is no way to become an immortal."

[121] Reading 玉 as 王.

[122] For this incident see *Shih chi* 28 (Vol. 4, p. 1385), which specifies that this was a "bronze vessel" (*t'ung-ch'i* 銅器) that belonged to Duke Huan of Ch'i (reigned 685-643 B.C.), and that when Li Shao-chün made the identification "the whole palace was amazed and considered him to be a spirit, several hundred years old." Li Shao-chün was the famous "magician" (*fang-shih* 方士) employed

Answer to the Refutation

the world to Hsü Yu, but Yang Hsiung said this was made up by some lover of tall tales.[123] In all such cases as these, [those who doubt], above [the surface] take the Duke of Chou and Confucius as their point of pivot, and their entire wills are completely sincere, while underneath they are whipped on by cravings and desires, and though they wish to stop they cannot. They chase about among the worldly teachings, and compete in their craftiness between glory and disgrace. They lessen themselves to be in agreement with the many, while their thoughts never stray from position. To limit the unusual to what you can see, and restrict profound truth[124] to common opinion, and yet talk of understanding change[125] and penetrating the unseen—this is something of which I have never heard.

You have an enduring hatred for the quiet life, saying it is devoid of happiness. And you deeply resent going without cooked meats, saying this is [simply] imposing misery on oneself. You consider wine and women to be nourishing provisions, saying that long life is not to be relied on. Thus, what you consider to be happiness must be to have rows and rows of horse-drawn carriages and a hundred square feet of food [set out] before you. Those who are content only if they first have these, and say this is the "natural order" and "nature,"[126] all enslave themselves to things and lose their wills to their desires. The essential

---

by Emperor Wu of the Han (reigned 140–87 B.C.). He too has a biography in the *Shen-hsien chuan* (see *Li-tai chen-hsien shih-chuan* text, 6.23ab). The Mr. Juan 阮生 of the text is understood to be Juan Chung 種 (style Te-yu 德猷), a contemporary of Hsi K'ang. That it is he who is referred to by Hsi K'ang in this essay is confirmed by his [Juan Chung's] biography in *Chin shu* 52 (Vol. 5, p. 1444).

[123] We find almost these exact words in Chang Hua's *Po-wu chih* (4.1a). For Yao's offering of the empire to the recluse Hsü Yu see *Chuang-tzu*, Chapter 1 (p. 2, line 22). Yang Hsiung's 楊雄 reaction to the story—that "it was made up by some lover of tall tales"—is recorded in his *Fa-yen* 法言, "Wen-ming" 問明 chapter (6.4b).

[124] The 禮 of the Tai Ming-yang text should be 理.

[125] Following the Wu text in reading 變通 in reverse.

[126] The words of Hsiang Hsiu.

Answer to the Refutation

character of one's original nature and fate is encumbered by what you say.

It is only water that the thirsty man sees; only wine that the alcoholic looks for. Everyone knows that [these desires] arise because they are ill. But if you take following one's desires to be acting in accord with one's nature, then [constant] thirst and alcoholism are not diseases,[127] and wantonness and drunkenness are not excesses, and the disciples of Chieh and Chih are all following nature.[128] But this is not the way I would explain the meaning of the "ultimate order of things"[129] in this present essay of mine. The highest truths are truly subtle, and they are easily lost in the world. But you can perhaps comprehend them if you first look for them inside, and know them through examination of external things.[130]

In people's lives, as they pass from youth to old age, their   and   rise and fall,[131] and their loves and hates flourish and decline. In some cases, what gives one pleasure in one's younger years is rejected when one matures; [in others], what we thought little of at the beginning, we end up treating with respect. At the time that it gives us pleasure, we say we cannot do without it; and when we come to regard it as repulsive, we say it could not possibly make one happy. But when we move to a new city[132] or change lands, our feelings revert to what they were at the start. If our cravings and desires can change, how do

---

[127] I am not sure why k'o 渴, "thirsty" is considered a disease; perhaps "weakness" would better apply.

[128] Chieh 桀 is the dissolute, last ruler of the Hsia (reigned 1818–1766 B.C.). Chih 跖 is "Robber Chih," the famous brigand of antiquity that we meet up with in Chapter 29 of the *Chuang-tzu*.

[129] Note that the "ultimate order" (chih-li 至理) contrasts with Hsiang Hsiu's t'ien-li 天理, "natural order."

[130] Following the Wu text in omitting the 者 at the end of the sentence.

[131] The text does not show a lacuna. But I agree with Tai Ming-yang (p. 189) that since lung-sha 隆殺 ("rise and fall") is parallel to sheng-shuai 盛衰 ("flourish and decline"), there should be three characters preceding it. Something like hsi-nu yu lung-sha 喜怒有, "likes and dislikes rise and fall" is what is required.

[132] Following the Wu text in reading 成 as 城.

Answer to the Refutation

we know that what we are addicted to at present is not [in reality] something stinking and rotten, and what we have previously regarded with contempt is not [actually] something beautiful and rare? If a menial servant suddenly rose to the post of prime minister, he would leave behind with disdain people like the keeper of the gate. To speak from this perspective, whenever we regard something as unimportant, these are simply the feelings we have in one set of circumstances. Can it be that they definitely will not change?

Also, with someone who is starving for a meal, when he is about to get what he wants, it [food] pleases his feelings and rivets his mind. But when he is sated and full, he sets it aside with disinterest, and in some cases even loathes and detests [it]. This being so, then glory and honor and wine and women [must also] have their times when they can be set aside.

Pythons are treasured in the region of Yüeh [southeast China]; but if we meet one in the Middle Kingdom, we hate it: embroidered robes are valued in China, but [people] in the Kingdom of the Naked[133] take them and throw them away. Where things have no use, they are all [like] the pythons of China and the embroidered robes in the Kingdom of the Naked. If[134] you take the Great Harmony as Perfect Joy[135] then glory and honor will not be worth your concern: if tranquillity and contentment are for you the Perfect Taste, then wine and women will not be worthy of respect. If what brings satisfaction depends on the place,[136] then the things vulgar people delight in are all nothing but dung and dirt. How could they be worth longing for?

The present speaker [Hsiang Hsiu], not seeing the true nature of Perfect Joy, delights in diminishing his years and harming his

---

[133] *Lo-kuo* 裸國: where people wear no clothes. The Kingdom of the Naked is located by several texts simply someplace in the South (南方).

[134] The 若 is added in the Wu text.

[135] *Chih-lo* 至樂, the title of Chapter 18 of the *Chuang-tzu*.

[136] *Ti* 地 perhaps means more here than "geographic area," i.e., where one places one's values.

Answer to the Refutation

life, so that he might do whatever he wishes. This is just like Li Ssu's turning his back on the scholars, to sacrifice his life for a moment's desire,[137] [and] Chu-fu [Yen's] working so industriously hoping to blend the flavors of the five cauldrons.[138]

Moreover, when one becomes used to the fish market, he disdains [the smell] of orchid and angelica, just as when the ocean bird faced the T'ai-lao sacrifice, he felt nothing but great sorrow,[139] and when Marquis Wen listened to classical music he blocked up his ears.[140] Thus to consider glory and honor as the means to life, and say that "[even if] one lived ten thousand

---

[137] Li Ssu 李斯 studied with the Confucian philosopher Hsün-tzu (born c. 312 B.C.). But having no desire for the scholar's life of poverty and mean status (and so he told Hsün-tzu), he sold his services to Ch'in Shih-huang-ti, becoming his prime minister. When Ch'in Shih-huang-ti died, Li Ssu was slandered at court and executed in 208 B.C. See his biography, *Shih chi* 87 (Vol. 8, pp. 2539–2563, especially pp. 2539 and 2562).

[138] Chu-fu Yen 主父偃 was an upright official in early Han who had the unfortunate habit of revealing others' secrets. When powerful officials tried to bribe him, he refused, saying that he had studied hard for over forty years, never mindful of self, family, or friends, and that "if a man does not eat from the five caldrons when his is alive, he will die being boiled in them." (See his biography in *Shih chi* 112: Vol. 9, p. 2961.) He became prime minister of Ch'i. But when the king of Ch'i committed suicide, being accused by Chu-fu Yen of fornicating with his sister, Chu-fu Yen and his entire family ended by being executed. The "five caldrons" (*wu-ting* 五鼎) were used in antiquity in sacrifice by the "officers" (*ta-fu* 大夫). Served in them were lamb, pork, beef, fish, and venison (lists vary). "Boiled in the five caldrons" (*wu-ting p'eng* 烹) was a method of execution.

[139] See *Chuang-tzu*, Chapter 18 (p. 47, lines 33–35). Watson (*The Complete Works of Chuang Tzu*, pp. 194–195) translates: "Once a sea bird alighted in the suburbs of the Lu capital. The marquis of Lu escorted it to the ancestral temple, where he entertained it, performing the Nine Shao music for it to listen to and presenting it with the meat of the T'ai-lao sacrifice to feast on. But the bird only looked dazed and forlorn, refusing to eat a single slice of meat or drink a cup of wine, and in three days it was dead. This is to try to nourish a bird with what would nourish you instead of what would nourish a bird." The *t'ai-lao* 太牢 ("Great Sacrifice") consisted of offering a bull, a sheep, and a pig.

[140] In the *Li chi* ("Yüeh-chi" 樂記) we find: "The Marquis Wan of Wei asked Tze-hsia, saying, 'When in my square-cut dark robes and cap I listen to the ancient music, I am only afraid that I shall go to sleep. When I listen to the music of Kang [Cheng] and Wei, I do not feel tired; let me ask why I should feel so differently under the old and the new music.'" (Tr. by James Legge, *The Li Ki*, in F. Max Müller, ed., *The Sacred Books of the East*, Vol. 28, pp. 116–117.) For the text see *Li chi hsün-tsuan* 19.16b.

Answer to the Refutation

generations it would not be worth delighting in"[141]—these both [result] from lacking the essential on the inside, and relying on external things for your happiness. But although one's external things are abundant, one's sorrow is also complete.[142] If you have the essential inside, and with the inside enjoy the out, even though you have no bells or drums, your joy [music][143] is already complete. Therefore, to realize one's will does not mean [having] the carriage of an official and minister's caps,[144] and having Perfect Joy does not mean [to be] uncontrollably happy.[145] It is simply to be un-ensnared by gain or loss.

Moreover, when one's parents are ill, and they are in distress and then recover, anxiety and delight work together [i.e., the delight is tied to the previous anxiety]. To speak from this perspective, that this is not as good as having nothing to delight in in the first place [i.e., there being no previous anxiety] can certainly be known. This being so, then how can it be that the absence[146] of joy is not Perfect Joy? Therefore, to those who accord with the harmony of Heaven by means of nature, and take the Way and its Virtue as teacher and friend, who delight in the transformations of Yin and Yang, and attain the everlastingness that comes with long life, who leave everything to nature and trust their lives to it, who become one with Heaven and Earth and do not decay—who will make offering to these?

There are five difficulties in nourishing life. [The desire for]

---

[141] The words of Ssu-ma Hsiang-ju quoted by Hsiang Hsiu.

[142] If I understand him correctly, Hsi K'ang is playing on the double meaning of *pei* 備, "complete, perfect," but also "to prepare beforehand." So one's grief is also "complete," or "perfect," like his goods, and has been "prepared for" by his attachment to things.

[143] Playing on the double meaning of 樂: *lo*, "joy," but also *yüeh*, "music."

[144] Alluding to some lines at the end of Chapter 16 of the *Chuang-tzu* (p. 41, lines 17 and 18). Watson (*The Complete Works of Chuang Tzu*, p. 174) translates: "When the men of ancient times spoke of the fulfillment of ambition, they did not mean fine carriages and caps. They meant simply that joy was so complete that it could not be made greater."

[145] Reading 充屈 as 充詘.

[146] Agreeing with Lu Hsün (p. 63) and Tai Ming-yang (p. 191) that there must be a 無 at this point.

Answer to the Refutation

fame and profit is not extinguished; this is the first difficulty. Delight and anger are not banished; this is the second difficulty. Music and beauty are not expelled; this is the third difficulty. The rich flavors are not renounced; this is the fourth difficulty. And the spirit is emptied and the essence scattered;[147] this is the fifth difficulty. If these five are firmly maintained, then even though in your heart you hope for a "rare old age,"[148] and with your mouth intone the "Perfect Words,"[149] and suck and chew the rare plants, and breathe in and breathe out the Great Yang, you will be unable to prevent being turned from your purpose and dying young.

If these five are not found in your breast, then sincerity and obedience[150] will daily increase, and your mysterious virtue[151] will be daily more complete. You will have blessings without praying for happiness, and naturally live longer without seeking long life. This is the verification of the great principle of nourishing life.

But there are some who in their conduct go beyond Tseng and Min.[152] Ever mindful of benevolence and righteousness, their actions according with justice and peace,[153] and having no great

---

[147] Following the Wu manuscript reading—神虛精散.

[148] Literally "aging only with difficulty" (*nan-lao* 難老). This is mentioned in poem 299 of the *Shih* (p. 79, stanza 3). Karlgren (*The Book of Odes*, p. 256) translates: "The prince of Lu has come, by the semi-circular water he is drinking wine; he has drunk the good wine; for long there will be given him a rare old age."

[149] *Chih-yen* 至言. In *Chuang-tzu* Chapter 22 (p. 61, line 84) we find: "Perfect speech is the abandonment of speech; perfect action is the abandonment of action." (Tr. by Watson, *The Complete Works of Chuang Tzu*, p. 247.)

[150] *Hsin-shun* 信順—an allusion to the *I ching* (*Hsi-tz'u*, A.11: p. 44), where we find: "What Heaven helps is obedience; what man helps is sincerity."

[151] *Hsüan-te* 玄德—a common expression in the *Lao-tzu*.

[152] That is Tseng-tzu 曾子 and Min Tzu-ch'ien 閔子騫, both disciples of Confucius, and both noted for their filial piety. For example, in *Analects* 11:5 (p. 20) Confucius says: "What a good son Min Tzu-ch'ien is! No one can find fault with what his parents and brothers have to say about him." (Tr. by D. C. Lau, *Confucius: The Analects*, p. 106.)

[153] *Chung-ho* 中和. This might also be the "centrality and harmony" mentioned at the opening of the *Chung-yung* 中庸 (The Doctrine of the Mean).

Answer to the Refutation

attachments, they say that [in this] the principles of humanity[154] are already complete, and on this account indulge in self-praise. But [to do this] and yet not cleanse oneself of delight and anger, and calm spirit and breath, and still desire to stave off old age and extend one's years—of this I have never heard.

Others set their ambitions high and emulate the past. And since they find no glory in fame and position, they see themselves as standing above those who chase after [these things]. [Still] others use their intelligence to manage the world, and think highly of themselves since they have not got caught up in disasters. But this is simply a case of young men and the ninety-year-old[155] elders of villages and towns—in the ways in which they use their bodies they are the same. To speak of preserving your life in this way—I am afraid there is still something missing.

Others leave the world and do not congregate with the masses. Their wills and breath are harmonious and pure. But they do not eliminate the five grains and eat [instead] the fungi. [Thus], this in no way increases their short spans.

[Finally] there are those who have stored up their provisions of agate [for the journey],[156] and harnessed the six breaths.[157]

Wing-tsit Chan (*A Source Book in Chinese Philosophy* [Princeton: Princeton University Press, 1963], p. 98) translates: "Before the feelings of pleasure, anger, sorrow, and joy are aroused it is called equilibrium (*chung*, centrality, mean). When these feelings are aroused and each and all attain due measure and degree, it is called harmony." For the text see *Li chi hsün-tsuan* 31.1a.

[154] Following the Wu text and others in reading 仁 as 人.

[155] Following Tai Ming-yang's suggestion (p. 193) of filling the lacuna here with *ni* 齯. A *ni-ch'ih* 齯齒 is an elder of ninety; literally someone who has the teeth that grow in after all of one's adult teeth have fallen out.

[156] Like Ch'ü Yüan: see note 96 above.

[157] The "six breaths" (*liu-ch'i* 六氣) are understood to be Yin and Yang, wind and rain, and night and day. *Chuang-tzu*, in Chapter 1 (p. 2, line 21), says of Lieh Tzu: "If he had only mounted on the truth of Heaven and Earth, ridden the changes of the six breaths, and then wandered through the boundless, then what would he have had to depend on?" (Tr. by Watson, *The Complete Works of Chuang Tzu*, p. 32.)

Answer to the Refutation

And they are able[158] to contain their light and look within, congeal their spirits[159] and return to simplicity,[160] rest their minds on the shores of the mysterious and profound, and hold in their breath on the banks of nothing greater. Thus, there are [cases] where old age can be staved off and [one's] years can be extended.[161]

All of these various things are useful when combined, but one will not work without the others, just as you cannot have a single part—the shaft, the axle, the wheels, the linchpin—missing from a carriage. But people are all[162] one-sided in their views, and each prepares for that which he fears. Shan Pao forgot the outside in attending to the in;[163] Chang I lost the inside in

---

[158] The original Wu manuscript has a 不 after the 而, giving "But they are unable to...." This would be in keeping with the pattern of Hsi K'ang's argument at this point—although these people master certain techniques, they still leave out certain others. But then we would not expect him to say at the end of this "Thus there are cases where old age can be staved off and [one's] years can be extended."

[159] *Chuang-tzu*, Chapter 19 (p. 48, line 21), explains that "to use the will undividedly, is to be congealed in spirit."

[160] *Fu-p'u* 復樸—*p'u* being the "uncarved block" of *Lao-tzu*. In Chapter 12 of the *Chuang-tzu* (p. 31, lines 68–69) we find Confucius speaking of "A man of true brightness and purity" as one who "can enter into simplicity, who can *return to the primitive* [italics added] through inaction, give body to his inborn nature, and embrace his spirit, and in this way wander through the everyday world." (Tr. by Watson, *The Complete Works of Chuang Tzu*, p. 136.)

[161] Or does he mean to say—in keeping with the spirit of the paragraph that follows—that "these people can *in part* stave off old age, and *to a degree* extend their years," but that this too is not by itself a totally perfect method? (The Chinese is 則有老可卻, 有年可延也.)

[162] Reading the variant 皆 in place of 若.

[163] Following the Wu text in reading 忘外 in place of 致斃—but this too ("brought on his death") makes sense. For Shan Pao 單豹 see *Chuang-tzu*, Chapter 19 (p. 49, lines 29–32). Watson (*The Complete Works of Chuang Tzu*, p. 201) translates: "In Lu there was Shan Pao—he lived among the cliffs, drank only water, and did not go after gain like other people. He went along like that for seventy years and still had the complexion of a little child. Unfortunately, he met a hungry tiger who killed him and ate him up.... Shan Pao looked after what was on the inside and the tiger ate up his outside."

Answer to the Refutation

chasing after the out;[164] Ch'i suffered defeat in [solely] taking precautions against [attack from] west of the Chi;[165] Ch'in wore itself out preparing against the Jung and the Ti [barbarians].[166] These are all disasters that resulted from not being comprehensive.

To "accumulate goodness"[167] and "tread sincerity"[168]—the world constantly hears of these. To be "cautious in word and speech, and restrained in eat and drink"[169]—this the scholars know. [But] "to go on beyond this, [that] no one seems to

---

[164] For Chang I 張毅 see the same place in *Chuang-tzu*—Chapter 19 (p. 46, lines 29–32). Watson (*The Complete Works of Chuang Tzu*, pp. 201–202) translates: "Then there was Chang Yi—there was not one of the great families and fancy mansions that he did not rush off to visit. He went along like that for forty years, and then he developed an internal fever, fell ill, and died.... Chang Yi looked after what was on the outside and the sickness attacked him from the inside."

[165] Ch'i was defeated in 284 B.C. at Chi-hsi 濟西 (west of the Chi river, Ch'i's western boundary) by the combined forces of Ch'in 秦, Chao 趙, Han 韓, and Yen 燕 (see *Shih chi* 44: Vol. 6, p. 1853). Holzman (*La Vie*, pp. 120–121, note 7) feels that this is being referred to here. I should think this refers instead to the final defeat of Ch'i by Ch'in in 221 B.C., when Ch'i sent troops to intersect Ch'in in the west, but Ch'in attacked from Yen to the north (see *Shih chi* 6: Vol. 1, p. 235).

[166] The Ch'in 秦 dynasty was short-lived, lasting only from 221–209 B.C. The Jung 戎 were the barbarians to the west, the Ti 狄, barbarians to the north. In *Shih chi* 6 (Vol. 1, p. 253) we read the following: "In the thirty-third year [214] those who had evaded conscription, men living with their wives' families, and tradesmen were conscripted to conquer Luliang; then the provinces of Kueilin, Hsiangchun, and Nanhai were created and convicts sent to garrison them. The Huns in the northwest were driven back. The region from Yuchung to east of the Yellow River was incorporated with Yinshan, making thirty-four counties. Ramparts were built along the river as frontier defences.... Outposts and defences were set up to resist the tribesmen [literally, the Jung] and convicts were sent to populate the new counties.... In the thirty-fourth year [213], officers of justice who had done wrong were sent to build the Great Wall or to Southern Yueh." (Tr. by Yang Hsien-yi and Gladys Yang, *Selections from the Records of the Historian by Szuma Chien*, p. 176.) Most important against the Jung and Ti would be the efforts of Ch'in on the Great Wall.

[167] In the *Wen-yen* 文言 on *k'un* 坤 in the *I ching* (p. 4) we read: "The family that accumulates goodness is bound to have a surplus of blessings."

[168] Again an allusion to the *I ching*, *Hsi-tz'u* A.11 (p. 44), where "tread sincerity" (*lü-hsin* 履信) is mentioned right after the words: "What Heaven helps is obedience; what man helps is sincerity."

[169] Also mentioned in the *I ching* as the *hsiang* 象 to hexagram 27 (p. 18).

Answer to the Refutation

understand."[170] Please allow those who are first enlightened to instruct those who will be enlightened in the future.[171]

---

[170] Borrowing words from the *I ching* (*Hsi-tz'u* B.3: p. 46), but replacing the 未 with 其. The context is not without relevance. Legge (*I Ching: Book of Changes*, ed. by Ch'u Chai and Winberg Chai [New York: Bantam Books, 1964—originally published in 1899 as Vol. XVI of *The Sacred Books of the East*—], p. 390) translates: "(So), when we minutely investigate the nature and reasons (of things), till we have entered into the inscrutable and spirit-like in them, we attain to the largest practical application of them; when that application becomes the quickest and readiest, and all personal restfulness is secured, our virtue is thereby exalted. *Going on beyond this, we reach a point which it is hardly possible to know* [italics added]. We have thoroughly comprehended the inscrutable and spirit-like, and know the processes of transformation;—this is the fulness of virtue."

[171] Echoing the words of Mencius in *Mencius* 5A:7 (p. 37): "Heaven, in producing the people, has given to those who first attain understanding the duty of awakening those who are slow to understand; and to those who are first to awaken the duty of awakening those who are slow to awaken." (Tr. by D. C. Lau, *Mencius*, p. 146.)

HSI K'ANG

Music Has in It Neither Grief nor Joy

(Sheng wu ai-lo lun)

∷

Translator's Comments. *This is a brilliant essay: the thesis is imaginative and well argued. The standard Chinese view of music is that it is a carrier of emotion: which is to say it both conveys the mind and feelings of the performer/composer, and transfers its own emotional quality to the listener. Hence the fear of lewd and licentious tunes; they can pervert the audience. Hsi K'ang, speaking here as the "Host of Tung-yeh" (東野主人), rejects that position, arguing that "music has in it neither grief nor joy." Or, to put it another way, there is no such thing as happy or sad music; the emotion is in the listener, not in the music.*

While Chang Shih-pin 張世彬 *is right in saying this recognizes music as an "independent art" and gets it out of the realm of morality and politics,*[1] *we must not fail to see that for Hsi K'ang there is something at stake. If music could be said to be happy and sad, and thus capable of producing those emotions, it would lose its place as a means for nourishing life. For, as we have seen, emotions such as grief and joy are not beneficial to health. Music does have its own essential quality; but it is not emotion, it is "harmony" (ho* 和*). And harmony does not* cause *emotion, it* releases *emotion that is already there. Thus music, and especially that of the lute, has a cathartic effect. Moreover, this explains why two people can listen to the same song and respond in emotionally different ways.*

The essay is in the form of a debate between the Host of Tung-yeh

---

[1] See Chang Shih-pin, "Hsi K'ang: yin-yüeh tu-li ti wei-ta kung-ch'en" 嵇康：音樂獨立的偉大功臣, *Ming-pao yüeh-k'an* 明報月刊, 91 (July, 1973), pp. 22-23.

Music . . . Neither Grief nor Joy

and a guest from Ch'in (秦客), with the guest defending the traditional view. Hsi K'ang apparently plays both roles; the entire essay is written by him. Juan K'an, the author of "Residence is Devoid of Good and Bad Fortune," was once on his way to Tung-yeh when Hsi K'ang wrote him a poem, and Tai Ming-yang identifies this Tung-yeh with Ying-ch'uan prefecture to the south of Lo-yang.[2] But that all seems irrelevant here.

The title—Sheng wu ai-lo lun 聲無哀樂論—appears to be a pun on a thesis proposed by Ho Yen 何晏 (d. 249), Sheng-jen wu hsi-nu ai-lo lun 聖人無喜怒哀樂論, "the sage lacks the emotions of delight and anger and grief and joy."[3]

There was a guest from Ch'in who asked the host of Tung-yeh: "I have heard that a previous discussion says that 'the songs of a well ordered age are peaceful and happy, but the songs of a doomed state are sad and melancholy.'[1] Whether there is order or chaos in the state depends on the government, but the music corresponds to it. Therefore, feelings of grief and melancholy are expressed in metal and stone;[2] signs of peace and happiness take form in pipes and strings.[3] Also, when Confucius heard the *Shao*, he understood the virtue of Shun,[4] and when Chi Cha

---

[2] See Tai Ming-yang, *Hsi K'ang chi chiao-chu*, p. 70. The poems exchanged by Hsi K'ang and Juan K'an are in *Hsi K'ang chi chiao-chu*, pp. 66–72.

[3] See Ho Shao's 何劭 biography of Wang Pi, cited by P'ei Sung-chih in his notes to Chung Hui's biography in *San-kuo chih* 28 (p. 795).

[1] From the "Great Preface" to the *Book of Poetry* (Mao shih). See Legge's translation with the text in *The Chinese Classics*, Vol. IV, *The She King* (London: Oxford University Press, 1935), p. 34. This section of the preface begins with "The feelings go forth in sound" (Legge's translation), 情發於聲. The host will argue that feelings are *released* by music which, in fact, is another possible translation of this line.

[2] I.e., bells of metal and the musical stones.

[3] I.e., flutes and whistles and the stringed instruments like the lute and the zither.

[4] The *Shao* 韶 was the music of Shun. This probably alludes to *Analects* 3:25 (p. 5) which D. C. Lau translates: "The Master said of the *shao* that it was both perfectly beautiful and perfectly good." See D. C. Lau, *Confucius: The Analects*, p. 71.

Music ... Neither Grief nor Joy

listened to the strings, he knew the dispositions of the various states.[5]

"These are things that are already so; things former worthies did not doubt. You alone, sir, feel that music has in it neither grief nor joy. What is the reason for this? If you have some fine announcement to make please allow us to hear the explanation."

The host responded: "Our understanding of this has for long been obstructed, and no one has been willing to come to the rescue. This has caused successive generations to be in error with respect to name and reality. Let me lead you out of ignorance now by discussing one corner of it.[6]

"Heaven and Earth united their virtues and the ten thousand things by this[7] were born. Cold and hot succeeded one another, and the five elements as a result came to be. These[8] became manifest as the five colors and issued forth as the five tones. The arising of musical sounds is like the presence of odors in the air; they are either good or bad. And though they get mixed in with other things, they remain in essence what they are and don't change. How could love or hate change the melody, grief or joy alter the beat?

"Coming to C and D together and in sequence,[9] and sounds and tones in harmony—this is the great delight of man's mind, what the feelings and desires love. But the ancients knew that

---

[5] See *Tso chuan*, Duke Hsiang, 29th year (pp. 326–327). In Legge's translation (*The Chinese Classics*, Vol. V, Part II), see pp. 549–550. Chi Cha was sent to Lu from Wu. In Lu he heard the songs from the *Book of Poetry*—the *feng*, or "airs of the states" from the fifteen states, the *ta-ya* and *hsiao-ya*, "greater elegant" and "lesser elegant," and the *sung*, "ritual hymns"—and right away knew the character and/or fate of the state of origin.

[6] Alluding to *Analects* 7:8 (p. 12), where Confucius says, "When I have pointed out one corner of a square to anyone and he does not come back with the other three, I will not point it out to him a second time." (Tr. by D. C. Lau, *Confucius: The Analects*, p. 86.)

[7] Reading the Wu text variant 資, "depends on this," where other texts have 貴, "value."

[8] Following the Wu text in omitting the "Therefore" (故) at the start of the line.

[9] Reading the Wu text variant 比, "put in order," for 化, "transform".

Music... Neither Grief nor Joy

feelings cannot go unrestrained and desires cannot be taken to the limit. Thus,[10] in accord with its effect, each thing was regulated. They made it that grief did not go to the point of self-injury and joy did not go to the point of licentiousness.[11]

"In accord with the event, we give it a name; things have their designations. When we cry we call it grief; when we sing we call it joy. This is generally true. But when we say 'music, music'—do we mean no more than bells and drums?[12] When we say 'grief, grief'—do we mean no more than crying and weeping? To speak from this perspective, presents of jade and silk are not the reality of rites and respect, and song and dance are not the essence of grief and joy.[13]

"How can I make this clear? Different regions have different customs; singing and crying are not done the same. If we mix them up and use them, some hear crying and are pleased; others listen to singing and become sad.[14] But their feelings of grief and joy are the same. Now if you use feelings that are the same to produce completely different sounds, is this not because music has no constant [relation to emotion]?

"However, sounds in harmony and sequence are what move people most deeply. 'Those who labor sing of their woes';[15] those who are happy dance about their achievements.[16] If inside

---

[10] The 故 is added in Wu.

[11] Alluding to Confucius' remark (*Analects* 3:20, p. 5) on poem 1 in the *Book of Poetry*, "In the *kuan-chü* there is joy without wantonness, and sorrow without self-injury." (Tr. by Lau, *Confucius: The Analects*, p. 70.)

[12] Quoting *Analects* 17:9 (p. 36). Lau's translation goes: "The Master said, 'Surely when one says, "The rites, the rites," it is not enough merely to mean presents of jade and silk. Surely when one says "Music, music," it is not enough merely to mean bells and drums.'" (Lau, *Confucius: The Analects*, p. 145.)

[13] Following Tai Ming-yang's suggested emendation of 悲哀 to 哀樂. That is to say, the ritual propriety and respect lie in the presenter; the grief and joy are in the performer.

[14] Reading the variant 慼 for 感. But either would apply.

[15] This line apparently was found in the no longer extant *Han-shih* 韓詩 (Han Ying's version of the *Book of Poetry*). Li Shan cites the *Han-shih* as the source for this line in his commentary on Hsieh Hun's 謝混 poem, "Yu hsi-ch'ih" 游西池 (*Wen hsüan* 22.5a).

[16] Perhaps an oblique allusion to Han Ching-ti's 漢景帝 remark: "Dancing is what is used to manifest accomplishments" (舞者，所以明功也). See *Han shu* 5 (Vol. 1, p. 137).

one's heart is pained and grieved, then words bitter and sad are aroused. Words in sequence become poetry; sounds in sequence become music. We blend the words and chant them, put together the sounds and listen to them. The heart is moved by harmonious sounds, the feelings touched by anguished words. The sigh has not yet ceased when our tears flow down in streams.

"The grieved heart is stored inside.[17] When it encounters harmonious sounds, only then is it released. Harmonious sounds have no sign, but the grieved heart has its essence. If you make the grieved heart that has an essence depend on the harmonious sounds that have no sign, then all you understand is the grief. How could you know, further, that 'it blows differently through the ten thousand things but causes each to be itself'?[18]

"The currents of customs and manners fulfill and complete the government. For this reason the state scribes, understanding the successes and failings of government teachings, and having examined the flourish and decline of customs in the states, 'chanted and intoned their feelings to admonish their superiors.'[19] Therefore [the 'Great Preface' to the *Book of Poetry*] says, 'the songs of a doomed state are sad and melancholy.'

"Now delight and anger, grief and joy, love and hate, and shame and fear—these eight emotions are the means by which living people relate with things and transmit their feelings. However, they are distinguished by category and cannot be confused.[20] Let us take the case of Mr. A, who is a worthy man that I love, and Mr. B, who is a fool that I hate. The love and hate appropriately belong to me; the worthiness and ignorance appropriately belong to them. Can we say this is a 'love' person

---

[17] Agreeing with Lu Hsün that this should read "藏於內," not as most texts have it, "藏於苦心內."

[18] Quoting *Chuang-tzu*, Ch. 2 (p. 3, line 9), where Tzu-ch'i says this of the pipes of Heaven. For Watson's translation see *The Complete Works of Chuang Tzu*, p. 37.

[19] The whole paraphrases a passage in the "Great Preface" to the *Book of Poetry*, and the last line is a direct quote. For Legge's translation see *The Chinese Classics*, Vol. IV, p. 36.

[20] The line "Now flavors are called either sweet or bitter," occurs here. I feel this is out of place and put it several lines further on.

Music . . . Neither Grief nor Joy

because I love him or a 'hate' person because I hate him? Flavors are called sweet or bitter. If I like a certain flavor is it to be called 'like'? Or if I am angered by a flavor, is it to be called 'anger'? To speak from this perspective, inner and outer are different functions, and self and other have different names. Since music must naturally have being good or bad as the essential thing, it has no relation to grief or joy; and since grief and joy must naturally be such that they are only released after the emotions are moved,[21] they have no connection with music.[22] When name and reality are kept apart, then this can be fully seen.

"Moreover, when Chi Cha was in Lu he collected poems and observed the rites to distinguish the 'Airs' from the 'Elegant.'[23] How could it be that he relied solely on the music to decide good and bad? And when Confucius heard the *Shao*, what he praised was its complete perfection, and therefore he sighed. Why must it be that he praised its beauty only after knowing the virtue of Shun by means of his music? Now I have roughly clarified one corner of this, but I am sure you can think through the rest on your own."[24]

The guest from Ch'in rejected this, saying: "The eight regions may have different customs, and crying and singing might be totally different. But people's feelings of grief and joy can certainly be perceived. When the heart is moved on the inside, then music comes forth from the heart. Although you entrust it to other tones, or express it with a surplus of sounds, the skilled listener and examiner will necessarily understand it; this will not cause him to err. In ancient times Po Ya strummed his lute and

---

[21] Adding in the variant characters 而後發 after 情感.

[22] Or punctuating differently—"Music is what it is; since the essential thing about it is that it is either good or bad, it has no relation to grief or joy. And grief and joy are what they are; since they are only released after the emotions are moved, they have no connection with music."

[23] Referring to the *kuo-feng*, *ta-ya* and *hsiao-ya* in the *Book of Poetry*.

[24] The host here paraphrases a line from the *I ching* (*Hsi-tz'u* B.7, p. 48)—"When one with intelligence sees the judgment, he can think through over half" (知者觀其彖辭則思過半矣).

Music ... Neither Grief nor Joy

Chung Tzu-[ch'i] knew what was on his mind.[25] The criminal laborer struck the musical stones, and Tzu-ch'i[26] knew he was grieved.[27] The person from Lu cried in the morning, and Yen Hui sensed it was a case of 'parted while yet alive.'[28] How could it be that these men further relied for their wisdom on the constancy of the tones, or found their evidence in the tempo of the song? When the heart is forlorn, the body shakes because of it; when the feelings are grieved, the sounds one makes are sad. This is a natural response and cannot be avoided. But only those with spirit-like insight are able keenly to perceive it. If you have the gift, then even a profusion of sounds will present no difficulty. But if you lack the talent, even a few sounds make it no matter of ease. But you cannot conclude, simply because you have never met a skilled listener, that music has no principles to be examined, or because you see the many variations in regional custom, that music has in it neither grief nor joy.

"You also say that 'it is not proper to call someone who is worthy "love," or someone who is stupid "hate".' But it is only with someone worthy that love arises, and only with someone stupid that hate begins. It is simply not appropriate to use the same name for both [the feeling and the cause]. The arising of grief and joy also has that which makes it so. This means that [some] sounds make me sad, and [other] sounds make me happy.

---

[25] If he was thinking of a mountain Tzu-ch'i knew it; if he had his mind on a river, Tzu-ch'i knew it. The anecdote is recorded in various sources. See for example *Lieh-tzu*, "T'ang-wen" 湯問 (in SPPY ed., 5.16ab). A. C. Graham translates the passage in *The Book of Lieh-tzu* (London: John Murray, 1960), pp. 109–110.

[26] Emended by Tai Ming-yang. The text says Tzu-ch'an 子產.

[27] The story is recorded in *Lü-shih ch'un-ch'iu*, "Ching-t'ung" 精通 (9.9b–10a). He was grieved because his father had been executed for killing a man, his mother was forced to make wine for the state, and he was forced to strike the musical stones. Moreover, he had not seen his mother for three years and could not afford to ransom her back.

[28] See *K'ung-tzu chia-yü*, "Yen Hui" 顏回 (SPPY 5.1b). The person (mother?) is crying because the father has died, and a child had to be sold and then sent away to pay for the funeral. But Yen Hui knew this from the sound of the cry alone.

Music ... Neither Grief nor Joy

If the grief and joy come from the music, then all the more must it be that the music has the reality in it.[29] How can it be that 'name and reality must be kept apart'?

"You also say that 'Chi Cha collected poems and observed the rites to distinguish the "Airs" from the "Elegant."' And that 'Confucius praised the complete perfection of the *Shao*, and therefore he sighed.' Where does it say this?[30]

"Moreover, music master Hsiang played[31] the lute melody, and Confucius saw the form of King Wen.[32] Music master Chüan respectfully presented a tune [to Duke P'ing of Chin], but Tzu-yeh knew this was the song of a doomed state.[33] Would you again prefer to say that they discussed the poetry and only then spoke, or studied the rites and only then made their judgments? These are both cases of spirit-like, unique perception. They had no need to sit and listen for days on end and only then decide its good or bad fortune. Therefore, former historians considered these praiseworthy anecdotes. But you, with your niggling, modern knowledge, are limited to seeing everything as the same. Thus, can you do anything but slander the understanding of the

---

[29] Referring back to the host's claim that the reality (feelings) is not in the outward sign, just as the reality of the rites (the feelings of respect) is not in the outward show of giving presents.

[30] In *Analects* 3:25, at least about Confucius (see note 4 above). But the guest is right about Chi Cha.

[31] Reading 奏 for 奉 as Tai Ming-yang suggests.

[32] The reported composer. This we read in *Han-shih wai-chuan*, Chapter 5. For the translation see J. R. Hightower, *Han Shih Wai Chuan: Han Ying's Illustrations of the Didactic Application of the Classic of Songs* (Cambridge, Mass.: Harvard University Press, 1952), pp. 168–169. Confucius says of the composer: "Darkly black, and grandly tall he rules the empire and attracts to his court the feudal lords; it can be no other than King Wen."

[33] The story is recorded in more than one source. See, for example, *Shih chi* 24 (Vol. 4, pp. 1235–1236). This is translated by R. H. van Gulik, *The Lore of the Chinese Lute* (Tokyo: Monumenta Nipponica Monographs, 1940), pp. 136–138. Duke Ling of Wei, on his way to Chin to visit Duke P'ing, hears some music in the middle of the night which he has master Chüan record. Master Chüan then plays this for Duke P'ing, but music master K'uang (Tzu-yeh) stops him, saying "That is the music of a doomed state; one must not listen to it." (Tr. by van Gulik.) It turns out to be a tune composed by a master Yen of the Shang to please the tyrant Chou.

Music ... Neither Grief nor Joy

subtle that former worthies had, and reject Confucius' mysterious powers of observation?"

The host replied: "You say in your refutation that 'although crying and singing are totally different, skilled listeners and examiners will necessarily understand it. They need not rely for their wisdom on the constancy of the tones or find their evidence in the tempo of the song. And followers of Chung Tzu[-ch'i], etc., etc., are examples of this.' This means that one whose heart is grieved, even though he chats and smiles and drums and dances, or one whose feelings are pleased, even though he beats his breast, laments and sighs, still cannot control his outward appearance to hide his true feelings, cannot deceive the examiner such that he has doubts. So you feel that even though the sounds are not constant, [the skilled listener] could still say who is happy and who is sad. [However], you also say that 'Chi Cha listened to *the music and by that knew the dispositions of the various states; music master Hsiang played the lute tune and Confucius saw the form of King Wen.*' Now, according to what you say *here*, this means that the meritorious virtue of King Wen, and the flourish and decline of state customs, can both be detected in music. The seriousness or levity of the music can be passed on to later generations, and with the skill of a music master Hsiang or Chüan we can discover it in the future. If this is true, then perhaps the ages of the Three August Ones and the Five Emperors[34] are not cut-off from the present. Why must this be limited to just a few things? But if this is really true, then the songs of King Wen must have a constant rhythm, and the notes of the *Shao* and the *Wu*[35] must be in number fixed. One cannot mix them up by adding in changes or play them with extra notes. But then your former notions—that music need not be constant, and that Chung Tzu [-ch'i] could infer from analogy—by this are overturned. Are

---

[34] Variously identified. One list would be: Three August Ones—Fu Hsi, Shen Nung and Nü Wa; Five Emperors—Huang-ti, Chuan Hsü, Ti-k'u, Yao, and Shun. But there are many different lists.

[35] The music of King Wu.

such things as the incontancy of music and Chung Tzu[-ch'i]'s using analogy really true? Then Confucius' understanding of the subtle and Chi Cha's skilled listening are definitely also false. These are both false records [made up by] vulgar pedants. They fabricated these accounts, wishing to make sacred their affairs. They wanted the whole world to misunderstand the way of music, so they did not speak what is reasonable and natural. Drawing our inference by exhausting this, they made it 'spirit-like' and 'mysterious,' 'difficult to understand.' Hating the fact that they had not met this rare listener in their own time, they longed for the ancients and sighed with admiration. This is the way they deluded later generations.

"If we are going to draw inferences and distinguish things, we must first seek the truth in terms of natural principle. If the principle is established, then, and only then, do we make use of ideas from the past to clarify it. But you have not yet got it in your mind and instead are relying heavily on statements made in the past, considering these verification of your remarks. If you go on from this, I am afraid that 'even a skilled reckoner will not be able to keep track of it all.'[36]

"You also refute me by saying that grief and joy are like love and hate which arise through association with the worthy and the stupid. 'This means,' [you say,] 'that [some] sounds make me sad, and [other] sounds make me happy. If the grief and joy come from the music, then all the more must it be that the music has the reality in it.' Now in matters of the five colors we say it is beautiful or ugly; with the five tones we call them good or bad. This is the natural state of things. But turning to love or not love, delight or displeasure,[37] the basic fluctuations in human feelings and the principles we use in common for all things, come

---

[36] Alluding to *Chuang-tzu*, Ch. 2 (p. 5, line 54), where Chuang-tzu says this about arguing for the oneness of all things. Watson (*Complete Works*, p. 43) translates, "The one and what I said about it make two, and two and the original one make three. If we go on this way...."

[37] Following Lu Hsün's recommended addition of 喜與不喜.

Music ... Neither Grief nor Joy

down to these and these alone. However, none of these exists beforehand on the inside; they come into being through contact with things. To turn to grief and joy, these naturally collect because of events and first build up in the heart. But with harmonious sounds they spontaneously manifest themselves and are released. Therefore, in my previous remarks I already made it clear that they have no constant [relation to music]. Let me here further take advantage of this discussion to rectify name and designation. You cannot say that the *release* of grief and joy by music is like the *production* of love and hate by worthiness and stupidity. Rather, the stimulation of men's hearts by harmony is in fact like the uninhibiting effect that wine has on their natures.[38] The primary characteristic of wine is that it is either sweet or bitter, but the effect on drunks is either delight or anger. To see that happiness and sadness are released by music and say that music has grief and joy in it, is like[39] seeing[40] that delight and anger are caused by wine and saying that wine has in it the principles of delight and anger."

The guest from Ch'in objected as follows: "Observing one's air and expression is a common practice in the empire. When the feelings change on the inside, one's expression corresponds on the out. This can clearly be seen, and therefore you do not doubt it. Now music is what stimulates the breath. The heart, responding to this stimulation, is moved, and music in accord with the change in feeling comes forth. The heart has its periods of flourish and decline; music too rises and falls. But both serve one and the same body. Why is it only with music that you must have doubts? If delight and anger show in one's expression and looks, then grief and joy ought also to appear in his sounds. Music

---

[38] Following the Wu manuscript with 性 where others have 情.
[39] The 猶 is omitted in most texts, but the original Wu has it.
[40] All texts have 不可, "one cannot see," here. But it makes better sense to omit this. The alternative would be to add these two characters at the beginning of the argument—"*One cannot*, seeing that happiness and sorrow are released by music, say that...."

Music ... Neither Grief nor Joy

naturally must have grief and joy in it, but stupid people are unable to recognize this.

"To turn to the followers of Chung Tzu[-ch'i], even though they encounter music that is not constant, they rise above the common lot[41] with their unique perception. If you have a blind musician face a wall he will not see a thing. But Li Lou[42] could discern the tip of an autumn hair at 800 feet. From this we can say that the blind and the clear-sighted have different abilities. You cannot doubt the powers of a Li Lou on the basis of your own meagre measurements; nor should you question Chung Tzu[-ch'i]'s sharp ear on the basis of your own mediocre listening faculties, and then say these are all false records made up by the ancients."

The host replied: "In your refutation you say that 'the heart, responding to the stimulation, is moved, and music in accord with one's changes in feeling comes forth. The heart has its periods of flourish and decline; music, too, rises and falls. Feelings of grief and joy must be expressed in sounds. With followers of Chung Tzu[-ch'i], even though the music they hear is not constant, they rise above the common in their unique perception.' If it is necessarily as you say, then if we took the satisfied feelings of the Cho's and the Chih's,[43] the hunger of Shou-yang,[44] the frustration of Pien Ho,[45] the sorrow of Po

---

[41] Reading 頴 as 穎.

[42] The standard representative of superior eyesight in antiquity. In some texts he is called Li Chu 離朱.

[43] See *Shih chi* 129 (Vol. 10, p. 3282). Here Ssu-ma Ch'ien notes the rise to fame and fortune of various men/families from meager states or demeaning occupations and says at one point: "Sharpening knives is a mean craft but the Chih's ended up eating from cauldrons. Making dried sheep's stomach is simple and crude but the Cho's [commanded] rows and rows of cavalry." Ssu-ma Ch'ien has 邟 for Chih; Hsi K'ang follows the *Han shu* account with 質.

[44] Alluding to Po I and Shu Ch'i, the two famous recluses who starved to death on Mt. Shou-yang at the beginning of the Chou dynasty, refusing to serve King Wen, whom they regarded as a usurper.

[45] Who twice had his feet cut off when the uncarved jade he took to the kings of Ch'u was declared mere stone by experts. Finally King Wen had it cut, and this became one of the famous treasures of Warring States times. See *Han-fei-tzu*, Ch. 13, "Mr. Ho" 和氏, pp. 4.10b–12a.

Music ... Neither Grief nor Joy

Ch'i,[46] the concealed anger of [Lin] Hsiang-ju,[47] the fearful respect of [Ch'en] Pu-chan[48]—people with completely different feelings and attitudes—and had each sing a single chord from a song, or together pluck a few subtle notes on the lute, then a follower of Chung Tzu[-ch'i] could in each case discover their true feelings. But does not someone who makes a practice of listening to music think differently when a few notes are produced as opposed to many? And does not someone who examines feelings differentiate between great emotion and little? When everything comes from one and the same person, you can hope to understand it. But if the music comes from an entire region,[49] then even a follower of Tzu-yeh will have repeatedly to regulate the pitch-pipes and test the bamboo tuning tubes in order to examine their music [and thus be able] to know from the airs of the South, which state will flourish and which decline,[50] and

---

[46] For Po Ch'i 伯奇 Tai Ming-yang (p. 206) cites Yang Hsiung's 揚雄 "Ch'in ch'ing-ying" 琴清英 found in the commentary on "Chiang-shui" 江水 in the *Shui ching chu*. Slandered by his stepmother, he jumped into the river, where in a dream he saw a water nymph who gave him the drug of immortality. Thinking of caring for his parents, he sang a mournful song which was copied down by a boatman.

[47] Referring to Lin Hsiang-ju's 蘭相如 dealings with the king of Ch'in over the Pien Ho jade. When he saw that the king did not intend to hold to his part of the bargain—trading fifteen Ch'in cities to Chao for the jade—he angrily seized the jade and threatened to smash it and his own head against a pillar. See his biography in *Shih chi* 81 (Vol. 8, 2439-2452). This has been translated into English by Yang Hsien-yi and Gladys Yang in *Selections from Records of the Historian by Szuma Chien*, pp. 139-151.

[48] Ch'en Pu-chan 陳不占 was a man from Ch'i who sought to avenge his lord (Duke Chuang) when he was assassinated by Ts'ui Chu 崔杼. However, he was so afraid that, setting off to attack Ts'ui, his hand slipped off the railing when he mounted his carriage, and he died of fright when he heard the battle drums. His story is cited from the *Han-shih wai-chuan* (not found in present editions) by Li Shan in his commentary on Ma Jung's 馬融 "Ch'ang-ti fu" 長笛賦 in *Wen hsüan* 18.17b.

[49] Following the original Wu text which has 從下出 for 從下. The reading of 從下出 as 從地出 is Tai Ming-yang's (p. 207) suggestion.

[50] The *Tso chuan* (Duke Hsiang, 18th year: p. 288) records that Chin heard of an army from Ch'u moving against them, but they were assured of success by music master K'uang (Tzu-yeh) because he had recently been singing a song from the south and it was non-combative (不競) and had many sounds of death (多死聲). For Legge's translation see *The Chinese Classics*, Vol. V, Part II, p. 479.

distinguish the uprightness of the 'Elegant' from the lewdness of the Cheng.[51]

"Eating acrid things brings on hysterical laughter; smoke in your eyes causes grief-struck sobbing. In both ways tears are produced. But even if you have a Ti Ya[52] taste them, he definitely will not say that the happy tears are sweet and the sad tears bitter. This can certainly be known. How does this work? The tissues secrete water and it beads up in the flesh; when pressure is applied it comes out. It is not controlled by grief or joy. It is just like the process of straining wine through a cloth sack. Although the device used to press it through may differ, the flavor of the wine is unchanged. Musical sounds are all produced by one and the same source. Why must they alone contain the principles of grief and joy?

"*Hsien-ch'ih* ["Complete Pond," the music of the Yellow Emperor], *Liu-ching* ["Six Stems," the music of Chuan-hsü], *Ta-chang* ["Great Manifestation," the music of Yao], *Shao* [the music of Shun], and *Hsia* [the music of Yü]—this is the perfect music of the former kings. By means of this they moved Heaven and Earth and stimulated ghosts and spirits.[53] Now if we must say that there is no music that does not intimate the nature of its source or convey the composer's mind, then we must also say that, this being Perfect Music, it could not be entrusted to blind scribes.[54] We must have a sage to pull on the strings and blow on the pipes; only then will these elegant songs achieve their perfect form. But Shun ordered K'uei to 'beat the musical stone, to strike it, and thus the eight sounds could be harmonized, and

---

[51] That the "Elegant" songs in the *Book of Poetry* are "upright" or "correct" (正) is a claim made in the "Great Preface" to that work. See Legge's translation, *The Chinese Classics*, Vol. IV, p. 36. The *locus classicus* for the lewd nature of the music of Cheng is Confucius' remark to that effect in *Analects* 15:11 (p. 31). Ya 雅, "elegant," also refers in general to classical music.

[52] Ti Ya 狄牙 is better known as I Ya 易牙. From the state of Ch'i in spring and autumn times, he is the noted expert in all culinary matters in ancient China.

[53] This power is claimed for poetry in the "Great Preface" to the *Book of Poetry*. See Legge, *The Chinese Classics*, Vol. IV, p. 34.

[54] Musicians were usually blind in ancient China.

spirits and men by this could live in peace.'[55] On the basis of this, though Perfect Music comes into being only with a sage, it need not be controlled by the sage himself. Why? Because music has a natural harmony; it is unrelated to human feelings. Lovely, harmonious tones are produced from the metal and stone; sounds of Perfect Harmony come from the pipes and strings. It is true that a fine thread and a strand of hair each has its form that can be distinguished. Therefore Li Lou and a blindman will have different results with their clear-sightedness and lack of vision. But if you simply 'mix water with water'[56] who can tell the difference?"

The guest from Ch'in objected as follows: "Although my many examples might not have been clear, and this is sufficient to invite your criticism, still, the main principle must be accepted. Ko-lu heard a cow bellow and knew that her three offspring had been sacrificed.[57] Music master K'uang [Tzu-yeh] blew on the pitch-pipes and knew that the airs of the south were non-

---

[55] Taken from the *Shu*, "Shun tien" 舜典. Legge/Waltham translate the relevant passage as follows: "The sovereign said, 'K'uei, I appoint you to be Director of Music.... Poetry is the expression of earnest thought; singing is the prolonged utterance of that expression; the notes accompany that utterance and are harmonized by the standard tubes. In this way the eight different kinds of musical instruments can be adjusted so that one shall not take from or interfere with another, and spirits and men are brought into harmony.' K'uei said, 'I smite the musical stone, I gently strike it, and the various animals lead on one another to dance.'" (This is the translation of James Legge updated by Clae Waltham in Clae Waltham, *Shu Ching: Book of History* [Chicago: Henry Regnery Company, 1971], p. 17.) For the text see *Shang-shu chin-ku-wen chu-shu* 尚書今古文注疏, 1B.20b.

[56] I.e., it is one and the same harmony in every piece of music. Thus there is nothing to be distinguished by the listener. For the host, harmony is the essential character of music, not some kind of emotion. "Mix water with water" alludes to a story in the *Tso chuan* (Duke Chao, 20th year: pp. 402–402), where Yen-tzu 晏子 rebuked the Marquis of Ch'i for thinking that Tzu-yu 子猶 was in harmony (和) with him. Yen-tzu says he is merely an assenter (同). But since he agrees with everything the Marquis does, it is hard to tell the difference, for "if you mix water with water, who can taste the difference?" For Legge's translation of the anecdote see *The Chinese Classics*, Vol. V, Part II, p. 684.

[57] Reported in the *Tso chuan* (Duke Hsi, 29th year: p. 137). Legge's translation is in *The Chinese Classics*, Vol. V, Part I, p. 214.

Music ... Neither Grief nor Joy

combative, that the army of Ch'u would be defeated.[58] Yang-she's mother heard the baby crying and knew he would bring ruin to the clan.[59] These several events were all verified in previous ages, and therefore they have all been recorded in the books. To draw our inference from this, flourish and decline and good and bad fortune are all present [in some way] in music. Now if you still want to call these false and lies, then anything said in the past and all records of the past must be thrown away; we cannot use them. But to talk in this way about those 'thorough discussions'—I am still uneasy about it. If you can explain the reason for this,[60] or clarify how this comes about, and arrange it that both theories [yours and that of the ancients] succeed, I would like to hear more about it."

The host responded: "Of someone who can come back with the other three corners,[61] we say he 'gets the meaning and forgets the words.'[62] Therefore in my previous remarks I talked generally and did not go into detail. But you keep bothering me with these criticisms that go round and round. Do I dare not to completely exhaust my ideas?

"If that cow from Lu knew that her calves had been sacrificed one by one,[63] and was able to grieve that her three children no longer existed, to hold in her sorrow through the years and bellow her lament to Ko-lu, then this is a case of having the heart and mind of a human; she differs only in her animal form. But this is something about which I have doubts. Cattle are not of the

---

[58] See above, note 50.

[59] See *Tso chuan* (Duke Chao, 28th year: p. 426). Legge's translation is in *The Chinese Classics*, Vol. V, Part II, p. 727. The story is also recorded in the *Kuo-yü*, in the "Conversations of Chin."

[60] Reading 其 for 斯, i.e., 其所以.

[61] See above, note 6.

[62] The Wu manuscript is correct in adding the 忘 before the 言. This is a quotation from *Chuang-tzu*, Ch. 26 (p. 75, lines 48–49). Watson translates, "Words exist because of meaning; once you have gotten the meaning, you can forget the words. Where can I find a man who has forgotten words so I can have a word with him?" (*The Complete Works of Chuang Tzu*, p. 302.) The allusion implies an insult—the host has not found in the guest someone he can talk to.

[63] Agreeing with Tai Ming-yang that 犠厤 should be 厤犠.

Music ... Neither Grief nor Joy

same species as man; there are no paths of communication between the two. If you say that birds[64] and animals are both able to speak,[65] and that Ko-lu received a special nature by which he alone could understand them, then this is a case of discussing their affairs by interpreting[66] their language, like translating and transmitting a foreign tongue. Since it is not a matter of knowing someone's feelings by examining their music, this is not a valid criticism of my position.

"If you say someone who is wise will thoroughly understand something as soon as he comes into contact with it, and that there is nothing he will not know, then let me first discuss what I find strange about this. May I ask, if a sage all of a sudden found himself in the lands of the Hu barbarians would he understand their language or not? My opponent must say that he would. Now how can we explain the principle involved in his knowing it? Let me borrow your illustration and with it set out the boundaries of examination and knowledge. Must he have repeated contact and exchange with them, and then get to know their language? Or, will be blow on the pitch-pipes and play the bamboo tuning tubes and in this way examine their music? Or, will be observe their manner and examine their facial expressions and in this way know their minds? This [the latter] would be a matter of knowing one's mind naturally from his air and appearance. Even though he himself said nothing, you could still know his mind. Thus the way of knowing does perhaps not rely on words. If you can blow on the pitch-pipes and examine their music, and in this way know their minds, then even if someone had his mind on a horse but by mistake said 'deer,' the examiner would definitely know[67] from 'deer' that he meant 'horse.' This means that one's mind is not related to what one says: and what

---

[64] Reading 鳥 for 鳴.
[65] The text has a lacuna here for which several variants exist. Of these 言 seems to be best.
[66] Reading the variant 解 for 稱.
[67] Reading 知 for 弘.

Music ... Neither Grief nor Joy

one says is perhaps not sufficient to verify what is on his mind. If one can know a language only through repeated contact and exchange, then this is a case [like] children learning language from their teacher and only then knowing it. But then what value is there in being wise [like a sage]?

"Language is not something that is by nature fixed. The five regions have different customs; the same thing has different designations. We simply select one name and use it as a sign. Now the sage exhausts the principles. This means that whatever is natural can be examined; there is no obscurity that cannot be illuminated. But if the principle involved is hidden, then you will not see it even if you are close by. Therefore, the language of a different land cannot be forcibly understood. To draw our inference from this, can Ko-lu's failure to understand the cry of that cow be anything but complete?

"You also criticize me by saying that 'music master K'uang blew on the pitch-pipes and knew that the airs of the south were non-combative, that the music of Ch'u had in it many sounds of dying.'[68] This is also something about which I have doubts. May I ask, when music master K'uang blew on the pitch-pipes, was it truly an air from Ch'u?[69] But they [Chin and Ch'u] are separated by a thousand li and sound cannot reach that far.[70] If you maintain that he truly knew this was an air[71] of Ch'u that came and entered his pitch-pipes, then I would point out that south of Ch'u are Wu and Yüeh and to the north are Liang and Sung: if he did not see the source, how could he know it [for

---

[68] This is not exactly what the guest had said. But it does agree with the original anecdote. See above, note 50.

[69] The host here plays on the double meaning of *feng* 風—a "tune," or "folksong," but also more generally the "air," or "wind." In the original anecdote K'uang *sings* a southern song (南風). But the host has more the idea of wind coming from Ch'u—wind touched by the current mood of the state—and entering into the pitch-pipes of K'uang.

[70] The point being that for the "southern song" (南風) to indicate the present condition of Ch'u it must come from Ch'u at the time.

[71] Reading the variant 風 for 國.

Music ... Neither Grief nor Joy

sure]? When the Yin and Yang are stirred and aroused, only then does wind arise; the mutual stimulation of the breaths touches the ground and sets it [wind] off.[72] How could something that arises in a Ch'u courtyard come and enter Chin?

"Moreover, the six Yang pitches and the six Yin pitches[73] divide the breaths of the four seasons. When the time arrives, the air moves; the pitch-pipes respond and the dust scatters.[74] These are all natural relationships; they do not rely on man to make them work. The ascending and descending notes[75] divide equally the harmony of the five tones[76] and set out in order the

---

[72] That is to say, if I am correct in my interpretation, the inner *ch'i* (breath, spirit, energy) of the leaders of Ch'u, which lacks the combative spirit, influences the *ch'i* in the earth, which then gives rise to wind. It is the wind which would indicate Ch'u's lack of fighting spirit, which has to make its way to Chin and into the pitch-pipes of music master K'uang.

[73] Literally the *lü* 律 and the *lü* 呂. The twelve pitch-pipes were distinguished in the Han, if not before, as six Yang and six Yin and then correlated with twelve months of the year, with half the year dominated by Yang and half dominated by Yin. Thus each month has a pitch appropriate to it. On this see *Han shu* 21 (Vol. 4, pp. 955–1026), "Lü-li chih" 律曆志 (Treatise on the Pitch-Pipes and the Calendar). The theory is also discussed in Fung Yu-lan's *History of Chinese Philosophy* (Princeton: Princeton University Press, 1953), tr. by Derk Bodde, Vol. II, ch. 3, especially pp. 118–123.

[74] This refers to a method for divining seasonal change. Ashes from the reed were put into the pitch-pipes. When the air (*ch'i*) outside had changed with the season, the dust would blow out of the appropriate pitch-pipe.

[75] According to one scheme, the twelve tones started with the lowest pitch and ascended to the highest through the twelve-month course of the year. But another scheme (described in the *Huai-nan-tzu*) had them starting with the highest (*ying-chung* 應鐘, Yin) at the winter solstice and descending for six months, and then the lowest (*huang-chung* 黃鐘, Yang) took over and the pitches gradually ascended. This more accurately reflects the Yin-Yang cycle in nature. See Fung Yu-lan, *History of Chinese Philosophy*, Vol. II, pp. 120–122.

[76] The "five tones" (*wu-sheng* 五聲) and the "twelve pitches" represent two different musical scales used in ancient China. The pentatonic scale corresponds to the notes C, D, E, G, A. The twelve pitches equal the twelve half-tones in the octave of the untempered chromatic scale. Here the two are being harmonized since the year can also be broken up in accord with the "five tones"—matching the *wu hsing* 五行 theory so popular in the Han—with any four of the tones controlling the four seasons and the fifth underlying all, or the fifth representing a "middle" season between summer and fall.

Music ... Neither Grief nor Joy

domains of firm and yielding.⁷⁷ However, the twelve pitches have fixed sounds. Though you blow *chung-lü*⁷⁸ in the winter, its tone will be naturally full and not diminish.⁷⁹ So if we blow on a pitch-pipe which itself will not diminish with the breath of someone from Chin, how can the wind from Ch'u come and enter into it and share the role of making the sound?⁸⁰ Since wind has no form and there is no connection between music and pitch-pipe, you will find nothing in wind and pitch-pipe relevant to the examination of principles. Is this not correct? Could it [not] be that master K'uang alone was widely learned in many things and himself possessed the knowledge to recognize the signs of victory and defeat, but, wishing to set the minds of the masses at ease, he attributed it to the divine and mysterious—like Po Ch'ang-ch'ien in his guarantee of long life to Duke Ching?⁸¹

"You also criticize me by saying that 'Yang-she's mother heard the baby crying and knew he would bring ruin to the clan.' May I once again ask, how did she know that? Was it a case of having spiritual intelligence and special understanding so that she could deal with hidden meaning? Or, had she once before heard a child cry with disastrous results of this magnitude, and, on the basis of the similarity in sound of the former and present cries, knew he would ruin the clan? If it was spiritual intelligence

---

⁷⁷ The marks of *ch'ien* 乾 and *k'un* 坤, the first two hexagrams of the *I ching*. The twelve pitches meshed with the hexagrams in that the twelve months of the year were also thought in the Han to be controlled by the lines of these two hexagrams: the first line of *ch'ien* prevails in the eleventh month, the second line in the twelfth, etc., with the first line of *k'un* taking over in the sixth month. Again see Fung Yu-lan, *History of Chinese Philosophy*, Vol. II, pp. 122–123.

⁷⁸ The pitch for the beginning of summer, according to the "Yüeh ling" 月令 (Monthly Commands) section of the *Li chi*. See *Li chi hsün-tsuan* 6.14a.

⁷⁹ Reading the variant 損 for 韻.

⁸⁰ Literally "wax and wane," or "advance and retreat" (*ying-su* 盈縮) with it.

⁸¹ See *Yen-tzu ch'un-ch'iu*, "Nei-p'ien tsa-hsia" 內篇襍下, 6.1b–2b. Po Ch'ang-ch'ien 伯常騫 told Duke Ching of Ch'i that he would add seven years to his life by prayer and sacrifice, and that the earth would move as a sign. But Yen-tzu got Po to confess that he knew the earth would shake whenever the stars *wei* (three stars lying behind the handle of the dipper) and *shu* (the "pivot," the first star in the handle of the dipper) disappeared.

Music ... Neither Grief nor Joy

and special understanding, the proper match for hidden meaning, then this was not something attained by reason. Although you say she 'listened' to the cry, she took no evidence from the sounds of the child. If it is rather that she knows the present cry will lead to evil because the one she heard before had, then this is a case of using sound A as the measure for examining cry B.

"The relationship of music to mind[82] is like that of body to mind. There are those with physical features the same whose feelings differ, and there are those who differ in appearance but who are the same in mind. How can I explain this? Sages are equal in intelligence and virtue, but their physical forms are not the same. If the mind is the same but the appearance different, then how can you speak of observing the form and knowing the mind?

"Moreover, how does the mouth's stimulation of breath to make sound differ in any way from the flutes[83] whistling by being filled with breath? That the good or evil of the sound of a cry does not come from the good or bad fortune of the baby's mouth is just like the fact that the clarity or muddledness in the sound of a lute or zither does not lie in the skill or clumsiness of the player. That the mind can distinguish principles and carry on skilled conversation but still cannot make a flute[84] play smoothly, is just like the fact that a musician can be skilled in rhythms but cannot make his instrument sing pure and clear. An instrument is good with no dependence on the refined musician; the flute is harmonious but not because of the intelligent mind. This being so, then mind and music are clearly two separate things. Since the two are truly this way, then one who is seeking to know someone else's feelings does not spend time observing his appearance and form, and examining the mind does not rely

---

[82] Reading the variant 心 for 音.
[83] Literally the *lai-yüeh* 籟籥, which one can understand as either the *lai* flute, or the *lai* and *yüeh* flutes. Both *lai* and *yüeh* are described as a short, three-holed flute or whistle. *Yüeh* is sometimes used as the generic name for flutes.
[84] Reading the variant 籟 for 內.

Music ... Neither Grief nor Joy

on listening to sounds and tones. If an examiner wishes to know the mind by means of music, is he not indeed off the track?

"Now this mother from Chin has as yet no evidence to go on from the child's growing up. She solely believes in a sound she has heard before and uses it to verify today's cry. How could this not be some lie originating in a former age that curiosity-lovers[85] followed and reported?"

The guest from Ch'in objected: "I have heard that one who is defeated is not ashamed to run away;[86] this is how he keeps himself intact. But my mind is not yet satisfied and I have expressed myself in my objections.[87] Let me move on to what remains.

"If you have someone who is peaceful and calm listen to the *cheng*,[88] or the *ti* whistle, or the *p'i-p'a*,[89] his form will become restless and his will jumpy. But if he hears the music of the lute or the zither, his body[90] is tranquil and his mind serene.[91] Even with one and the same instrument, the effect of songs is different in each case, and the feelings change accordingly. If we play the music of Ch'in, we sigh with admiration and become resolved and dedicated: with the songs of Ch'i and Ch'u, the feelings are united and thoughts concentrated: If we let go with a little ditty, then happiness is released and our desires satisfied. The heart is changed by music: the examples of this are many. If restlessness and tranquillity come from music, then why do you draw the line

---

[85] Literally a *hao-ch'i che* 好奇者, lover of the strange and unusual.

[86] The guest perhaps has in mind Ts'ao Chih's 曹植 (A.D. 192–232) statement in his "Ch'ing chao hsiang chiang-tung piao" 請招降江東表: "A skilled debater is not embarrassed to concede; a skilled fighter is not ashamed to flee." See Yen K'o-chün, *Ch'üan shang ku ... wen*, "San-kuo wen," Vol. 2, p. 1134, top.

[87] Following Tai Ming-yang's suggested emendation of putting the 於, which the Wu manuscript has before the 難, after it.

[88] The *cheng* 箏 is similar to the zither (*se* 瑟) but generally has only twelve or thirteen strings to the latter's twenty-five. On the various stringed instruments mentioned in the essay—the *ch'in*, the *se*, *cheng*, and *p'i-p'a*, see R. H. van Gulik, *The Lore of the Chinese Lute*, Chapter 1, pp. 1–21.

[89] A five- or six-stringed guitar-like instrument.

[90] Reading the variant 體 for 聽.

[91] Reading the variant 閑 for 閒.

Music ... Neither Grief nor Joy

with grief and joy, simply saying that the music of Perfect Harmony affects all things? To attribute the Great Unity[92] to music, while entrusting the manifold changes to the emotions of man—can this be anything but [a case of] having no knowledge of *that* and not understanding *this*?"

The host responded: "In your refutation you say that the *p'i-p'a*, the *cheng*, and the *ti* whistle make people restless and jumpy. And you also say that 'the effect of songs is different in each case, and the feelings change accordingly.' These are indeed things that cause people to be affected in always the same way. With the *p'i-p'a*, the *cheng*, and the *ti*, the intervals are close togehter[93] and the notes are high, the changes [in melody, tempo?] are many and the beat fast. With high notes in charge of fast beat, the body is restless and the will jumpy, just as wind chimes startle the ear, and bells and drums frighten the mind. Thus, 'When we hear the sound of war drums, we are aroused to take command.'[94] Thus it appears that as the noise is great or little in music, the effect is ferocity or tranquillity.

"The essence of the lute and zither is that the intervals[95] are far

---

[92] The "Great Unity" (*ta-t'ung* 大同) is a phrase which occurs in both the *Chuang-tzu* and the *Lieh-tzu*. Presumably another name for the Tao, it stresses the unifying nature of the one force in all things. In *Chuang-tzu*, Ch. 11 (p. 28, lines 64–66), we find the following said of the Great Man: "He dwells in the echoless, moves in the directionless, takes by the hand you who are rushing and bustling back and forth, and proceeds to wander in the beginningless. He passes in and out of the boundless, and is ageless as the sun. His face and form blend with the Great Unity, the Great Unity which is selfless." (Tr. by Burton Watson, *The Complete Works of Chuang Tzu*, p. 124.)

[93] Or possibly the "spacing," the space between bridges or frets on the *p'i-p'a* and the *cheng*; with the *ti* whistle, the space between the holes. The word is *chien* 間. The *p'i-p'a* has five or six strings and is shaped like a mandolin with frets on the handle. The *cheng* has twelve or thirteen strings and is relatively short. *Chengs* are sometimes pictured with one or two sets of bridges. The *ti* is a short pipe of bamboo with seven holes close together.

[94] *Li chi* 19, the "Record of Music," (*Yüeh-chi* 樂記). In *Li chi hsün-tsuan*, see 19.19b

[95] Reading the variant 間 for 閑. The lute has no bridge on the body of the instrument save one at the top, where the seven strings pass through; thus the strings stretch the length of the instrument with no break. The zither does have a movable bridge for each string, but the instrument is so long that there is still much space between bridge and the ends of the instrument.

Music ... Neither Grief nor Joy

apart and the notes are low, the changes are few and the sounds pure and clear.[96] With low notes controlling few changes, if you do not empty your mind and listen tranquilly you will not exhaust the limits of purity and harmony. Therefore the body[97] is tranquil and the mind serene.

"That the effect of songs is different in each case is just like the music of different instruments. The songs of Ch'i and Ch'u have much repetition and therefore the feelings are one; the changes are few,[98] and therefore one's thoughts are concentrated. The music in a little ditty pours forth with the beauty of the many notes and brings together the harmony of the five tones. Ditties are rich in substance and broad in effect; therefore the mind is beset[99] with many thoughts. The five tones are brought together; therefore happiness is released and the desires satisfied. However, in all of these cases, the essential factor is that the music is simple or complex, high or low, or good or bad, and the emotions respond by being restless or tranquil, concentrated or scattered, just as when you go sight-seeing in the capital your eyes overflow and your feelings are scattered, but when you sit quietly and study songs, your thought are tranquil and your appearance correct.[100] This means that the essential thing in music is that it is simply either relaxed or intense; the response of the emotions to music is also limited to restlessness or tranquillity.

"That the effect of songs is different in each case, and that the feelings note the change, is just like the fact that the flavors each have a different beauty but the mouth in each case knows it. The

---

[96] Robert van Gulik (*Lore of the Chinese Lute*, p. 1) says of the music of the lute: "... its music is not primarily melodical. Its beauty lies not so much in the succession of notes as in each separate note in itself. 'Painting with sounds' might be a way to describe its essential quality."

[97] The text has 聽, "listening is tranquil." But Tai Ming-yang is surely correct in emending this to 體 on the basis of what the guest said earlier.

[98] Reading 少 instead of 妙 on the basis of what is said in the text later on.

[99] Reading the Wu variant 役, literally "to serve," "to be a slave to," for *ch'ih* 侈, "to go to excess."

[100] The "just as ..." passage is added in the Wu manuscript.

Music ... Neither Grief nor Joy

five flavors are completely different, but they find their great union in beauty; song variations though many also find their great union in harmony. In beauty there is sweetness and in harmony there is joy. But the feelings that change with songs are cut off from the domain of harmony, and the mouth that responds to sweetness is severed from the realm of beauty.[101] How could we find grief and joy in it?

"However, people's feelings are not the same. We each[102] take our own view as the correct one and then express what we feel. If you say that peace and harmony and grief and joy are all on the same level, then there is nothing that is first there and then released. Therefore you end up with nothing but restlessness or tranquillity. But if there is emotion that is released, then this is controlled from the inside, not by peace and harmony. To speak from this perspective, restlessness and tranquillity are the effect of music; grief and joy are the controllers of emotion. You cannot say that grief and joy both come from music simply because you have seen that music produces the responses of restlessness and tranquillity.

"Moreover, though music may be fierce or tranquil, fierce and tranquil both have the same harmony. And whatever is moved by harmony is spontaneously released. How can I make this clear? A party of guests fills the hall. Drunk with wine, they play the lute. Some are delighted and happy; others become sad and weep. It is not that they were led to grief by one thing and brought to joy by another. There has been no change in the song from what they were playing before, yet sorrow and happiness both result. Is this not a case of 'blowing differently through the ten thousand things'?[103] It can only be that it has no control over delight and anger, and no control over grief and joy. Therefore

---

[101] The text says the reverse—i.e., "the mouth that responds to *beauty* is severed from the realm of sweetness." But the analogy seems to demand this correction.

[102] Reading the Wu variant 名 for 自.

[103] Again the allusion to *Chuang-tzu*, Ch. 2 (p. 3, line 9).

Music . . . Neither Grief nor Joy

happiness and sorrow simultaneously appear. If we were using a song that was emotionally one-sided and fixed, containing sounds all of one kind, then the emotions released and manifested would in each case match the music. Then how can this simultaneously control a host of different ideas, and together release many different emotions? To speak from this perspective, peace and harmony is the substance of music, but it moves things in different ways; dependence on something else is the essential character of mind and will; they are released in response to stimulation. This being the case, the relationship of music to mind is one of separate roads and different paths; they do not intersect. How can you stain the Great Harmony with happiness and sorrow, combine the Void Name with grief and joy?"

The guest from Ch'in objected as follows: "In your statement you say that 'fierce and tranquil have both the same harmony. And whatever is moved by harmony is spontaneously released. Therefore drunk with wine they play the lute but happiness and sorrow both result.' This says that strong feelings inclined one way or another[104] first build up inside. Therefore, one who nourishes pleasant thoughts will express those feelings when he hears a sad song, while one who is sad inside will be moved by a happy song.

"Now music must naturally be fixed when it comes to grief and joy. But the transformation brought on by music is slow to take effect. It cannot be hurried, and it cannot come up against its opposite and right away change it. But strongly inclined feelings are aroused the moment they come into contact with something. Thus, this is why grief and joy simultanously respond. But although the two feelings appear together, in what way does this harm the claim that music has fixed principles?"

The host responded: "You criticize me by saying that 'grief and joy naturally have fixed sounds but strongly inclined feel-

---

[104] The text says 偏拜之情. Lu Hsün says this must be 偏重 —"strongly leaning in one direction"—and I have followed him, even though Tai Mingyang says both will work.

ings cannot be quickly changed. Therefore one who harbors feelings of sorrow will be sad, even when he hears a happy song.' If things are as you say, then there are fixed types of music. Now let us suppose someone repeatedly plays "The Bleating Deer"[105]—a happy song indeed—and someone consumed by sorrow hears it. Even though music's transformation is slow to take effect, it would never be able to make him change and be happy. And how could it increase his grief? It is like having the heat from a single torch: although it could never warm up an entire room, it certainly would not, to the contrary, increase the cold. Fire is not the thing to magnify the cold; music is not the means to increase the grief. If you pluck the strings in the banquet hall and happiness and sorrow both result, this is truly because Perfect[106] Harmony has released pent-up emotions and drawn out people's feelings. Therefore, I make it to be simply the case that, having been aroused by external things, one is able to exhaust his inner self.

"In your criticism you say that 'strongly inclined feelings are aroused the moment they come into contact with something. Thus, this is why grief and joy simultaneously respond.' Now those who speak of grief, some see bench and cane[107] and weep; others are overcome by the sight of carriage and robes.[108] It is just that they are moved that the people are gone while their possessions remain, pained that memories are still vivid while their physical bodies are lost from view. But in all of these cases,

---

[105] Poem 161 in the *Book of Poetry*. For Waley's translation see Arthur Waley, *The Book of Songs* (New York: Grove Press, 1960), p. 192. the last stanza reads: "Yu, yu cry the deer, Nibbling the wild garlic of the fields. I have a lucky guest. I play my zitherns, small and big, Play my zitherns, small and big. Let us make music together, let us be merry, For I have good wine, To comfort and delight the heart of a lucky guest."

[106] Reading the Wu text variant 至 for 主.

[107] Reading 机 as 几. This is a sign that one's parents are getting old. The *Li chi* (1.5a in *Li chi hsün-tsuan*) says that you must carry a bench and cane with you when you are discussing matters with an elder.

[108] Presumably those left behind by deceased parents. Tai Ming-yang cites a passage from *Shih chi* 30 (Vol. 4, p. 1420) where the expression "carriage and robes" (*yü-fu*) is used in this way.

Music ... Neither Grief nor Joy

there is naturally something that causes these feelings. If it is not that the grief arises from contact with a [memorable] spot, then the tears appear when they face their [parents'] mats. But in the present case of someone who has tears flowing from listening to a happy[109] song, with no[110] bench or cane to stir his emotions— is this not because whatever harmony moves is spontaneously released?"

The guest from Ch'in objected: "In your [previous] statement you said 'Drunk with wine they play the lute, but happiness and sorrow both result.' I wished to understand this, and therefore I replied that it is simply that strongly inclined feelings are released when they are moved by something. But now let me say what is really on my mind, and I will make my point clear with proven results. Now the mind of man [is such that] if it is not happy then it is sad; if it is not sad then it is happy. These are the great extremes of emotion and will. However, crying shows the pain of sorrow, while a smile is the sign of happiness. Now when someone listens to the songs of Ch'i and Ch'u, I have seen on their faces grief and tears, but I have never seen the expression of laughter or a smile. This must mean that the songs of Ch'i and Ch'u have grief as their essence. Therefore, those who are moved by them all respond to the degree [of emotion]. How could it be merely a matter of 'much repetition' and 'few changes,' and thus 'the feelings are one and thinking concentrated'?[111] If this can truly bring you to tears, then that music has in it grief and joy can conclusively be known."

The host replied: "Although feelings are moved[112] by grief and joy, of grief and joy there can be much or little, and the extremes of grief and joy do not necessarily show in the same way. With a little grief the expression is crestfallen, but with great sorrow you weep. This is the direction of grief. With a little

---

[109] The text says *ho* 和, "harmony," but *lo* 樂, "joy," makes better sense.
[110] Reading the Wu variant 無 for 見.
[111] Referring back to what the host had said earlier.
[112] Reading the variant 感 in place of 慼.

Music ... Neither Grief nor Joy

happiness the face lights up, but with extreme joy the mind is contented.¹¹³ This is the principle of joy. What can I use to explain this? When members of your own family are safe, secure, and happy, then you are quiet, and natural, for this makes you feel self-attained. But when there is a crisis and they narrowly escape harm, then the clapping of your hands cannot keep up with the dancing of your feet. To speak from this perspective, that this dancing is not as good as the former self-attainment—how can it not be true?¹¹⁴

"To turn to smiles and laughter, though they come from happy feelings, nonetheless they are naturally the result of causes, they are not natural responses to music.¹¹⁵ This means that in the response of joy to music, self-attainment is the key thing, whereas in the response of grief to stimulation, weeping is the result. When you weep your body shakes and this can be recognized. But when the self is attained, one's spirits are united and there is no [visible] change.¹¹⁶

"Therefore, you have observed where they differ but do not understand where they are the same. You have distinguished their external features but not yet examined the inner states. This being the case, how can the fact that smiles and laughter fail to appear with music be limited to the tunes of Ch'i and Ch'u?¹¹⁷

"You do not seek for joy in the realm of self-attainment, and you say that grief is the very essence of [the music] of Ch'i and

---

[113] The Wu text reads that with extreme happiness (至樂) you smile (而笑). Tai Ming-yang says this is correct. But the form of the host's coming argument is that extreme joy, as opposed to extreme grief, is something internal that does not show in facial expressions.

[114] That is to say, self-attainment (*tzu-te* 自得) represents a higher form of joy even though it does not show.

[115] Tai Ming-yang's text after "although they come from happy feelings," reads 然自然應聲之具也, which seems contrary to what the host wants to say. The Wu text has 然自以理成，又非自然應之聲具也, which I have followed, moving the 之 to follow 聲.

[116] Reading the Wu variant 變 for 憂.

[117] The host's point being that some people may be happy when they hear this music, but their happiness being the extreme form of self-attainment, there is no sign of this in their expression.

Music . . . Neither Grief nor Joy

Ch'u, simply because no one laughs or smiles. Is this not because you have no knowledge of grief and do not understand joy?"[118]

The guest from Ch'in asked the following: "There is the saying by Confucius—'For improving customs and bettering traditions there is nothing better than music.'[119] But if things are as you say, and none of the many different kinds of grief and joy are to be found in music, then what in the end are we to use for improving customs and bettering traditions? Also, the ancients were cautious with delicate and lovely airs, and they restrained the use of music that was pleasing to the ear. Therefore they said, 'Do away with the music of Cheng and keep your distance from flatterers.'[120] This being the case, then 'the songs of Cheng and Wei [lead the mind to lascivious thoughts],'[121] but 'we strike the musical stone to bring harmony to spirits and men.'[122] May I presume to ask,[123] since the two kinds of music, Cheng and 'Elegant,' represent the extremes of what is glorious and what is corrupt, in improving and bettering customs and

---

[118] Mimicking the guest's earlier question: "Can this be anything but [a case of] having no knowledge of *that*[harmony in music] and not understanding *this* [man's emotions]?"

[119] See the *Hsiao ching*, Ch. 12 (p. 4).

[120] Confucius says this in *Analects* 15:11 (p. 31). D. C. Lau translates: "Banish the tunes of Cheng and keep plausible men at a distance. The tunes of Cheng are wanton and plausible men are dangerous." (*Confucius: The Analects*, pp. 133-134.)

[121] The line in brackets does not occur in any text. But Tai Ming-yang and Lu Hsün were both agreed that something here is missing. I have followed Tai Ming-yang's suggestion (see his note on p. 221) that what is missing is 使人之心淫, making this a quote from the *Hsün-tzu*, Ch. 20 (p. 77, lines 25), "Yüeh-lun" 樂論.

[122] The whole is probably a quote from the *Shu*, but only the first half of the line occurs in present versions of that work. In the "I chi" 益稷 chapter we find "K'uei said, 'When the musical stone is tapped or struck with force [戛擊, 鳴球]; when the lutes are strongly swept or gently touched to accompany the singing; then the progenitors of the sovereign come to the service....'" (Tr. by Legge/Waltham, *Shu Ching: Book of History*, p. 34.) Shun does say in the "Shun tien," in his charge to K'uei to be Director of Music: "In this way the eight different kinds of musical instruments can be adjusted so that one shall not take from or interfere with another, and spirits and men are brought into harmony."

[123] The Tai Ming-yang text mistakenly prints 閒 for 問.

Music ... Neither Grief nor Joy

traditions with which would we succeed? I would like[124] to hear more about this so that my doubts might be removed."[125]

The host responded in this way: "One who speaks of improving customs and bettering traditions must come after a period of decay and decline. The kings of antiquity, carrying on the work of Heaven in bringing order to things, necessarily venerated teachings that were simple and easy, and controlled by means of the government of non-action. The ruler was tranquil above and his ministers submissive below. Mysteriously things transformed and in hidden ways interfused. Heaven and man were united and at peace.[126] Those species subject to withering and decay were immersed and nourished in life-giving fluids. All within the six directions[127] were bathed and purified by the Vast Stream,[128] washed and cleansed of all defiling impurities. All forms of life were secure and at ease, 'bringing to themselves many blessings.'[129] Silently they followed the Way, cherishing loyalty and holding righteousness dear, unaware of the reason why things were so. Filled with a harmonious heart on the inside, they manifested a harmonious manner on the out. So they sang to express their wills and danced to make known their feelings. After that they refined it [music] with stylish ornament, and

---

[124] Following the original Wu manuscript, which has 願 here for 幸.

[125] More playful banter between host and guest. The host had said, it might be remembered, at several points, "This is something about which I have doubts" (wu chih so i yeh 吾之所疑也). Now the guest comes back with "so that my doubts might be removed" (i wu so i 以悟所疑).

[126] Probably a take-off on the "image" to Hexagram 11 in the *I ching* (p. 9) which begins 天地交 · 泰. Wilhelm translates "Heaven and earth unite. The image of Peace." See Richard Wilhelm, tr., *The I Ching or Book of Changes* (Princeton: Princeton University Press, 1950, tr. by Cary F. Baynes), p. 49. Here the Chinese is 天人交泰.

[127] The *liu-ho* 六合; the four cardinal directions plus up and down—i.e. the limits of the universe.

[128] The "Vast Stream" (*hung-liu* 鴻流) being an image used for the Tao, for the Tao is all-encompassing, a source of nourishment and life to all things and the on-going force of change in all things.

[129] Quoting a line from poem 235 "Wen wang" in the *Book of Poetry* (p. 58, stanza 6).

Music ... Neither Grief nor Joy

displayed[130] it in the 'Airs' and the 'Elegant';[131] they spread it by means of the eight kinds of sound,[132] and responded to it with Great Harmony. They guided their spirits and breath, nourished them and brought them to completion; they welcomed their feelings and nature, took them to the limit and made them shine. They caused mind and principle to accord with one another and made harmony[133] and music mutually respond. United they merged together, making their beauty complete. Thus happy feelings were manifested by [instruments] of metal and stone; 'comprehension vast and illumination great'[134] showed themselves in their music. To go on from this,[135] all the states in the empire had the same customs, fragrant and flourishing, one[136] in their luxuriousness, with the aroma of the autumn orchid. Without seeking it, people were sincere; without making plans, things were brought to completion.[137] Respectfully things loved one another. [Looking at this period of time] is like unrolling an embroidered tapestry or displaying colored silk; thus the dazzling beauty can be seen. Of the flourishing periods of the Great Way, none was greater than this; of the accomplishments of the Great Peace, none was more illustrious than this. Therefore [Confucius] said: 'For improving customs and bettering traditions, nothing is better than music.' However,[138] the essence of music is such that the mind is the central thing. And therefore, music that has no sound is the father and mother of the

---

[130] Preferring the variant 昭 to 照.

[131] Two of the sections in the *Book of Poetry*, although the host might here have in mind types of music rather than these specific songs.

[132] Of the eight kinds of musical instruments.

[133] The Wu text has *ch'i* 氣, "breath." But "harmony" seems to me correct.

[134] A line from the "judgment" on Hexagram 2 of the *I ching* (p. 3). Wilhelm translates (*The I Ching*, pp. 386–387), "It embraces everything in its breadth and illumines everything in its greatness."

[135] All texts read 若以往, but Tai Ming-yang is surely correct in adding the 此 after the 若.

[136] Reading 齊 instead of 濟.

[137] Reading the Wu variant 成 for 誠.

[138] Adding the 然 in accord with the Wu text.

people.¹³⁹ To turn to the united harmony of the eight kinds of sound, this is what people delight in, and we also generally call this music. However, the improving and bettering of customs and traditions does not, fundamentally,¹⁴⁰ lie in this.

"Sounds in harmony and sequence—this is something that cannot be completely experienced by the emotions. For this reason the ancients, knowing that the emotions cannot be set free, restrained those that would get away, and knowing that desires cannot be taken to the limit, took themselves as examples of the extreme.¹⁴¹ [On this basis] they made the respectable rites and created music which would lead and guide. The mouth does not exhaust the possibilities of flavor; music does not exhaust the possibilities of sound. They estimated the proper mark between beginning and end, and calculated the mean between worthy and fool and made this the rule, making far and near have the same customs which could be used without end. It was also in this way that they founded loyalty and sincerity; they were set forth as things not to change. Therefore the village schools and those of families and towns, all follow them,¹⁴² having silk and

---

¹³⁹ So the text reads. But perhaps it should be "The one who thoroughly understands the music that has no sound...." In the opening of *Li chi*, Ch. 29 ("K'ung-tzu hsien-chü" 孔子閒居), Tzu-kung asks Confucius who deserves to be called the father and mother of the people. The reply is that it is the one who thoroughly understands the origin of the rites and music so that he can transmit the five perfections and put into practice the three "have-nots." The three "have-nots" are then explained as music that has no sound, rites that have no form, and funerals that have no mourning regulations. See *Li chi hsün-tsuan* 29.lab. Legge's translation is in Müller, *The Sacred Books of the East*, Vol. 28, pp. 278–283. As an example of the music that has no sound, Confucius cites the line from poem 271 (p. 74) of the *Book of Poetry*: "Night and day he enlarged its foundations by his deep and silent virtue." Thus, music that has no sound would seem to be that inner harmony or virtue that is not necessarily expressed. But this inner state of mind is superior to the music that is then produced.

¹⁴⁰ Adding the 本 that is found in the Wu text.

¹⁴¹ Follwing the Wu text reading of 自以爲致. The other texts have 因其所自. The translation is tentative.

¹⁴² Tai Ming-yang's text here has "change in accord with them" (隨之變). But the Wu text has 使 instead of 變, and this must start the next section, not end this one.

Music ... Neither Grief nor Joy

bamboo present together with meat stand and platter,[143] and feather and hair-adorned banners[144] used together with bowing and yielding, and proper speech [as in ritual] and harmonious music come together. If you are about to listen to *this* song, then you must hear *these* words; if you are going to observe *these* movements [in dance] then you must honor *this* rite. Matters of ritual are like those between guest and host; they first ascend and descend [the hall?], and only then is the exchange of toasts carried out.

"Therefore, regulation of word and speech, rhythm of sound and tone, the proper form for bowing and yielding, the number of times you move and stop, the mutual dependence of advance and retreat, these are all in substance the same. The ruler and his ministers use them at court; nobles and commoners use them in their homes. We practice them when we are young and do not neglect them when we are grown. When with mind secure and will resolved we follow the good day after day, only then will we approach them[145] with respect. And when we can maintain them[146] for a long time and not change, only then are we transformed and perfected. This was the intention of the former kings in using music. Therefore at court feasts and guest parties, the finest music must be present. For this reason state scribes in examining the flourish and decline of customs and traditions entrusted the joy to musicians, who made known the results by means of pipes and strings.[147] Those who spoke the words of the songs were held without blame; those who heard the songs

---

[143] I.e., on occasions of sacrifice. "Silk and bamboo" are musical instruments made of the two—i.e., stringed instruments and flutes.

[144] Reading 毛 as 旄, in accord with the Wu text; banners or flags decorated with animal tails. "Feathers and banners" were used in dancing.

[145] I am not sure what the "them" refers to, the "rites and music" most likely.

[146] Lu Hsün feels that a word is missing here.

[147] Referring to the well-known tradition that in the Chou dynasty the king sent out musicians to collect folksongs by which he could see the quality of life in his various states.

Music ... Neither Grief nor Joy

considered this sufficient evidence for self-admonishment. This was also the intention of the former kings in using music.

"Now as for the music of Cheng, this is actually the most exquisite music of all. But exquisite music moves people in the way that a beautiful face confuses the will. Addicted to pleasure and driven crazy by wine, it is easy to lose all that you have. If it is not the Perfect Man, who is able to stay in control?[148]

"The former kings were afraid that the whole world would get lost [in pleasure] and never return. Therefore they made use of the eight kinds of sound, making music that would not be defiling. But they cut off the Great Harmony without exhausting its different forms. They did away with music that was lovely and alluring, making it 'joyful without being licentious.'[149] But it is like the unblended Great Broth[150]—it does not reach the heights of the flavor of the peony.[151] If it is simply common and vulgar,

---

[148] Reading the Wu variant 御 for 禦.

[149] Alluding to Confucius' statement in *Analects* 3:20 (p. 5) where he says (D. C. Lau tr., *Confucius: The Analects*, p. 70), "In the *kuan-chü* [poem 1 in the *Book of Poetry*] there is joy without wantonness, and sorrow without self-injury."

[150] *T'ai-keng* 太羹 was used in sacrifice to the former kings. It was plain meat-broth, with no salted vegetables added in. In the "Yüeh-chi" 樂記 section of the *Li chi* (*Li chi hsün-tsuan* 19.3b) a remark is made that the host probably has in mind. Legge translates: "Hence the greatest achievements of music were not in the perfection of the airs; the (efficacy) of the ceremonies in the sacrificial offerings was not in the exquisiteness of the flavours. In the lutes for the Khing Miao the strings were of red (boiled) silk and the holes were wide apart; one lute began, and (only) three others joined it; there was much melody not brought out. In the ceremonies of the great sacrifices, the dark-coloured liquor took precedence, and on the stands were uncooked fish, while the grand soup had no condiments; there was much flavour left undeveloped." (See Legge's translation of the *Li chi*, in Max Müller, *The Sacred Books of the East*, Vol. 28, pp. 95–96.)

[151] The analogy is quite apt. The "Great Broth" compares well with the "Elegant" music—the "proper" music used at court functions; and the peony (*shao-yao* 勺藥), like the music of Cheng, was thought to be an aphrodisiac of sorts. Waley glosses poem 95 in the *Book of Poetry*—where in courtship a girl gives her lover a peony—in this way: "The peony has, of course, a great reputation for medicinal and magical powers, both in the West and in China. It shares some of the mythology of the mandrake. It was probably the root rather than the flower that first interested the Chinese; for the second element in the name (*Shao-yao*) means "medicinal herb," and it is the root of the peony that has

Music ... Neither Grief nor Joy

then music is not worth delighting in and is also not what we enjoy.

"If superiors lose the Way and the state loses its laws, and men and women chase after one another, and licentiousness and depravity know no limit, then customs because of this will change and manners will develop in accord with people's delights. If what is esteemed is whatever is willed, then the masses can abandon themselves to it; if they are allowed to delight in what they are accustomed to, then how can you punish them?

"If you rely on harmonious music and develop them with this as their companion, then their sincerity will be moved by words and their hearts moved by harmony, and customs and traditions will be completely reformed. It is because of this that it has its name.[152] However, the music so-named does not contain[153] lewdness and perversity. Licentiousness and uprightness are both in the mind. Thus the true nature of 'Elegant' and Cheng can also be seen."

---

always been used in medicine. It probably figured in courtship first as a love-philtre, and later (as in this poem) merely as a symbol of lasting affection, like our rosemary." (Waley, *The Book of Songs*, pp. 28–29.) But the peony is also thought by the Chinese to be the perfect blend of the five flavors.

[152] Its reputation for being able to "improve customs and better traditions."
[153] Following the Wu text which has 中 here. The Huang text has a lacuna.

HSI K'ANG

Dispelling Self-interest

(Shih-ssu lun)

::

Translator's Comments. This is a good exposition of Taoist moral theory, which might be thought of in the light of this essay as a morality of openness. The main thesis is that it is morally better to do and say what one genuinely feels, even if what one says or does goes against standard moral norms, than to hide one's feelings out of concern for what others might think. In this way one at least avoids hypocrisy; moreover, by being open, it is easier to change and correct one's faults.

The word ts'o 措 *is important in the essay; the key thing is to be* wu-ts'o 無, *without ts'o. For ts'o, Holzman has* s'engage *(to engage oneself, get involved) and also* action intéressée.[1] *I translate it "concern," so the important thing is to be "without concern," i.e., unconcerned with whether one's feelings and actions are right or wrong in standard terms, and unconcerned with what others might think. In modern Chinese* ts'o-i 措意 *means "to pay attention to," or "to mind."*

Kung 公 *in the essay is "unselfish," and* ssu 私 *is "self-interest." But Hsi K'ang also uses* kung *to mean "be open," "go public," while* ssu *means to keep things to oneself. The reader must keep this double meaning in mind.*

When we speak of the "Gentleman" we mean someone whose mind is unconcerned with right and wrong, whose actions are not opposed to the Way. How can I explain this? One whose breath is tranquil and spirit empty has a mind which does not

---

[1] See Holzman, *La Vie et la Pensée de Hi K'ang*, p. 122, note 2.

Dispelling Self-interest

dwell on arrogance and self-praise; one whose substance is pure and mind penetrating has feelings which are not attached to that which he desires. Since arrogance and self-praise do not exist in his mind, he can transcend the moral teachings[1] and follow nature; since his feelings do not cling to that which he desires, he can carefully examine noble and mean and thoroughly understand the essential nature of things. Since the nature of things is followed and understood, the Great Way will not be opposed. Since he transcends fame and follows his heart, he will not be concerned with right and wrong.

For this reason, when we speak of the Gentleman, we take "lack of concern" [with right and wrong] as the central thing, and understanding things as his point of beauty. When we speak of the Small Man—that he hides his feelings is his error, and his opposition to the Way is his defect. Why? Because hiding the feelings, pride, and stinginess are the worst evils of the Small Man, while the empty mind without concern is the sincere action of the Gentleman. Therefore the *Great Way* says:[2] "If I had no body what worries would I have?" [And] "To not consider life a thing of value[3] is better than valuing life."

To speak on the basis of this, the Perfect Man in his intentions definitely harbors no [self-]concern. Therefore, I Yin did not begrudge[4] his worth to T'ang of Yin, and the whole world was benefitted, and his name became well-known.[5] Tan of Chou [the Duke of Chou] paid no mind to the suspicions[6] and acted in

---

[1] The *ming chiao* 名教, literally the "name" or "fame" teachings; this is sometimes translated as the Doctrine of Names. The phrase is code at this time for the proper moral instruction of the Confucian gentleman, the one hoping for fame in government service.

[2] That is, the text of *Lao-tzu*, the *Tao te ching*. For these quotes see Ch. 13 (Part I, 7a in SPPY ed.) and Ch. 75 (Part II, 22a) respectively.

[3] This *kuei* 貴 is not found in extant versions of the *Lao-tzu* save one—the Fu I text has it.

[4] Reading the Wu variant 惜 for 借.

[5] I Yin 伊尹 served as minister to T'ang 湯, and with his help T'ang founded the Yin 殷 (or Shang) dynasty in (traditional chronology) 1766 B.C.

[6] Reading the Wu variant 嫌 for 賢. See below, the "Essay on Kuan and Ts'ai."

Dispelling Self-interest

secret; therefore he used the moment to assume the regency, and [the Chou] was transformed and flourished. I Wu [Kuan Chung] did not hide his talents[7] from [Duke] Huan of Ch'i; therefore his state established the hegemony, and his ruler was revered.[8] How could we say, with respect to their intentions, that they acted for themselves and clung to self-interest? Therefore the *Kuan-tzu*[9] says: "When the Gentleman practices the Way he forgets that he is an individual." These words are true indeed.

The Gentleman, in doing the worthy, does not first examine to see if this will bring him good fortune,[10] and only then act. He follows his heart without exhausting it;[11] he does not first debate the good and only then decide what is proper. He manifests his feelings with no concern [with what others might think]; he does not first discuss whether something is right and only then do it. For this reason, unrestrained he forgets about the worthy, and the worthy and good fortune[12] coincide. Indifferent to all else, he follows his heart, and his heart and the good come together. Forgetting himself, he has no concerns, and his actions are one with the right.

Therefore, in discussing unselfishness and self-interest, even though someone might have his will set on the Way and maintain the good and act[13] without wickedness and evil, if he keeps all that he cherishes to himself, we cannot say he is devoid of self-

---

[7] Reading the Wu variant *shan* 善 "his good points," for *ch'ing*, 情 "feelings."

[8] Huan of Ch'i 齊桓 became duke in 685 B.C., and became the first hegemon (*pa* 霸) with the help of his able minister Kuan Chung 管仲. For Kuan Chung's biography see *Shih chi* 62 (Vol. 7, pp. 2131–2134).

[9] Both Tai Ming-yang and Lu Hsün point out that these two characters do not occur in this passage as it is cited in Hsi K'ang's *Chin shu* biography (Vol. 5, p. 1370). Moreover, Tai Ming-yang adds that the two lines cited from the *Kuan-tzu* are not found in present versions of that work. Holzman (*La Vie*, p. 124, note 1) does note a passage in the *Kuan-tzu* that is close (6.9a in the SPPY ed.). This reads: "A man of worth, in cultivating his own person will forget about his name; a ruler in practicing the Way, forgets about his accomplishments and merit."

[10] Following the Wu manuscript variant of *ch'ing* 慶.

[11] Preferring the Wu variant of 窮 to 邪.

[12] Again following the Wu text in reading 慶 instead of 度.

[13] Tai Ming-yang notes a lacuna here for which there are many variant readings. Of these I prefer 行, but the 心 of the Wu text would also work well.

Dispelling Self-interest

interest; and even though someone wishes to boast of his abilities and his feelings go against the Way, if he reveals all that he holds dear, we cannot say he is not unselfish. If we hold to the principle that one must be open, to restrain the feelings that are not, that means that even though one is by nature[14] good, he may still not break away from selfish concerns; and, even though one desires to boast of his talents, he may still not sink into selfishness.

If one values his name and respects his mind, then he must make known his feelings of right and wrong. If [one's feelings] of right and wrong are revealed, one who is good will not have the fault of hiding his feelings, and one who is wrong will not add to it the greater wrong of not being open and frank. If one lacks this fault [in the first case], then all good qualities will be attained; and if one is without the greater wrong [in the second], the only fault he will have is that of being wrong, and thus, because of this, he can correct his mistake. Not only is this the way to be completely good, it also serves to stimulate [to good] those who are not. The good by this means are completely good, and those who are wrong can correct their mistakes. How much the more is this the case for those who are at the extremes of right and wrong?

Therefore, being good or bad [by nature] are the extremes of things. If one falls between the two, then in all that he does he will necessarily succeed if he is open [unselfish] and fail if he keeps it to himself. These people all have the same capacities, but some succeed and some fail. Being open and being private are the roads to success, [on the one hand], and failure, [on the other], and the gates to good and bad fortune.

Therefore, those who lie at the extremes and do not change are few;[15] those not at the extremes, [whose moral state] depends on how they use what they have, are many. If one is endowed with[16]

---

[14] Reading the Wu variant of 性 for 爲.

[15] Paraphrasing Confucius in *Analects* 17:2 (p. 35): "It is only the most intelligent and the most stupid who are not susceptible to change." (Tr. by D. C. Lau, *Confucius: The Analects*, p. 143. In Lau's translation this is 17:3.)

[16] Reading *chih* 質, "basic substance" as *tzu* 資, "native endowment," as Tai-Ming-yang suggests. But either word would work.

Dispelling Self-interest

the nature[17] of the average man,[18] then his fate will lie in the use made of his substance. If he rests his mind on the virtuous stalwarts of antiquity, and follows them in walking the path of openness, then if he speaks what is on his mind, his words will all be right, and if he acts as his feelings are moved, his actions will all be blessed [with good fortune].

Thus what others[19] are concerned about will not be his concern; what the common lot keep to themselves he does not consider as private. In speaking he does not calculate whether he will succeed or fail, and yet he encounters the good; in acting he does not weigh out right and wrong, and yet he meets with good fortune. How could this not[20] be because of the fixed nature of unselfishness bringing success and selfishness spelling defeat? This being the case, why would he further have any concerns?

Therefore, Li Fu admitted to being a thief, and [Duke] Wen of Chin was pleased;[21] Po Ti bewailed his crimes, and his loyalty

---

[17] The Wu text has *t'i* 體 instead of *hsing* 性. Again, the meaning is the same.

[18] Or "the man in the middle," the *chung-jen* 中人. The "average man" is mentioned by Confucius in *Analects* 6:21 (p. 11): "You can tell those who are above average [中人以上] about the best, but not those who are below average." (Tr. by D. C. Lau, *Confucius: The Analects*, p. 84.) But Hsi K'ang here has in mind the moral theory of Wang Ch'ung 王充 (A.D. 27-100?) who, based partly on things said by Confucius here and in 17:2 (see note 15), argued that some people are by nature good and some are by nature evil, while those in between (the *chung-jen*), the majority of people, are morally mixed by nature and can go either way. He says: "At bottom I consider Mencius' doctrine of the goodness of human nature as referring to people above the average, Hsün Tzu's doctrine of evil nature of man as referring to people below the average, and Yang Hsiung's (53 B.C. to A.D. 18) doctrine that human nature is a mixture of good and evil as referring to average people." (See his *Lun-heng* 論衡, (tr. by Wing-tsit Chan, *A Source Book in Chinese Philosophy*, pp. 295-296).

[19] The Huang text has *t'ung* 同. Lu Hsün says this must be *ch'ing* 情, "feeling", and Tai Ming-yang suggests it might be an error for *hsiang* 向, "the former." I think we can stay with *t'ung* in this sense; it parallels the *su* 俗, "common lot," in the next line.

[20] Agreeing with Tai Ming-yang that there should be a 非 here. But without this one could perhaps read this as "How could it be that he had calculated that openness brings success and being private defeat?"

[21] For this see *Tso chuan*, Duke Hsi, 24th year (p. 123). Li Fu 里鳧 (but in the *Tso chuan* called T'ou-hsü 頭須) attended Ch'ung-erh 重耳, the future Duke Wen of Chin, being in charge of his treasury. When Ch'ung-erh had to flee the

Dispelling Self-interest

was established and his life preserved;[22] Mu Hsien confessed his offense, and his words were accepted and his reputation praised;[23] [Kao] Chien-li told the truth, and the entire hall was moved to tears.[24] All of these men, because of disasters where they had risked their lives, came to critical junctures where the outcome was unpredictable. They revealed and disclosed what they knew in their minds, and yet[25] as a result they were safe and secure. How much the more [will this be true] for the Gentleman, who does not have the crimes of these men, and to the contrary has his virtue? To concern oneself with "being good" is truly a great defect.[26] "It is only because he recognizes his defects as defects, that he therefore has no defects."[27] To have the defect and be able to correct it is also better than [simply] having the defect.[28]

---

country, Li Fu also fled and took the treasury with him. But, he used the money to secure his lord's return, and he was forgiven by Ch'ung-erh. The story is translated in Legge, *The Chinese Classics*, Vol. V, Part I, p. 191.

[22] See the same reference to the *Tso chuan* (Duke Hsi, 24th year, p. 123). Po Ti 勃鞮 (called P'ei 披 in the *Tso*), chief of the eunuchs, was hired by Duke Hsien and then Duke Hui to kill Ch'ung-erh. When the latter took over the throne of Chin, P'ei was denied an interview. But he emphasized that he was only doing his job in serving his lords before, and now he wished to serve this lord, pointing out that there were again threats against the duke's life. For the translation see Legge, *The Chinese Classics*, Vol. V, Part I, p. 191.

[23] See *Shih chi* 81 (Vol. 8, pp. 2439–2440). This is translated by Yang Hsien-yi and Gladys Yang in *Records of the Historian*, pp. 139–140. Mu Hsien 穆賢 advised King Hui-wen of Chao to use his (Mu's) steward, Lin Hsiang-ju, as envoy to Ch'in in the exchange of fifteen Ch'in cities for the Pien Ho jade, because Lin Hsiang-ju had once correctly advised him (Mu) to admit to a crime and accept the punishment rather than flee to Yen.

[24] By his music. See *Shih chi* 86 (Vol. 8, pp. 2536–2537), translated by Yang Hsien-yi and Gladys Yang in *Records of the Historian*, p. 401. Kao Chien-li 高漸離 was the good friend and accomplice of Ching K'o 荊軻, the would-be assassin of the first emperor of Ch'in. When their mission failed, Kao Chien-li went incognito and became a waiter in Sung-tzu. But his identity was discovered when he passed comment on some music being played. He then assumed his true identity and was placed in the seat of honor and played for the guests, moving them all to tears.

[25] Reading the Wu variant 猶 for 獨.
[26] Following the corrected Wu manuscript which has 亦其所甚病.
[27] From the *Lao-tzu*, Ch. 71 (Part II, 20b).
[28] Following the Wu text reading of 病 for 療.

Dispelling Self-interest

However, there are also cases where something seems to be wrong but in fact is not, or appears to be right and in fact is not. These must be examined with care. Thus, in critical moments when one must adapt, some people who are arrogant become submissive, and others who are greedy become generous; the stupid as a result become wise, and the truculent perform acts of mercy. However, even [before], when they had been arrogant and stingy, we cannot say they [totally] lacked [this] magnanimity; and when their actions took the form of cruelty[29] and truculence, we cannot say they [totally] lacked benevolence. These are cases where something seemed wrong but in fact was not.

Others speak with slander but seem sincere; we cannot say they are [truly] genuine. And there are fierce thieves who seem loyal; we cannot say they lack self-interest. These are cases where something appears to be right but in fact is not.

Thus, if we are going to discuss someone's intentions, we must determine his inclinations; we must hold on to his words to[30] weigh his motives,[31] and examine his feelings to get to the bottom of his changes [in mood].[32] If we familiarize ourselves with where he begins and understand where he ends, then one whose feelings are controlled by self-interest will not be able to follow what seems to be right[33] while all the while tolerating inside his wrongs, and one whose heart is pure and good will not be able to pursue what seems to be wrong[34] while keeping to himself the fact that he is right.

Thus, what is actually right is revealed only by, first, temporarily, [appearing] to be wrong; and what is actually wrong

---

[29] Reading the Wu variant 猜 for 情.
[30] Reading the Wu variant of 以 for 而.
[31] Reading the Wu variant 理 for 禮.
[32] The phrase is *hsün ch'i pien* 尋其變.
[33] The text actually says *ssu fei* 似非, "seems to be wrong." But that makes little sense in the context of what precedes and what follows. I choose to change the *fei* 非 to *shih* 是.
[34] Changing the *shih* 是 to *fei* 非.

Dispelling Self-interest

only becomes clear by, first, temporarily, [appearing] to be right.[35] If unselfishness and self-interest are together revealed, then the one who acts for himself will have nothing to hope for, and the one who is pure and good will suffer no defeat. If the one who acts for himself has nothing to hope for, he will think of correcting his faults; if the one who acts for the public good[36] has nothing to fear, he will act without hesitation. This is the way of great order.

Thus, the head concubine overturned the [poisoned] wine, and for her crime she was disgraced;[37] Wang Ling contested at court, but Ch'en P'ing followed the imperial will.[38] Seen from this perspective, were these not cases where something seemed to be wrong but in fact was not?[39]

If one manifests the sincere action of the Gentleman, and shows where self-interest and unselfishness lie, those in the court and those on the stairs will all fix their eyes on him and say, "This is a good man indeed." But to one who turns his back and expresses his views in private, acting out of self-interest, they will not respond the same. One who cherishes his will[40] and hides his feelings without change, is truly, as a result, [one whose]

---

[35] One would expect Hsi K'ang to say, "Thus, what is actually right might seem temporarily wrong, but later it will be revealed," etc. But the syntax seems to demand this translation.

[36] Reading the Wu variant of 公 for 功.

[37] The story is told in the *Chan-kuo ts'e*, "Yen ts'e" 燕策, (29.3b–4a in SPPY). When a wife who is having an affair tries to poison her husband, his concubine saves his life without getting her mistress banished from the house by spilling the poisoned wine she is to serve. For this she is whipped. For the English translation see James Crump, *Chan-Kuo Ts'e* (Oxford: Clarendon Press, 1970), pp. 510–511.

[38] When Empress Dowager Lü 呂太后 (reigned 187–179 B.C.) wished to make members of her clan kings, Wang Ling 王陵 argued against it while Ch'en P'ing 陳平 and others agreed. But Ch'en P'ing was only acting expediently, and, after the death of Empress Dowager Lü, he had the various members of her clan executed and established on the throne Emperor Wen (Liu clan). See *Shih chi* 9 (Vol. 2, p. 400), and *Shih chi* 56 (Vol. 6, p. 2061).

[39] Agreeing with Tai Ming-yang that we need to add 而非 here. The phrase must be 似非[而非]非者.

[40] The Huang text has a lacuna at this point. There are several variants for this in other texts. Of these I favor *chih* 志.

Dispelling Self-interest

spirit will be lost in what moves[41] him, whose body sinks into moral platitudes.[42] His mind will be controlled by the things he fears, his feelings attached to that which he desires. All [such people] consider themselves to be in the right; no one is more virtuous than they. Having not yet experienced a sorrow that attacks the flesh[43] or a disaster that startles the mind, none is able to collect his feelings and look inside, to reject [mere] name and follow reality.

Thus in their minds they have their "rights," but out of self-interest they hide them; their wills are set on the "good," but their concern with it makes it evil. They pay no mind to that which they should and concentrate rather on what they should not. They seek not the principle that would free them from concern, but rather look for the "Way" that makes them concerned. Thus they clearly understand[44] what concerns them but are kept in the dark by their concerns. Therefore, for them, to be unconcerned is to be clumsy, to be concerned is to be skilled. Their only fear is that what is concealed is not obscure; their only worry, that what is hidden is not secret. Therefore, with an arrogant, defiant expression they look down on the common man; with speech pretentious and affected they seek their vulgar fame, saying that of the good models for all eternity none is greater than this, and though one might belabor his mind to the end of his days, he would never see anything that goes beyond this. Thus they are able to perfect their selfish forms while losing their natural substance.

Therefore, feelings hidden and concealed necessarily dwell in their minds; crafty and idle machinations are necessarily manifested in their actions. This being the case, their opinions on right and wrong being clear, the reality of their rewards and

---

[41] Preferring the Wu 惑 over the Huang 憨.
[42] A guess at what Hsi K'ang might mean by *ch'ang-ming* 常名, "constant, or common names."
[43] Reading the Wu characters 攻肌 for 功著.
[44] Following the Wu variant of 明 for 時.

Dispelling Self-interest

punishments is also great.[45] They do not know one can brave the shade without a shadow[46] but worry, rather, that their shadow is not hidden. They do not know they can be without concern with no fear of harm, but rather hate[47] their concerns not being used.[48] Is this not lamentable?

Therefore, Shen Hou was improperly favored, and got sent away by King Kung of Ch'u;[49] Chancellor P'i indulged his own interests, but ended getting his just deserts.[50] To speak from this perspective, there has never been anyone who cherished the hidden and looked out for himself whose person was established in a pure age; [and there has never been anyone who] hid his faults and concealed his feelings whose sincerity was made famous by a wise ruler.[51]

Therefore,[52] the Gentleman, already possessing the basic substance, further looks at these examples. What he values are

---

[45] I think Hsi K'ang has in mind people like Chancellor P'i about to be mentioned below. They might enjoy a temporary reward for their self-interested actions, but in the end they will get their due. Their rewards are heavy but so are their punishments.

[46] Reading the Wu variant 陰 for 廕; i.e. speaks openly in times of danger with no hidden feelings.

[47] Reading the Wu variant 恨 for 患.

[48] There is a variant 巧 in some texts for 以. This would give an equally plausible reading of "but hate (or regret) rather that their concerns were not skilfully presented (or disguised)."

[49] This is usually identified as King Wen of Ch'u. Shen Hou 申侯 was his favorite, and he gave him whatever he wanted though his demands were insatiable. When Wen was dying, he sent Shen Hou away with the warning that he would not be tolerated in other states. Shen Hou was eventually put to death. For this story see *Tso chuan*, Duke Hsi, 7th year (pp. 97–98). Legge translates this in *The Chinese Classics*, Vol. V, Part I, p. 149. Holzman (*La Vie*, p. 129, note 2) puts forth an alternate view, that this Shen Hou is the Shen Pao-hsü 申包胥 mentioned in *Tso chuan*, Duke Ting, years 4 and 5, who submitted to the state of Ch'in so that they would help Ch'u, but who refused to accept reward from the latter.

[50] Chancellor P'i 宰嚭 was bribed by Kou-chien 勾踐 of Yüeh to convince the king of Wu to accept Yüeh's entreaties for peace. He succeeded. But later Yüeh showed no mercy when Wu asked for it, and P'i ended up being executed. See *Shih chi* 41 (Vol. 5, pp. 1739–1745). This is translated by Yang Hsien-yi and Gladys Yang in *Records of the Historian*, pp. 47–52.

[51] Reading the variant 君 for 名.

[52] Added in the Wu text.

Dispelling Self-interest

purity and understanding; these he considers precious[53] and preserves. What he hates are arrogance and stinginess; these he rejects and puts far away. To have concerns [he sees as] completely wrong, and is ashamed of inside in his spirit; to have things[54] he conceals [he sees as] entirely deficient, and is embarrassed by outside in his form. In his words there is nothing improperly concealed; in his actions there is nothing improperly hidden. He does not improperly approve of something, simply because he likes it; nor does he improperly reject something, simply because he hates it. His mind has nothing of which it is proud, his feelings nothing to which they cling. His body is pure and his spirit upright, and his rights and wrongs are fit and proper.[55] Loyal and reverent is he to[56] the Son of Heaven, sincere and honest to the common people. He consigns ambition to the limits of space, and hands down contentment forever. Are these not the beautiful rarities of the noble conduct of the man of virtue and the Gentleman?

Someone might ask, "Did Ti-wu Lun act out of self-interest?" [When he himself was asked this question], he replied: "Formerly, when my elder brother's son was ill, I went to check on him ten times in one night, but when I went home I slept at ease. But when my own son was sick, although all morning long I did not go to see him, all night I was unable to sleep."[57] Can something like this be called self-interest?[58] Or is it not self-

---

[53] Reading the variant 希 for 布.

[54] Agreeing with Tai Ming-yang that the 殿 here should be so 所, "that which."

[55] An important phrase which unfortunately could be read in several ways. The Chinese is *erh shih-fei yün-tang* 而是非允當. One could also say, "and he approves and rejects what is fitting and proper," or "and he lets right and wrong fall where they may."

[56] Agreeing with Lu Hsün that the 明 here is a mistake, and that a 於 is needed for the parallelism.

[57] All of this paraphrases what is said in Ti-wu Lun's 第五倫 biography in *Hou Han shu* 41 (Vol. 5, p. 1402). But Ti-wu Lun was a man known for his unselfishness.

[58] This is Hsi K'ang speaking now, but he continues to paraphrase Ti-wu Lun who went on to say, "If I act like this, how could I say I have no self-interest?"

Dispelling Self-interest

interest? My answer is that it is not: this is not self-interest. Self-interest gets its name from being unwilling to speak [about it]; unselfishness is so-called because everything is confessed; the essence of being good is the absence of being stingy;[59] the substance[60] of being wrong is having one's concerns. Ti-wu Lun revealed his feelings; this is acting without self-interest.[61] That he was proud of himself for going [to see his brother's son] and not sleeping [when his own son was sick]; that is wrong. To act without self-interest and yet be wrong is to set your mind on lack of concern [with what others might think]. To say that someone lacks this concern is not the same as saying [his actions] are necessarily completely [right]; and to say that someone is very stingy is not the same as saying he simply will not speak.

Therefore, to be very stingy is wrong; to have no concerns is right. But the reason why lack of concern is right is that there is nothing esteemed by the will, and nothing desired by the mind. If he thoroughly understands the essential nature of the Great Way, and his actions are one with nature, there is no way he could do anything wrong. If he cherishes the One and lacks concern, he is devoid of self-interest. And if this is combined with not being wrong, he will have both principles, and thus be totally good.

If one is wrong but able to talk about it, this is better than the self-interested action of saying nothing. To be wrong but not concerned [about what others might think] is truly a minor error.[62] Ti-wu Lun was wrong, but he was able to reveal it; we cannot say he was not unselfish. And [when we look at] the rights and wrongs he revealed, we cannot say he was concerned. If

---

[59] Reading the Wu variant 吝 for 名.
[60] Agreeing with Tai Ming-yang that 負 should probably be 質.
[61] The 非 before the 無私 is to be omitted.
[62] I think Tai Ming-yang is correct in seeing this as the reverse of what Hsi K'ang said earlier about "greater error." This requires some emending of the text. It now reads "非無情以非之大者也." Tai Ming-yang suggests "有非無措亦非之小者也," which is what I have followed.

Dispelling Self-interest

someone says someone is self-interested [simply] because he does something wrong, we would have to say that person is confused. These are the principles of unselfishness and self-interest.[63]

---

[63] Or punctuating in a different way: "If someone says someone is self-interested simply because he does something wrong, we would have to say that person is confused about the principles of unselfishness and self-interest."

HSI K'ANG

An Essay on Kuan and Ts'ai

(Kuan Ts'ai lun)

::

Translator's Comments. Shortly after the Chou conquest of the Shang (or the Yin) in *1122* B.C. (traditional dating), King Wu died. And since his son, King Ch'eng, was too young to rule, the Duke of Chou, one of King Wu's brothers, assumed control of the government. With that, Kuan and Ts'ai (Kuan-shu Hsien 管叔鮮 and Ts'ai-shu Tu 蔡叔度), two other brothers of King Wu, joined forces with the last descendant of the Shang, Wu Keng 武庚, and revolted—according to one account.[1] According to another, they spread rumors about what the Duke of Chou intended, so that he fled to the Eastern Capital of the Chou in Lo-yang, only to be recalled and returned to glory when King Ch'eng discovered that he (the Duke of Chou) had once offered to sacrifice his own life if the ailing King Wu would be spared.[2]

Kuan and Ts'ai are usually made out to be evil culprits. But Hsi K'ang argues that they were upright and moral, and simply misunderstood the actions of the Duke of Chou; they assumed he was taking the throne for himself, so they acted to save the dynasty.

Hsi K'ang's essay can be dated to *256* or shortly thereafter. For in that year, as Hou Wai-lu has noted,[3] the emperor, Kao-kuei hsiang-kung 高貴鄉公, went to the Imperial Academy and asked the scholars about the Kuan and Ts'ai affair,[4] and Hsi K'ang seems to

---

[1] See *Shih chi* 35: Vol. 5, pp. 1563–1565.
[2] This according to the "Chin-t'eng" 金縢 (Metal-bound Coffer) chapter of the *Shu*.
[3] See Hou Wai-lu, et al., *Chung-kuo ssu-hsiang t'ung-shih*, Vol. 2, pp. 163–164.
[4] See *San-kuo chih* 4 (pp. 135–138).

Kuan and Ts'ai

allude to that discussion when at the end of his essay he mentions "the present debate" (時論).

Moreover, the striking similarity between the rebellion of Kuan and Ts'ai and that of Kuan-ch'iu Chien and Wen Ch'in in 255 was noted already in the Ming by Chang Ts'ai 張采.[5] Ssu-ma I, like the Duke of Chou, had been a regent to the throne, and Kuan-ch'iu Chien, like Kuan-shu Hsien (even their names sound somewhat alike), was killed, while Wen Ch'in, like Ts'ai-shu Tu, was banished. Thus, in justifying the revolt of Kuan and Ts'ai, Hsi K'ang was justifying as well the revolt of Kuan-ch'iu Chien and Wen Ch'in.

Someone asked: "According to the records, Kuan and Ts'ai spread baseless rumors and revolted in the Eastern Capital.[1] The Duke of Chou marched against them and quelled the uprising, punishing them severely for being wicked and perverse. Their recalcitrance and evil is well known and established; for this they have been famous for a thousand years.[2]

"But they had a wise father and a sagacious older brother, and even[3] they were unable[4] to perceive this wickedness and evil[5] in the young and immature, or sense this lack of good in their sons [in the one case], and their brothers [in the other]. In fact, they put them in charge of the defeated and exhausted masses of rebellious Yin, glorifying them with honor and noble rank in the

---

[5] See his *San-kuo wen* 三國文 cited by Tai Ming-yang in *Hsi K'ang chi chiao-chu*, p. 248.

[1] The "Eastern Capital" (*tung-tu* 東都) would normally mean Lo-yang, where the Duke of Chou had a second capital built for the Chou, and where, according to some accounts, he is said to have fled when he was slandered by his brothers. But, along with Tai Ming-yang, I would take this to mean here the old capital of the Yin, where Wu Keng had been granted power, which was indeed to the east of the first Chou capital.

[2] Reading the Wu variant 載 for 里.

[3] Following A. C. Graham's suggested interpretation of the particle 曾, "even this," which works quite well here. See A. C. Graham, "The Chinese Particle *Tseng* 曾," *Early China*, 3 (Fall, 1977), pp. 31–35.

[4] Following the Wu text, which adds a 能 at this point.

[5] Again following the Wu text, which has 惡 instead of 愚. But either fits.

Kuan and Ts'ai

feudal states. This let their evils build up and their vices develop, and in the end they met with disaster and harm.

"This does not accord with reason, and my mind is not at ease. I would like to hear how it is to be explained."

[My] response is this: "Great indeed is your question! Formerly, Wen and Wu's employment of Kuan and Ts'ai was based on the actual facts, and the Duke of Chou's punishment of Kuan and Ts'ai was because of a matter of expediency. The matter of the moment is well known, but the actual facts are hidden. Thus, this has caused our contemporaries all to say that Kuan and Ts'ai were recalcitrant and wicked. Now I will discuss the matter for you.

"Kuan and Ts'ai obeyed the [moral] teachings and were committed to duty to the point of sacrificing their lives. Loyalty and sincerity were natural to them. Therefore King Wen gave them rank and made them prominent, and Fa [King Wu] and Tan [the Duke of Chou], the two sages, recommended them for office and gave them official duties. It is not that they favored them because of special feeling for kin. This was how they honored their virtue and showed respect for their worthiness in saving the defeated people of Yin and pacifying and aiding Wu Keng. Because their achievements were meritorious in reforming[6] the recalcitrant and vulgar, by successive generations they were not rejected; their fame capped their age, and they ranked as feudal ministers.

"When Wu died, the throne went to Sung [King Ch'eng], who was still a young boy. So the Duke of Chou assumed control of the government and took the lead in meeting with the feudal lords at court. He thought only of glorifying the [deeds of the] former years, to make the kingship flourish. But Kuan and Ts'ai, obedient to the teachings, did not comprehend the expedient actions of the sage. And when they suddenly encountered this momentous change, they were unable to understand. "With loyalty in[7] their hearts, their thoughts were on the royal

---

[6] Reading the variant 興 for 與.
[7] Following the Wu text variant of 于 for 疑.

house."[8] As a result, they spoke out in opposition and stirred up the masses, wishing to eliminate this menace to the state. To protect and preserve the Son of Heaven, they were willing to slander Tan. Thus they were ignorant but sincere, and vented their frustrations, and it was this that called down the disaster.[9] But King Ch'eng was greatly enlightened,[10] and the Duke of Chou was restored to prominence.

"When the species is one, the customs must be the same. Justice called for showing no mercy. So though inside he [the Duke of Chou] was sincere and forgiving,[11] on the outside he could not allow their actions to stand. For they had raised troops and rebelled, and led many astray. Therefore, patiently bearing his suffering, he bestowed the penalty; with flowing tears he carried out the punishment. When you set an example with punishment and reward, you cannot omit your relatives. Those made prominent by honor and rank must be those with abundant virtue; those treated to whipping and execution must be the ones who have the crime. This, then, is the true substance[12] of the teachings, the illustrious justice of past and present.[13] Kuan and Ts'ai, even though they embraced loyalty and cherished

---

[8] Literally the passage says "with loyalty in your hearts" (乃心). This alludes to the statement in "K'ang wang chih kao" 康王之誥 of the *Shu*: "Though your persons be distant, let your hearts [乃心] be in the royal house." (Tr. by Legge/Waltham, *Shu Ching*, p. 218.) For the text see *Shang-shu chin-ku-wen chu-shu* 25B.11a.

[9] Reading the Wu variant 禍 instead of 福. This probably refers to the warning sent by Heaven when the Duke of Chou was slandered. In the *Shu*, "Chin-t'eng" 金縢, we find: "In the autumn, when the grain was abundant and ripe but before it was reaped, Heaven sent a great storm of thunder and lightning, along with wind, by which the grain was broken down and great trees torn up." (Tr. by Legg/Waltham, *Shu ching*, p. 137.) For the text see *Shang shu chin-ku-wen chu-shu* 13.7ab.

[10] Presumably when he opened the "Metal-bound Coffer" and read how earlier the Duke of Chou had offered himself as a substitute for the ailing King Wu.

[11] Following the Wu manuscript, which has 恕 where the Huang text separates the two elements of the character to give 如心.

[12] Following the Wu text in adding 體 after the 正.

[13] Following the Wu text reading of 古今之明義也. The Huang text has 今之朝議—"what is being discussed at present at court"—which would also make sense.

Kuan and Ts'ai

being sincere, had to be punished for their crime. [But] once their crime and their punishment became well known, it was impossible to get back to the truth. With their true feelings[14] hidden and concealed, their crime and its evil stood out. The roads of hidden and manifest are far apart, and this has brought it about that successive ages have not yet learned the truth. This being the case, my opponent,[15] genuine in name and sincere in conduct,[16] regards Kuan and Ts'ai as evil, not understanding that the evil of Kuan and Ts'ai is precisely the thing that makes it then necessary to regard the three sages as unwise.

"If the three sages were not unenlightened, then as sages they would not have aided the evil and employed the recalcitrant and wicked. If the recalcitrant and wicked are not tolerated in an enlightened age,[17] then Kuan and Ts'ai received no favoritism from their father and older brother, and that they were employed must be because of their loyalty and virtue. And in that case the two Shu's were definitely pure and good.

"If we start from the premise that the three sages were enlightened in their employment [of Kuan and Ts'ai], and keep in mind the actual reasons for their conferring [on them] great honors, and expand this in terms of loyal and worthy men being in the dark about a matter of expediency, and discuss it as one of the great records of the state, then the virtue of the two Shu's will be obvious, and their employment by the three sages justified.[18] There was a reason for the rumors they spread, but their punishment by the Duke of Chou was the right thing to do. Moreover,

---

[14] Reading the Wu variant 心 for 必.

[15] Literally *lun-che* 論者, "the debater," "the one presenting the thesis." However, the extension could be wider, i.e., something like "those who have discussed the point."

[16] The Wu text has 承 instead of 誠. Perhaps the line should read, "carrying on the established line and believing in what has been said."

[17] Following the Wu line which has 明世 for 時世 and adds the "obstinate and perverse" at the beginning of the sentence.

[18] Following Tai Ming-yang's suggested emendation of 用也以 to 用有以.

Kuan and Ts'ai

when the Duke of Chou assumed the regency, the Duke of Shao was [also] displeased.[19]

"To draw our inference from this, Kuan and Ts'ai harbored doubts; they were never unworthy. But it is possible that the loyal and worthy do not understand matters of expediency. The three sages were never in the position of using evil men, and the Duke of Chou had no choice but to punish them. This being the case, the men employed by the three sages were sincere and good; the punishment carried out by the Duke of Chou was just and proper; and the minds of Kuan and Ts'ai were in accord with reason. This being so, then the main ideas can be understood, and inner and outer can both be explained.[20] Since there is nothing here to attack or refute, the present debate ought to be greatly resolved with all misunderstandings cleared up.

---

[19] See *Shih chi* 34 (Vol. 5, p. 1549), the "hereditary family" account of Duke Shao of Yen. There we find "King Ch'eng being young, the Duke of Chou assumed regency of the government and ruled the court. The Duke of Shao was suspicious about it and wrote 'Prince Shih' [one of the documents in the *Shu*]."

[20] Referring, I think, to the fact that, externally, both the sages and the Shu's did the right thing, and internally, the sages were wise and the uncles virtuous.

HSI K'ANG

An Essay on Wisdom and Courage

(Ming tan lun)

::

Translator's Comments. The problem of the relation of wisdom to courage must be seen as part of the general problem in Confucianism of the relation of knowledge to action.[1] *The issue here is, can one know the right thing to do, but lack the courage to do it? Lü An (the Master Lü of the essay) says no, but Hsi K'ang says yes, and Hsi K'ang probably speaks from experience.*

The debate is set up by the Analects *(14 : 28) where Confucius identifies benevolence (*jen 仁*), wisdom (*chih 知*), and courage (*yung 勇*) as the three virtues of the Gentleman, and where he also says (*Analects *14 : 4): "A benevolent man is sure to possess courage, but a courageous man does not necessarily possess benevolence,"*[2] *a statement which is paraphrased by Lü An.*

That Hsi K'ang's position—that wisdom and courage are separate things—is the same as that of his contemporary Liu Shao 劉邵 *in his study of personality types,* Jen-wu chih 人物志, *is a point noted by Hsiao Teng-fu as well.*[3] *Moreover, the authors of* Chung-kuo ssu-hsiang t'ung shih *correctly connect this essay to the ongoing debate of the times on the relation of* ts'ai 才 *(talents) to* hsing 性 *(nature).*[4]

---

[1] See David Nivison, "The Problem of 'Knowledge' and 'Action' in Chinese Thought Since Wang Yang-ming," in Arthur F. Wright, ed., *Studies in Chinese Thought* (Chicago: University of Chicago Press, 1953), pp. 112–145.

[2] Translated by D. C. Lau, *Confucius: The Analects*, p. 124.

[3] See Hsiao Teng-fu, *Hsi K'ang yen-chiu*, pp. 140–141. The relevant chapter in Liu Shao is Chapter 8, "Ying-hsiung" 英雄 (Heroes), B.6a–7b in SPPY. For an English translation see J. K. Shryock, *The Study of Human Abilities: The Jen wu chih of Liu Shao* (New Haven: American Oriental Society, 1937), pp. 127–130.

[4] See Hou Wai-lu, *et al.*, *Chung-kuo ssu-hsiang t'ung-shih*, Vol. 2, pp. 164–172.

Wisdom and Courage

There was a certain Master Lü, a man of refined intelligence who delighted in pondering the Way, a man who examined with great care issues of right and wrong. He felt that if a man has courage he may perhaps lack[1] wisdom, but if he has wisdom then he will [also] have courage. Mr. Hsi felt that wisdom and courage are different functions, they cannot produce one another. He presented his thesis as follows:

"The Primal Vapors [of creation] were molded and mixed, and the many forms of life received their allotments from them. In the giving and receiving, some got much and some got little; therefore, in talents and in nature there are those who are dull and those who are bright. It is only the Perfect Man who uniquely combines all unblemished beauties, who unites and embraces both inner and outer, who has nothing that is not final and complete. Moving down from this, [all things] are probably deficient. Some are wise in understanding things, others courageous in making decisions. The human emotions, greed and honesty, each has its dwelling place. 'We can compare it to the grasses and trees; they are distinguished by their differences.'[2] One who combines all traits is widely versed in [all] things; but one whose gifts are one-sided [simply] maintains his lot. Therefore, I would say that wisdom and courage are different breaths; they cannot produce one another.

"With wisdom one can understand things; with courage one can make decisions. If you have only wisdom without courage; then even though you are perceptive, you will not be decisive. If you have only courage without wisdom, then[3] [your actions] will go against[4] reason, and you will miss the opportune moment. Thus Tzu-chia was weak and vacillating and was trapped into [agreeing to] the assassination of his ruler;[5] the Master of the

---

[1] Reading the variant 無 for 棄.
[2] Quoting Tzu-hsia in *Analects* 19:12 (p. 40).
[3] The 則 is added to the Wu text.
[4] Reading the Wu variant 違 for 達.
[5] The story is recorded in *Tso chuan*, Duke Hsüan, 4th year (p. 184). Duke Ling of Cheng was going to kill a certain Tzu-kung 子公 for dipping his finger

Wisdom and Courage

Left was indecisive and ended up being threatened by Hua Ch'en.[6] These are both cases where their intelligence was up to it,[7] but their courage didn't match.

"This principle is perfectly clear; it is not something that should stand in your way.[8] Thus I have just briefly raised one corner of it,[9] thinking you should have no further doubts."

[Master Lü then said:][10] "I have carefully examined your essay. This could be called something that even instruction[11] could add nothing to. Your analysis of the principles observes economy of expression and yet completely covers the essentials. But why must you still [say] what is false and vile and talk in such an exaggerated why?

"In your essay you cite the chaotic, primal [vapors] by way of illustration. How distant they are and ill-defined! Therefore, my

---

into a turtle stew without being asked. But Tzu-kung decided to turn the tables and kill the duke. He planned this together with his friend Tzu-chia 子家, but the latter disapproved, pointing out that "Even an animal which you have long kept about you, you shrink from killing; how much more should you shrink from killing your ruler!" (Tr. by Legge, *The Chinese Classics*, Vol. V, Part I, p. 296.) Tzu-chia was persuaded to let Tzu-kung proceed when Tzu-kung threatened to make up charges against him.

[6] *Tso chuan*, Duke Hsiang, 17th year (p. 285). When Hua Ch'en 華臣 killed the steward of his brother's son for personal reasons, the Master of the Left objected. But when the Duke of Sung proposed to expel Hua Ch'en for this the Master of the Left said it would look bad for the state. Legge's translation (*The Chinese Classics*, Vol. V, Part II, p. 475) continues: "Shih [Ch'en] accordingly was let alone; but the master of the Left made himself a short whip, and whenever he passed Hwa Shin's gate, made his horses gallop."

[7] 智及之 is probably an oblique reference to *Analects* 15:33 (p. 32) where D. C. Lau (*Confucius: The Analects*, p. 136) translates: "The Master said, 'What is within the reach of a man's understanding [知及之] but beyond the power of his benevolence to keep is something he will lose even if he acquires it.'" This is an appropriate allusion since this speaks of having one good trait but lacking another.

[8] Following the Wu text reading, 非所宜瀋.

[9] See note 6 to "Music Has in It Neither Grief nor Joy."

[10] The three characters 呂子曰 do not occur in either the Huang text or the Wu, but they are found in others and need to be added for clarity.

[11] Reading the Wu variant 誨 for 海. Tai Ming-yang feels the character should be 論. From his notes, he would seem to read this line: "This could be called an essay which cannot be topped by other essays."

Wisdom and Courage

response will be direct, using what is most fitting and most vital from the realm of human affairs. Mr. Chia [Chia I] of the Han made proposals [at court] that were to the point and direct, and vigorously spoke out with words that were dangerous to the extreme.[12] When he thus acted resolutely, it was because he had carefully examined it with his wisdom. When fearing the owl he wrote his rhapsody, he was confused by his ignorance.[13] How could it be that courage in one and the same person waxes and wanes? I suspect it is [rather] that people are either perceptive or they are not, and thus there are those who decisively act and those who do not. Tzu-chia and the Master of the Left were both stupid and deluded, shallow and corrupt. Their wisdom was not penetrating and thorough. Therefore, they were confused by what they did not clearly understand and ended meeting with disaster and harm. How could one see something clearly and examine it with care, and yet in his courage be indecisive?

"Therefore, Huo Kuang was a man of great bravery who discharged the duties of Supreme General; but he trembled with fear at the affair of King Ho.[14] [T'ien] Yen-nien was a cultured

---

[12] Tai Ming-yang at this point cites Chia I's 賈誼 (201–169 B.C.) *Han shu* biography (*Han shu* 48, Vol. 8, p. 2230), which says that when he was appointed tutor to King Huai of Liang by Emperor Wen, he frequently memorialized the throne advocating change and reform.

[13] Chia I's *fu* on "The Owl" (鵩鳥賦) is recorded in his *Shih chi* biography (*Shih chi* 84, Vol. 8, pp. 2496–2502). For an English translation see Burton Watson, *Chinese Rhyme-Prose* (New York: Columbia University Press, 1971), pp. 25–28. This was written after Chia I had been slandered at court and banished, in a way, to Ch'ang-sha to be the tutor of that king—in 174 or 173. Chia I was in poor health, and an owl coming to rest in his house was considered an inauspicious sign. He asked the owl: "Where is it I must go? Do you bring good luck? Then tell me! Misfortune? Relate what disaster! Must I depart so swiftly? Then speak to me of the hour!" (Tr. by Watson, *Chinese Rhyme-Prose*, p. 26.)

[14] More precisely, Liu Ho 劉賀, king of Ch'ang-i 昌邑, who served for a short while as emperor in the Han following the death of Emperor Chao in 74 B.C. Huo Kuang 霍光 is the prominent Han statesman who served Emperors Wu, Chao, and Hsüan. His biography is recorded in *Han shu* 68 (Vol. 10, pp. 2931–2969). This is translated into English in Burton Watson's *Courtier and Commoner in Ancient China* (New York: Columbia University Press, 1974), pp. 121–157. To explain the "King Ho affair"—when Emperor Chao died in 74 B.C. he left no

Wisdom and Courage

scholar who previously had no reputation for prowess; but he spoke of duty with rousing words and his courage soared to the clouds.[15] This is the proof.

"Coming to Ch'i's [Fan Yü-ch'i] giving up his head,[16] and Ling's [Wang Ling] mother falling on her sword[17]—these belong to the class 'wise and courageous.' There are ten thousand cases like this. If we wanted to record them in detail we simply could not mention them all. How much the more [plentiful] are those who see a level road but lack the courage to walk it, [or those who] climb paths through the clouds thinking they will in this way reach heaven![18]

"If someone in the class of 'stupid[19] and dishonest' is talented,

---

heir. The choice fell on Liu Ho, a grandson of Emperor Wu. But, to quote Watson's translation, "After he had assumed the position of emperor, Liu Ho behaved in scandalous and disorderly fashion" (p. 129). Thus, all were in favor of deposing him, but Huo Kuang, with good reason, was hesitant to take this step.

[15] Watson translates from the biography of Huo Kuang: "... Liu Ho behaved in scandalous and disorderly fashion. Ho [Huo] Kuang, deeply distressed, discussed the matter in private with the minister of agriculture T'ien Yen-nien, a close friend who had once been attached to Ho Kuang's staff. T'ien Yen-nien said, "General, you are the pillar and foundation stone of the state. If it appears to you that this man will not do, why do you not propose to the empress dowager that a more worthy person be selected and set up in his place?" "That is just what I would like to do," replied Ho Kuang, "but are there any precedents in antiquity for such an action?" T'ien Yen-nien said, "When Yi Yin was prime minister of the Yin dynasty, he deposed T'ai-chia in order to insure the safety of the ancestral temples, and later ages have all praised him for his loyalty. If you are able to carry this out, you will become the Yi Yin of the Han!" Ho Kuang recommended T'ien Yen-nien for the honorary rank of steward of the palace." (Watson, *Courtier and Commoner*, p. 129.)

[16] Fan Yü-ch'i 樊於期 slit his own throat so that his head could be used as an exchange present by Ching K'o 荊軻 in his attempt to get an interview with, and thus assassinate, the king of Ch'in. See *Shih chi* 86 (Vol. 8, pp. 2532-2533). This is translated by Burton Watson in *Records of the Historian* (New York: Columbia University Press, 1969), pp. 60-61.

[17] Wang Ling 王陵 threw his forces behind Liu Pang 劉邦 in the struggle between Liu Pang and Hsiang Yü 項羽 that led to the founding of the Han. Hsiang Yü kidnapped Wang Ling's mother in an attempt to bring him over to his side. But Ling's mother killed herself to allow Wang Ling the freedom to do what he wished. See *Han shu* 40 (Vol. 7, pp. 2046-2047).

[18] Tai Ming-yang notes (p. 250) that this refers to those who are lacking in both wisdom and courage.

[19] Following Lu Hsün's recommended emendation of 思 to 愚.

Wisdom and Courage

he will keep to places that are dark and hidden and risk his life in snares and pitfalls, like Robber Chih, who hid himself in the mouth of a tiger, or the thief who bores holes in walls, who sticks his head into ditches and canals. They [are brave enough] to seize a tiger bare-handed and walk on water.[20] Thus there are those who belong to the group 'stupid but brave.'

"Therefore I say that when wisdom is lacking, courage can stand on its own.[21] This is an easily understood principle; there is no need for copious illustrations. So I will not cite far-off things or go on with a lot of words. If you still cannot return with the other three corners and continue to have doubts, let me receive your honored instruction. You will receive a speedy reply."

[Hsi K'ang responded]: "In discussing and reasoning about human nature and the emotions, analyzing[22] and drawing out [the implications] of differences and similarities, one must[23] certainly search for the ultimate starting point from which we receive [these things], and push back to the source from which comes our allotment of breath. When you move from the root to the very tip of the branch, only then will there be no error. But now you wish to dispense with the chaotic, primal [vapors] and hold on to what you can see. This is to delight in laying out the details while hating to hold on the essentials.

"My thesis is that the two breaths are not the same; wisdom does not produce courage. If we wish to discuss the extreme, then we must suppose the case of a man who has been banished who lacks the courage to satirize [his superiors], but who has the

---

[20] Alluding to poem 195 in the *Book of Poetry* (p. 45). Karlgren translates: "One dare not overpower a tiger, one dare not without boat cross the river." (Bernard Karlgren, *The Book of Odes*, p. 143.)

[21] Omitting the second occurrence of the characters 無膽 because they do not occur in the Wu text in Hsi K'ang's quote of this line later on. As it stands, the Huang text has 是以余謂明無膽, 無膽能偏守, out of which I can get nothing that would correspond to Lü An's stated position.

[22] Reading 折 as 析.

[23] Adding the 當 found in the Wu manuscript.

Wisdom and Courage

wisdom to see what is going on. Therefore, in this case there will necessarily be harm resulting from his lack of decision. I do not mean[24] a man of the middling sort who is lacking in foolhardy daring,[25] but to the contrary, one who has wisdom as part of his native endowment. If the two breaths are present in one body, then wisdom can *move* courage. Chia I is an example of this. The wisdom and courage of Chia I were complete and interrelated. Therefore he was able to be useful in [state] affairs. Whoever said he was completely lacking in courage and relied solely on wisdom to carry things out? You made this up yourself because it matches your thesis. When he [Chia I] feared the owl and was in the dark and confused, this was something not encompassed by his wisdom; how does this interfere with his being courageous?[26] It is simply that if wisdom has understood something, then courage is able to carry it out. But how can courage decide what wisdom cannot see?

"In advance and retreat they support one another; this could be called[27] waxing and waning. If we speak like this, then when Mr. Chia made his proposals [at court] it was because he understood with his wisdom; when fearing the owl he wrote his rhapsody, he was confused by his ignorance.[28] This being the case, his wisdom was penetrating in the former case, but his ignorance confused him in the latter.[29] Thus wisdom[30] has periods when it

---

[24] The original Wu manuscript adds a 焉 after the 非; Tai Ming-yang reads this as 謂 giving 非謂中人.

[25] Tai Ming-yang (p. 253) points out that a "middling" man might lack "foolhardy daring" (*hsüeh-ch'i* 血氣) but not necessarily be completely devoid of the "courage to satirize" (*tz'u-feng chih tan* 刺諷之膽).

[26] Tai Ming-yang points out that Lü An's interpretation was that Chia I lacked courage here *because* he lacked understanding. Hsi K'ang, rather, sees it as simply a matter of lacking understanding; courage is not involved.

[27] The Wu text has 何謂 for 可謂, and Tai Ming-yang affirms this variant. From what follows I feel that 可 is correct.

[28] Mimicking—and saying much the same thing—the statement made earlier by Lü An.

[29] Both Lu Hsün and Tai Ming-yang see this sentence as a question. I find nothing to indicate this in the grammar.

[30] The 明 is added in the Wu manscript.

Wisdom and Courage

waxes and wanes. If wisdom can advance and retreat, how can it be that courage cannot also stand on its own?[31]

"You say[32] that Huo Kuang was a man of great bravery, but he trembled at [the thought of] deposing the king. So this bravery[33] has that to which it yields. And yet you [also] say 'How could it be that courage in one and the same person waxes and wanes?' This, then, is true. Mr. Chia did not understand about the owl, because there are things that can stand in the way of wisdom. [Huo] Kuang feared deposing the king, because there are things that make bravery yield. It is only Perfect Wisdom that can never be confused and Perfect Courage that can never be diminished. If one is not like this,[34] then who does not have his moments of weakness? But we must simply deal in general with those who have it [wisdom or courage] and those who do not, and proceed to discuss them.

"In [all] things, we take what we actually see to be central. Yen-nien was aroused, and his bravery and sense of duty rose up to the clouds. This was certainly courage. And yet [you] say that he 'previously had no reputation for prowess.' This is to believe in a former reputation and doubt what has actually occurred. When Yen-nien made his speech, it was because he understood with his wisdom. When his valor was aroused and fierce, it was the result of the decisiveness of his bravery.[35] This can certainly be seen.

"You also say 'when widsom is lacking, courage can stand on

---

[31] I would agree with Tai Ming-yang in taking this to mean that courage, too, can wax and wane on its own—which is opposed to what Lü An had argued.

[32] The text says 然, which perhaps could be read as "affirm." But Tai Ming-yang's suggestion that this might be an error for 言 gives a reading that seems superior.

[33] Adding the 此勇 from the Wu text.

[34] The 苟 at the head of the sentence is not necessary and is omitted in the Wu text.

[35] The point being that he possessed all along both courage and wisdom. It is not, as Lü An argued, that his wisdom *gave rise to* his courage.

Wisdom and Courage

its own.'[36] According to what you say, if there is a man who is solely courageous [not wise], this is also courage, and it comes uniquely from the single breath. Now[37] the five elements dwell in the body, and each produces certain things. Wisdom results from the dazzling rays of Yang; courage comes from the congealing of Yin. How can you say[38] that it is Yang [wisdom] that produces Yin [courage], and yet maintain that it is possible to be without Yang?[39] Although they [Yin and Yang] rely on each other to unite their powers, it is essential that each be a different breath.

"As for the rest of your various statements—Yü-ch'i, Ling's mother, confronting a tiger bare-handed, etc., etc.—these are ten thousand words that all come to the same thing. What were you hoping to show? I trust you will think this over carefully again and not make such a waste of words."

---

[36] Following the Wu manscript. The Huang text repeats 無膽 giving 子又曰言明無膽無膽能偏守.

[37] Adding the 夫 found in the Wu text.

[38] Following the Wu variant of 猜 for 為.

[39] Tai Ming-yang feels there is something missing in this sentence. It seems to me to make perfectly good sense.

CHANG MIAO

People Naturally Delight in Learning

(Tzu-jan hao hsüeh lun)

∷

Translator's Comments. The author of "People Naturally Delight in Learning" is Chang Miao 張邈 *(style, Shu-liao* 叔遼*). About him we know very little. He was at one time prefect of Liao-tung, and he died in 291 before assuming a new appointment as prefect of Yang-ch'eng (in present-day Honan).*[1]

Delight and anger, grief and joy, love and hate, desire and fear—this is the lot of man's emotions.[1] When we get what we want we are delighted; when we meet opposition we are angered. Rebellion and separation make us sad; compliance and harmony cause joy. Birth and nurture we love; opposition to what we like we hate. When we are hungry we want to eat; when oppressed, we are frightened[2] and afraid. All eight of these are "things we can do without being taught" as [Mencius] says in his discussion.[3] They are natural.

Before people knew how to keep meats from spoiling by cooking, they drank the blood and ate the fur to fill their empty bellies.[4] This was the beginning of food. But when they applied[5]

---

[1] This is from Hsün Cho's 荀綽 *Chi-chou chi* 冀州記, cited by P'ei Sung-chih in his commentary on *San-kuo chih* 11 (p. 354).

[1] Following the Wu text, which adds 情 after 人.

[2] Following the Wu variant of 悉 for 欲.

[3] A guess on my part about what Chang Miao has in mind with "若論所云." Mencius says, in 7A:15 (p. 51), "What a man is able to do without having to learn it [不學而能者] is what he can truly do." (Tr. by D. C. Lau, *Mencius*, p. 184.) The text here is 不敎而能.

[4] Chang Miao probably has in mind the passage in the *Li chi*, "Li yün" 禮運, which goes: "Formerly the ancient kings ... knew not yet the transforming power of fire, but ate the fruits of plants and trees, and the flesh of birds and

Delight in Learning

heat to it, and blended in bits of fragrant tangerine, even though they had never tasted it before, they of course praised it as soon as they tasted it, because it was pleasing to the palate.

With clumps of soil[6] for drumsticks and drums made of earth[7] they tapped their tummies[8] and sang; they stepped to it and danced to it[9] to add pleasure to their delight. This was the original substance of music. But when they added to it pipes and strings, and mixed in feathers and hair [i.e., ornaments used in dance], although this was something they had never heard before, they definitely loved it the moment they experienced it, because it agreed with their minds.

People are born to be upright.[10] But if you bring them together [to form a society] and fail to teach them [anything], each will indulge his own mind, and there will be a clash of wills, and the eight feelings will necessarily arise. Delighted, they will necessarily want to give things to others; angered they will necessarily

---

beasts, drinking their blood, and swallowing (also) their hair and feathers." (Tr. by Legge in Müller, *Sacred Books of the East*, Vol. 27, p. 369.) For the text see *Li chi hsün-tsuan* 9.3a.

[5] Reading the Wu variant 加 for 茄.

[6] Following Tai Ming-yang's suggested emendation of the Wu variant 凶 for 簣 (*k'uei*, "a straw basket") to 凷 (*k'uai*, "earthen clod").

[7] This line occurs in the "Li yün" chapter of the *Li chi* (*Li chi hsün-tsuan* 9.2b). Legge translates: "At the first use of ceremonies, they began with meat and drink...; they fashioned a handle of clay, and struck with it an earthen drum." (In Müller, *Sacred Books of the East*, Vol. 27, p. 368.)

[8] Perhaps an oblique allusion to *Chuang-tzu*, Ch. 9 (p. 23, line 17). That text says of people in the days of the ancient emperor Ho Hsü: "Their mouths crammed with food, they were merry; drumming on their bellies [鼓腹 where our text has 撫腹], they passed the time." (Tr. by Watson, *The Complete Works of Chuang Tzu*, p. 106.

[9] They "stepped to it and danced to it" (*tsu-chih tao-chih* 足之蹈之) comes from the "Great Preface" to the *Book of Poetry*. In a passage describing the origins of music and dance we read: "When those prolonged utterances of song are insufficient for them unconsciously the hands begin to move and the feet to dance [足之蹈之]." (Tr. by Legge, *The Chinese Classics*, Vol. IV, p. 34.)

[10] Paraphrasing Confucius in *Analects* 6:19 (p. 11). Interpretations of the line vary; I have followed Legge—"Man is born for uprightness." (See James Legge, *The Four Books* [Taipei: Culture Book Co., 1969], p. 194.) D. C. Lau (*Confucius: The Analects*, p. 84) has "That a man lives is because he is straight."

Delight in Learning

want to punish them. But they will lack the talons and fangs[11] needed to enforce their authority; and they will have no titles and rewards by which they could show their favor. They have no way to receive with respect those whom they love and cannot get rid of that which they hate. But if someone were to say to them: "Grey bamboo and rush—these you can use to express your grief;[12] moats and canals, high ridges and dangerous passes—these you can use to ease your fears;[13] strung-up branches [a bow] and sharpened metal [arrow tips, or possibly knives and swords]—these you can use to release your frustrations; abundant goods and rich possessions—these you can use to give to others"—who is there with lungs and intestines that would not become happy, with pleased expression and mind at ease? What further need would there be to eat gentian and horse-fly[14] or have this craving for pickled sweet flag?[15]

Moreover, in the daytime we sit and at night we sleep. When it is light we are active; when it is dark we rest. This is the constant way of the Way of Heaven and that which men follow and practice. If someone is in a dark room and sees the light of a small candle, he will still be delighted with what he sees, even though no one tells him he should be. His happiness would not be diminished by revealing to him that even[16] beyond this there is the white sun, comparable in size to the red gates [of his house], and that it will shine again at dawn. What greater happiness

---

[11] I.e., military and civil authorities.

[12] A staff made of "grey bamboo" (*chü-chu* 苴竹) and rush sandals were used in mourning.

[13] These make one's area easy to defend.

[14] *Tan-fei* 膽蜚 (Brave Roach?) remains unidentified. Tai Ming-yang (p. 258) speculates that the *tan* might refer to *lung-tan* 龍膽, the herbal flower "gentian" (see Read, *Chinese Medicinal Plants*, p. 42, item 169), which in the Chinese pharmacopoeia is thought to help memory. *Fei*, on the other hand, might mean *fei-meng* 蜚蝱, "horse-fly" (Read, *Chinese Materia Medica: Insect Drugs*, pp. 146–147, item 76), which as a drug is thought to cleanse one's arteries.

[15] *Ch'ang-p'u* 菖蒲, "calamus," or "sweet flag," has certain marvelous effects: it "opens the holes in the heart," "repairs the five organs," "makes the ear hear clearly and the eyes see well," etc. See the *Shen Nung pen-ts'ao ching* 1.10b.

[16] Reading the Wu variant 尚 for 向.

Delight in Learning

then, when after the long night of darkness [ignorance] he attains the illumination of the great sun [knowledge]; his feelings change from their former melancholy and his ignorance is dispelled.

Therefore, I feel that even though[17] it may be a secondary development, the response of the feelings is basic. Even if one only turns to study after[18] calculating the numerous glories associated with the Six Disciplines[19] and the various rarities of fame and profit, this would still do no harm to [my claim] that there is a natural delight [in it].

---

[17] Reading the Wu variant 雖 for 誰.
[18] Reading the variant 後 for 復.
[19] The *liu-i* 六藝 are usually listed as the six classic texts; the *I*, *Li*, *Yüeh*, *Shih*, *Shu*, and *Ch'un-ch'iu*—the *Book of Changes*, *Record of Rites*, *Record of Music*, *Book of Poetry*, *Book of History*, and *Spring and Autumn Annals*.

HSI K'ANG

A Refutation of Chang Miao's Essay—People Naturally Delight in Learning

(Nan Tzu-jan hao hsüeh lun)

::

Human nature is such that people love security and hate danger, love leisure and hate hard work. Therefore, if they are not disturbed their wishes are attained; if they are not oppressed they can follow their wills.

Formerly,[1] in remote antiquity, when the Great Simplicity had not yet gone into decline, rulers were uncultured above and the people uncontentious below. Things were complete and reason was followed; there were none that were not self-attained. When they had eaten their fill, they rested and slept; when they were hungry, they looked for food. Contented, they drummed on their bellies,[2] unaware this was the age of Perfect Virtue. This being the case, how could they have known the principles of benevolence and righteousness or the ornaments of ritual and law?

When the Perfect Man no longer existed, and the Great Way had deteriorated and declined—it was then they began to make writings in order to transmit their ideas. They differentiated and distinguished the many things, setting up "species" and "families". They created and established benevolence and righteousness to encircle and close in their minds. They instituted[3] titles and responsibilities [for officials] to keep a check on those outside. They urged people to study and lectured on their texts

---

[1] Added in the Wu text.
[2] See note 8 to Chang Miao's essay.
[3] The Wu reading of 制為 seems preferable to the Huang 制其.

A Refutation

to make their teachings sacred. Therefore [we have] the chaotic profusion of the Six Classics[4] and the teeming abundance of the one hundred schools.[5] They opened the road to profit and glory, and people, unaware, rush down it headlong.

Therefore birds that are greedy for life will eat the grain and beans in parks and [public] ponds; scholars in search of security will defy their wills and follow the vulgar. They grasp their pens and hold on to their boards,[6] with feet in a restful pose. They accumulate learning and elucidate the Classics in place of sowing and reaping.

Therefore, when people find themselves in straits—only then do they turn to study;[7] they study because it brings glory. They calculate [the benefits] and only then do they [begin to] learn; they delight in it, because with learning they can succeed. There is something about this that *seems* natural, and therefore it has brought you to say that it *is* natural.

But if we go back to the beginning—the essential features of the Six Classics are restraint and guidance; but what pleases human nature is following one's desires. Restraint and guidance thus go against our wishes, where by following our desires we attain the natural. This being the case, attainment of the natural does not come from the restraining and guiding Six Classics, and the root of perfecting one's nature does not rely on the laws and rituals which go against our feelings. Therefore benevolence and righteousness come into being with corruption of the natural order—they are not the vital methods for nourishing the real; modesty and yielding are produced by quarrel and struggle—they are not things that come from nature.

---

[4] Same as the "Six Disciplines." See note 19 to Chang Miao's essay.

[5] The various non-Confucian schools of thought.

[6] The word is *ku* 觚. Before the invention of paper writing was commonly done on silk, bamboo slips, and wood in ancient China.

[7] Hsi K'ang certainly has in mind Confucius' statement in *Analects* 16:9 (p. 34): "Those who are born with knowledge are the highest. Next come those who attain knowledge through study. Next again come those who turn to study after having been vexed by difficulties." (Tr. by D. C. Lau, *Confucius: The Analects*, p. 140.)

A Refutation

To speak from this perspective, birds do not [by nature] flock together[8] and seek to be tamed; animals do not [by nature] form a herd and ask to be tended. Thus the true nature of man is to be without intentional action; he will not[9] by nature crave ritual and learning.

In your essay you also say, of fancy foods and delicacies, that "even though they [the ancients] had never tasted them before, they of course praised them as soon as they tasted them, because they were pleasing to the palate." [And you also say] "If someone is in a dark room and sees the light of a small candle, he will be pleased in his heart without anyone telling him to be. What greater happiness, then, when after the long night of darkness he attains the illumination of the great sun; his feelings change from their former melancholy, and his ignorance is dispelled? Even though this may be a secondary development, the response of the feelings is basic, and thus this does not harm [my claim] that people naturally delight in learning."[10]

I object to this as follows: the mouth's relation to sweet and bitter and the body's relation to pain and itching is one of being aroused by stimulation, arising in response to the event. There is no need to study and only then be able to do it; it is not something that exists only in dependence on something else. This is a principle that is necessarily so, something we cannot change.[11] But you are using a principle that is necessarily so to illustrate the not necessarily so [matter of] delight in learning. I am afraid this is an argument that seems right but in fact is wrong. "[Delight in] learning" is like that discussion of hulled and unhulled rice;[12] it

---

[8] Following Lu Hsün's suggestion that *hui* 毀, "destroy," might be a mistake for *chü* 聚, "gather together."

[9] Agreeing with Lu Hsün that 正當 should be 不當. The alternative would be to place the 不 directly in front of 自然, giving "The true nature of man is correct and right [正當] when it is without intentional action, he does not by nature...."

[10] The quote is not exact.

[11] Or, reading 易 in the sense of 異, "I find nothing odd about it." The pattern is the same used by Hsi K'ang elsewhere in the reverse—吾所疑也—"This is something about which I have doubts."

[12] Tai Ming-yang (p. 262) is probably correct in concluding that the 一粟 should be 米粟.

A Refutation

is [simply] being placed in the context of something that is right.[13]

Now you set up the Six Classics as your standard and revere benevolence and righteousness as the central things, taking rules and regulations as the carriage you ride in and nursing on lecture and instruction. What follows this road you understand; what veers from this path you do not. [Though] you let your mind wander and look to the limit, you cannot see beyond this. To the end of your years you will chase about with thoughts on nothing but [official] position. You assemble your group and present your opinions, and only learning is of value; you grasp a book and select a sentence, look up and look down and sigh with admiration; to memorize[14] their words you consider honor and glory. Thus you call the Six Classics the great sun and lack of learning the long night.

But if you saw the lecture[15] hall as [nothing but] a grave hut,[16] and took all that chanting and reciting to be the words of ghosts; if you saw the Six Classics as [nothing but] overgrown weeds, and benevolence and righteousness as the stinking, rotting flesh; [if you realized that] all this staring at documents and records makes your eyes go weak,[17] and all this bowing and saluting makes you hunched over and crooked; [and if you realized that] wearing the insignia robes [showing one's rank in the official hierarchy] twists your muscles, and discussing the rites and canons makes your teeth rot—then you would reject the whole

---

[13] Tung Chung-shu 董仲舒 in his *Ch'un-ch'iu fan-lu* 春秋繁露 (10.6ab, SPPY ed.) says: "Therefore man's nature may be compared to the rice stalks and goodness to rice. Rice comes out of the rice stalk but not all the stalk becomes rice. Similarly, goodness comes out of nature but not all nature becomes good." (Tr. by Wing-tsit Chan, *A Source Book in Chinese Philosophy*, pp. 274-275.)

[14] Omitting the 使 at the head of the sentence on the basis of Tai Ming-yang's argument (p. 262). It is a mistake for 伏.

[15] The Huang text has a lacuna here. I follow the variant 講 found in various texts; the Wu text has 明.

[16] *Ping-she* 丙舍; a place where the coffin was temporarily placed.

[17] The word is *ch'iao* 瞧, "to glance at." But this must be read as 燋, from which we can get the meaning "worn out."

A Refutation

lot and begin anew with the ten thousand things. Then even if you delighted in learning without tiring[18] you would still find something lacking in it. Thus, the former lack of learning is not necessarily the long night, and the Six Classics are not necessarily the great sun.

There is a common saying: "A beggar does not find a horse-doctor insulting."[19] If you could get back to the uncultured state[20] of high antiquity,[21] you could have security without study and attain your will without having to labor. What then would you seek for in the Six Classics, and what would you want from benevolence and righteousness? To speak on the basis of this, how could it be that those who study at present do not turn to study only after calculating [the benefits]? If one takes action only after first making calculations, this is not a natural response. Given the things that you say, I am afraid you really need the sweet flag![22]

---

[18] Probably mimicking Confucius, who talked a lot about delight in learning, and who says in *Analects* 7:2 (p. 11): "Quietly to store up knowledge in my mind, to learn without flagging, to teach without growing weary, these present me with no difficulties." (Tr. by D. C. Lau, *Confucius: The Analects*, p. 86.)

[19] See *Lieh-tzu*, "Shuo fu" 說符, 8.15a. The story is translated by A. C. Graham in *The Book of Lieh-tzu*, p. 179. When some people ask a beggar if he is not disgraced to be working for a horse-doctor he replies: "There is nothing in the world more disgraceful than to beg. If even begging did not disgrace me, how can I be disgraced by a horse-doctor?" (Tr. by Graham.) I take Hsi K'ang's point to be that people should be insulted by the Six Classics and study, and would be were they not already in a low state.

[20] Reading the Wu variant 治 for 始, though either seems appropriate.

[21] Reading the Wu variant 古 for 有.

[22] Or perhaps, "If we follow what you say, I am afraid we will definitely need the calamus."

JUAN K'AN

Residence is Devoid of Good and Bad Fortune: You Must Rather Preserve Your Life

(Chai wu chi-hsiung she-sheng lun)

::

Translator's Comments on the Residence and Good Fortune Debate. No author is given for "Residence is Devoid of Good and Bad Fortune" in the Hsi K'ang chi. *Yen K'o-chün* 嚴可均 *attributes the essay to Chang Liao-shu (which should be Chang Shu-liao).*[1] *Mou Tsung-san* 牟宗三, *on the other hand, argues that since the idea of "preserving life" (*she-sheng 攝生*)— which is the same as "nourishing life"—is Hsi K'ang's thesis, the "Refutation" and "Answer" in the debate cannot be by him; in fact "Residence is Devoid of Good and Bad Fortune: You Must Rather Preserve Your Life" might have been written by Hsi K'ang using the name of Juan K'an.*[2] *But against Mou Tsung-san, the style of the "Refutation" and "Answer" is clearly that of Hsi K'ang; moreover, certain key Hsi K'ang expressions,* chih-li *(perfect reason) and* chien *(comprehensiveness), occur in these essays.*

That the author of the initial essay in the debate is Juan K'an 阮侃 *(style Te-ju* 德如*) is argued persuasively by Tai Ming-yang, who points out that a note to the Bibliography section of the* Sui shu *records an "Essay on Preserving Life" (*She-sheng lun*) in two* chüan *by one Juan K'an.*[3]

---

[1] See Yen K'o-chün, *Ch'üan shang-ku san-tai Ch'in Han san-kuo liu-ch'ao wen* 全上古三代秦漢三國六朝文 (Kyoto: Chūbun 中文, 1972), Vol. 2, p. 1337 top.
[2] See Mou Tsung-san 牟宗三, *Ts'ai-hsing yü hsüan-li* 才性與玄理 (Taipei: Jen-sheng 人生, 1963), pp. 320–321.
[3] See Tai Ming-yang, *Hsi K'ang chi chiao-chu*, pp. 265–266. And then see p. 86 in the *Chung-kuo li-tai t'u-shu ta tz'u-tien* 中國歷代圖書大辭典 (Taipei: Far East Book Co., 1956).

Residence

From a note to Shih-shuo hsin-yü *19:6, we know that Juan K'an and Hsi K'ang were friends (and we have the aforementioned poems exchanged between them), and that Juan K'an was skillful in logic, and at one time served as prefect of Ho-nei.*[4]

This is the longest of the debates, and it is an interesting debate indeed. While at the outset the issue is whether where one lives has any bearing on his good or bad fortune, the question that develops out of this is how is fate related to other things (morality, intelligence, effort, divination) in determining one's lot in life. Juan K'an argues that morality and divination—regular divination, that is, not divination of residence—are necessary to "complete" one's fate. Hsi K'ang never does take a position, preferring instead the role of devil's advocate.

*One assumes from the titles of these essays that they are about "geomancy" (*feng-shui 風水*), and they are indeed concerned with proper location of residence and grave to assure good fortune. Moreover, Needham shows that the general principles of geomancy were probably well known already in the Han.*[5] *However, the expression* feng-shui *itself is never used in the essays, and there is also no mention of the "white tiger" and the "green dragon" and the geomancer's compass,*[6] *things very important in* feng-shui *as it is commonly understood.*

One final note: if the initial essay reads smoothly, I have done my job too well. The Chinese in the original is awkward, unbalanced, and unclear.

One who is proficient at seeking long life and vigor must first know from whence come early death[1] and disease; only then can

---

[4] See Yang Yung, *Shih-shuo hsin-yü chiao-chien*, p. 511 where the *Ch'en-liu chih-ming* 陳留志名 is cited.

[5] Joseph Needham, *Science and Civilization in China*, Vol. 2, *History of Scientific Thought* (Cambridge: Cambridge University Press, 1956), pp. 359–363.

[6] For the "white tiger" and "green dragon" and a description of the geomancer's compass, see Ernest J. Eitel, *Feng-shui: or the Rudiments of Natural Science in China* (Hong Kong: Lane, Crawford & Co., 1873), pp. 22–44.

[1] Agreeing with Lu Hsün (p. 95) that the Wu variant of *yao* 夭 ("early death") for *tsai* 災 ("disaster") forms a better contrast with *shou* 壽 ("long life").

Residence

their arrival be prevented. If the calamity originates in one thing and the prevention is applied to another, the calamity will have no natural cure.

In this world there are the superstitions [associated with] placement of one's residence, [with] burial, [with] Yin and Yang, [with] measurements and numbers, and [with] punishments and rewards.² From what do these arise? From not understanding human nature and fate, and not knowing about calamity and blessing. Since people do not understand [them]; they pursue things falsely, and since they do not know about [them], they pray for luck. Therefore "the one who is good at holding on to life"³ understands what is proper to human nature and fate, and knows the causes of calamity and blessing; thus his search for them is correct, and his prevention of them is real.

If you drink a lot and then walk around, you will develop

---

²"Punishments and rewards" (*hsing-te* 刑德) should be done in accord with the seasons. Rewards are Yang and should be given out in the summer; punishments are Yin and should be done in the fall. Fung Yu-lan in his *History of Chinese Philosophy*, Vol. II, quotes Tung Chung-shu's *Ch'un-ch'iu fan-lu* as saying: "Thus with his [the good ruler's] beneficence he duplicates warmth and accords with spring, with his conferring of rewards he duplicates heat and accords with summer, with his punishments he duplicates coolness and accords with autumn, and with his executions he duplicates coldness and accords with winter" (p. 48). "Punishments and rewards" also refers to the good and bad fortune associated with certain celestial bodies and their positions in the heavens at certain times of the year. Donald Harper notes that "The idea that the year was divided into times of Punishments (*hsing* 刑) and times of Virtue (*te* 德) evolved out of the cosmological theories of the late Warring States period. Associated with the Yin and Yang cycles, it was sometimes stated that the motions of the moon and the sun determined the cycles of Punishment and Virtue respectively; and it was also believed that the Big Dipper was an indicator of cosmic Punishment and Virtue." (See note 47 to his article "The Han Cosmic Board (*Shih* 式)," *Early China* 4 [1978–79], p. 8.) In his "Explanation" to Hsi K'ang's "Refutation" of the present essay, Juan K'an refers to the "punishments and rewards" associated with the planet Jupiter.

³Quoting from Chapter 50 of the *Lao-tzu*, but the phrase "hold on to life" (*chih-sheng* 執生) occurs only in the Ma-wang-tui texts of the *Lao-tzu*. See *Ma-wang-tui Han mu po-shu* 馬王堆漢墓帛書, Vol. I (Peking: Wen wu, 1980), p. 104. Other texts here have *she-sheng* 攝生, "preserve life." Wing-tsit Chan (*The Way of Lao Tzu*, p. 188) translates: "I have heard that one who is a good preserver of his life will not meet tigers or wild buffaloes," etc.

Residence

painful limbs.[4] If you frequently travel about in the wind, you will nourish poisons.[5] If you sit for a long time in a damp place, your waist will ache and you'll become partially paralyzed.[6] If you delight in the inner [chambers—i.e., the women's quarters] without tiring, you will become blindly lost in the diseases of lust.[7] Things of this kind are the things that bring on disaster and the things that eliminate long life. And yet they dig out their graves[8] and build their houses, wasting their days and belaboring their bodies in search of it [long life and good fortune]. When the disease arises in the form and the cure is applied to earth and wood—this is a disease which there is no way to cure.

The *Book of Poetry* says: "Happy and pleased is our lord; in seeking blessings he does not go astray."[9] His being righteous and upright was not done to avoid slander and libel. Presumably [it was because] he knew that to go astray is not the way to seek blessings.

Therefore, for long life and vigor [you must] "concentrate your breath and make it extremely soft,"[10] "diminish self-interest and lessen your desires,"[11] directly follow that which is appropriate to feelings and nature, and act in accord with the

---

[4] The expression is *tan-chih* 澹支. But not much sense can be made from this *tan* ("tranquil, quiet"), unless it means that one's limbs fall asleep (?). Commentators are agreed on reading *tan* as an error for *t'ung* 痛, "painful," but an explanation for the sentence is still wanting. Tai Ming-yang (p. 267) has found one source that claims that "if you drink wine and sweat and then face the wind, your limbs and joints will hurt."

[5] Translation is tentative. I am reading *yang* 癢 ("itch") as *yang* 養, "nourish". But perhaps it should be "develop itching poisons" (?).

[6] Chuang-tzu says much the same in Chapter 2 (p. 6, line 67): "If a man sleeps in a damp place, his back aches and he ends up half paralyzed." (Tr. by Watson, *The Complete Works of Chuang Tzu*, p. 45.)

[7] Following the Wu text reading of 女疾, which I take to be "disease of lust," in place of 文房, "study."

[8] The Wu manuscript has *mu* 墓, "grave" here instead of *chi* 基, "foundation."

[9] Stanza 6 of poem 239 (p. 60). For Karlgren's translation see *The Book of Odes*, p. 191.

[10] From Chapter 10 of the *Lao-tzu* (part I, pp. 5ab). Chan (*The Way of Lao Tzu*, p. 116) translates the line: "Can you concentrate your vital force and achieve the highest degree of weakness like an infant?"

[11] Also words from the *Lao-tzu*; the last line of Chapter 19 (part I, p. 10b).

Residence

correct measures for nourishing life. Seek for them in the things you hold inside and you will get them.

Once there was a man who did not understand about silkworms. Everything he said and everything he did was done out of fear of evil spiritual influence. The more he failed to obtain silk from the silkworms, the more his fear of the spirits increased, as though he were personally offending them.[12] But then someone taught him about silkworm [cultivation], and he [began] to concentrate solely on the mulberry [leaves] and the fire [for warming], on hot and cold and dry and damp.[13] With that his one hundred fears came to an end of themselves, and he profited tenfold. Why? [Because] at first he did not know why things are as they are, and therefore his superstitious feelings abounded. But afterwards he understood why things are as they are, and therefore the techniques he used to seek his results were correct. Therefore, superstitions always arise from ignorance. If people understood human nature as they understand[14] silkworms, superstitions would have no place to stand.

If you have over-eaten and it will not digest, if you dispense with the Yellow Pill[15] and [instead] use divination and invocation to ask the spirits wherein lies the fault, or seek help from a

---

[12] For readers unfamiliar with the superstitions associated with silkworm cultivation in China, one can get a good sense of these in Mao Tun's short story, "Spring Silkworms." See his *Spring Silkworms and Other Stories* (Peking: Foreign Languages Press, 1956). pp. 1–26. There we read, for example, "The second day of incubation, Old Tung Pao smeared a garlic with earth and placed it at the foot of the wall inside the shed. If, in a few days, the garlic put out many sprouts, it meant the eggs would hatch well." And, "Even peasants normally on very good terms stopped visiting one another. For a guest to come and frighten away the spirits of the ripening eggs—that would be no laughing matter!" (From pp. 13–14.)

[13] Silkworms eat mulberry leaves, and a fire is kept going underneath the trays that hold them as they eat and grow. Presumably the "hot and cold and dry and damp" refers either to the conditions in the shed where they are raised, or to climatic conditions in general. Silkworm cultivation takes place in the spring around the time of the Clear and Bright festival.

[14] Following the Wu text in reading 知 for 如.

[15] The "Yellow Pill" (*Huang-wan* 黃丸) must refer to *ta-huang* 大黃, which Read (*Chinese Medicinal Plants*, p. 186, item 582) identifies as "rhubarb." The *Shen Nung pen-ts'ao ching* (3.7a) claims that rhubarb breaks up accumulations of food and drink in the stomach and intestines.

Residence

begging barbarian,[16] the common people will all laugh at you. Why? Because they are smart enough to understand that there is no calamity [caused by the spirits] involved. Therefore, superstitions all arise from ignorance. To speak from the point of view of someone who understands, they are all [about as effective as] begging barbarians.

Let us suppose the case of the residence of the three high ministers,[17] and let us have someone from the ignorant masses live in it. That he definitely would not become one of the three high ministers can be known. That long life and early death cannot be sought is even more certain than the fact that one's rank, high or low, [cannot be sought].[18] Thus you may auspiciously select your "one hundred years" palace and hope for the "old age" of a child who dies young. [On the other hand] you might build counter to the Bow[19] or Dipper K'uei,[20] yet hasten to the "early death" of a P'eng-tsu.[21] These are definitely not omens.

---

[16] Fukunaga Mitsuji 福永光司 argues that "begging barbarian" (ch'i-hu 乞胡) refers to itinerant Buddhist monks in China who begged for their food and cured diseases. See his article "Kei Kō to Bukkhō" 嵇康と佛教, Tōyōshi kenkyū 東洋史研究, 20:4 (1962), p. 101.

[17] The san-kung 三公 were the three highest-ranking ministers of state in traditional China. From the Latter Han onward, their titles were T'ai-wei 太尉 (Grand Marshal), Ssu-t'u 司徒 (Director of Instruction), and Ssu-k'ung 司空 (Director of Works).

[18] In Analects 12:5 (p. 22) Tzu-hsia says: "I have heard it said: life and death are a matter of Destiny; wealth and honor depend on Heaven." (Tr. by D. C. Lau, Confucius: The Analects, p. 113.) Tai Ming-yang (p. 269) cites the following line from Ts'ao Ta-chia's 曹大家 (Pan Chao 班昭) "Rhapsody on the Eastern Campaign," (Tung-cheng fu 東征賦): "High station and low, poverty and wealth—these cannot be sought for." (See Wen hsüan 9.14a.)

[19] Reading 孤 as 弧. The "Bow" is a constellation in the shape of a drawn bow, made up of the four stars below the "Wolf" (狼, Sirius). To "build counter" to it probably means to be situated facing the oncoming arrow—but I am not sure.

[20] The name is k'uei-kang 魁罡. K'uei is the first star in the Northern Dipper (our Big Dipper), and kang is the handle of the same. In the tenth month k'uei's energies or aura (氣) are in the direction of WNW (or possibly in the region of Aquarius—in hsü 戌); this is not a good time to build.

[21] Cleverly put. For P'eng-tsu, China's Methusaleh, who is reported to have lived over eight hundred years (although Juan K'an later says seven hundred), see note 116 to Hsi K'ang's "Answer to Hsiang Hsiu's Refutation of My Essay on Nourishing Life."

Residence

Someone might say: "[But] the ignorant masses definitely are not able to live a long time in the houses of nobles." This being so, there is truly no [influence] from residence. This is all [a matter of] one's nature and fate and what is naturally so; it cannot be sought.[22]

When a thief is about to arrive, if you do not quickly escape [to a place where you can be] safe and alone, then in a moment you will become the victim. This being so, in avoiding harm and pursuing blessing there is nothing better than following principle. Of the principles for avoiding a thief, none is better than rapid escape; [if you do this] the result will be good. Of the ways for nourishing life, none is better than putting harmony[23] first; [if you do this] you have done all that needs to be done. That in avoiding thieves it is proper to hurry is crystal-clear; thus [even] people of mediocre abilities do not find this difficult to see. [But] the principle for avoiding misfortune is dark and obscure; therefore [even] those who are wise do not with ease perceive it. But in so far as they originate in principle and cannot be falsely[24] sought, these [two] are one and the same.

[Once] Confucius was ill. The doctor said to him: "The place where you live seems agreeable and the food you eat is pleasant;[25] that you are sick must come from Heaven. How can I do anything to help?"[26] Therefore, "one who knows fate does not

---

[22] From what precedes we expect Juan K'an to answer the objection (an interesting one at that) that if a commoner lived *long enough* in the house of a noble, he might indeed share in good fortune. Instead we have only Juan K'an's conclusion.

[23] Emending the text to read *ho* 和, "harmony", instead of *chih* 知, "knowledge." It becomes clear from Hsi K'ang's reply that Juan K'an had said that "harmony" is all one needs to have. The original, unedited, Wu manuscript, according to Tai Ming-yang (p. 269), had: "Of the ways for nourishing life, none is better than profit; then harmony is all that you need to have."

[24] Following the Wu text in reading 妄 in place of 要.

[25] Reading the variant 樂 for 藥.

[26] The closest we come to documenting this story are the words of Kung-sun Ni-tzu 公孫尼子 preserved in *T'ai-p'ing yü-lan* 724 (Vol. 3, p. 3207 in the Chung-hua shu-chü edition [Peking, 1960]): "[Once] when Confucius was ill, Duke Ai sent a doctor to see him. The doctor asked: 'What are your dwelling

Residence

worry;"[27] he traces things to the beginning and follows them to the end, and thus he understands what is said about life and death."[28]

"Good times and lucky days" and "asking the spirits wherein lies the fault"—these are things the great kings of the past did not have, but that decadent kings [of later ages] love to follow. They make their "long life" palaces and get [in return] early death; they strive to have a hundred boys, but end up without [so much as] an adopted heir; they must divine to have a tomb that will not be opened, and the grass on their graves never has a chance to spread its roots.[29] Why? [Because] they live in their high towers and deep palaces, cutting themselves off from heat and cold, and they overindulge in sex and eat too much rich food, poisoning their essence. They lose it where it counts and seek it in what is in vain. Therefore, their natures and fates are not brought to completion. Someone might say: "The specialists [in divination] they consulted were not skilled." [To which I reply] "There is not a single skilled specialist in the world."[30]

Now with chickens that are all in one coop, or sheep that are all in one pen, when a guest arrives and some die, how could it be that their residence was different? Therefore, destinies are controlled. And one who understands fate is not impeded by the common and vulgar. Such things as Hsü Fu's predicting that [Ya

---

place and food like?' Confucius said: 'In the spring I live in Ko-ch'ung and in the summer I live at Mi-yang. In the autumn I do not [go out in the] wind, and in the winter I do not [sit before] a blazing fire. In eating I do not offer food as a gift to others, and in drinking wine I do not offer drinks as a toast to others.' The doctor said, 'This is good medicine indeed.'" Also, the Lü-shih ch'un-ch'iu ("K'ai-ch'un" 開春 chapter: 21. 1a) says: "If the food one eats and the place one lives are both agreeable, the nine cavities [of the body] and the one hundred joints and the one thousand arteries are all clear and sharp."

[27] From the I ching, Hsi-tz'u A.4 (p. 4): "He delights in Heaven and understands fate and therefore he does not worry."

[28] Also from the I: Hsi-tz'u A.3 (p. 4).

[29] Meaning that their tombs are constantly looted and desecrated. Su-ts'ao 宿草 is grass that has spread its roots—i.e., it has been there at least one year.

[30] Translation is tentative.

151

Residence

Fu] would become marquis of T'iao,[31] and Ying Pu's first being tatooed [as a criminal] and later becoming a king,[32] and P'eng-tsu's seven hundred years, and the early death of an infant—these are all [matters] of one's nature and fate.

If you divine about residence and [in this way] fix where to live,[33] [thinking that] if you move from east to west you will get it [good fortune]; to the contrary, this destroys what is proper to human nature and fate. "When Confucius ascended Eastern Mountain he thought that Lu was small. When he ascended Mt. T'ai, he thought the whole world was small."[34] When you stand on a high mound and survey where people live, then you will know to say that east and west are not [related to] calamity and blessing. But if you forget [the importance] of having a location that is high and clear,[35] and [instead] have a mind[36] that is restricted by screens and walls, what you see will be all the more narrow.

To look at it from the perspective of one who understands:

---

[31] See *Shih chi* 57 (Vol. 6, pp. 2073-2074). This happened in the early years of the Han. When Ya Fu 亞夫 was magistrate of Ho-nei, Hsü Fu 許負, through physiognomy, predicted that in three years he would become a marquis, and having been a marquis for eight years, become a general, and nine years after that die of starvation. All of this came true. In three years he was appointed marquis of T'iao 條.

[32] See *Shih chi* 91 (Vol. 8, pp. 2597-2608). When Ying Pu 英布 was young, someone predicted, again through physiognomy, that he would suffer criminal punishment but then become a king. He was tatooed for breaking the law under the Ch'in, but went on to become king of Chiu-chiang 九江 under Hsiang Yü and then king of Huai-nan 淮南 in the early years of the Han.

[33] Or possibly "determine the true substance of a place." The expression is *chih-chü* 質居.

[34] Quoted from the beginning of passage 7A.24 in the *Mencius* (p. 52). For Lau's translation see D. C. Lau, *Mencius*, p. 187.

[35] The importance of being in a place that is "high and clear" (*shuang-k'ai* 爽塏—also "high and dry," and "clear and dry" is a point made in the *Tso chuan* (Duke Chao, 3rd year: p. 349) where Duke Ching of Ch'i wanted to move Yen-tzu to such a place and away from the commotion of the market. (For Legge's translation of the anecdote see *The Chinese Classics*, Vol. V, part 2, p. 589.) But here Juan K'an also has in mind the necessity to raise one's horizons intellectually by seeing things from above.

[36] Reading the Wu variant 立 instead of 心.

Residence

"the Creative is firm and shows man ease; the Receptive is yielding and shows man the simple."[37] If Heaven and Earth are easy and simple and one fears them as being severe and exacting—this is to go against them all the more.[38] Therefore the Gentleman is enlightened in serving Heaven and circumspect in waiting on Earth.

The skilled specialists in this world, when they divine a completed house they [have] proof, but if you have them build a new one, they have no evidence. The people of the world, in many cases, because they have [successfully] divined about an old [house], seek [by this method] to build a new one. [But] this is [like] seeing that a boat can move on water and wishing to push it along on dry land.[39] This is not a wise plan.

The principle [involved] in old and new[40] [houses], is just like [that involved] in divination by tortoise shell and milfoil. By boring holes in the tortoise and counting the stalks you can *know* good and bad fortune; however, you cannot *make* good and bad fortune. Why? Because good and bad fortune can be known but they cannot be made. To first divine by milfoil a propitious hexagram and then do what it says without blessing, is just like first building a beneficial house and then living in it without reward. To divine about an old residence to determine the cause of evil influence is possible; but to lay out a new residence in such a way as to seek blessings is not possible. [Thus,] this is just exactly[41] like the theory behind divination by shell and milfoil.

---

[37] Quoting the *I ching*, *Hsi-tz'u* A.1 (p. 45). The "Creative" and "Receptive" are the first two trigrams (and hexagrams) in the *I ching* (*ch'ien* 乾 and *k'un* 坤); they are also male and female, Heaven and Earth. "Creative" and "Receptive" are the names assigned by Wilhelm. See Richard Wilhelm, *The I Ching or Book of Changes*, pp. 3 and 10.

[38] Or possibly "turn them into things that oppose you" (更所以爲逆也).

[39] A paraphrase of a statement made in *Chuang-tzu*, Chapter 14 (p. 38, lines 36–37). Watson (*The Complete Works of Chuang Tzu*, p. 159) translates: "Nothing is as good as a boat for crossing water, nothing as good as a cart for crossing land. But though a boat will get you over water, if you try to push it across land, you may push till your dying day and hardly move it any distance at all."

[40] Reading the Wu variant of 新 instead of 斷.

[41] Following the Wu text in reading 即 instead of 則.

Residence

Among the common people, for both cutting out clothes and planting grains, they [must] select the right [propitious] day.[42] [But] those who [make] clothes [in this way], are hurt by the cold, and those who plant [in this way], miss the time when the soil is moist. When the Fire-star has gone down and the cold has arrived, then you must give out the clothes;[43] [and when] the seasonal rains have fallen, then you must sow the seeds; [and when] a thief is about to arrive, then you must quickly run away. But now [people] reject the true and pursue the false, and therefore the three adversities accordingly arrive.[44] Whoever manages his household by means of superstition, seeks for wealth[45] but ends up impoverished. Therefore, there is the saying: "Whoever believes in the stars will not have clothes to cover his back." The words of the ancients are not false. They must be studied with care.

---

[42] According to Wang Ch'ung's *Lun-heng* ("Chi-jih" 譏日 chapter: 24.3b) there was in fact a book which noted the days of good and bad fortune for cutting out clothes. The *Sui chih* (Bibliography section of the Sui History) lists a *Ts'ai-i shu* 裁衣書 of one *chüan* which was still extant in the Liang. (See *Chung-kuo li-tai i-wen chih*, p. 99.)

[43] The "must" (當) is added in in the Wu text. This is said against the background of the opening line of *Shih* 154 (p. 41). Karlgren (*The Book of Odes*, p. 97) translates: "In the seventh month there is the declining Fire-star; in the ninth month we give out the clothes." The "Fire" (火) is glossed as *ta-huo* 大火, or "Scorpio," and Waley (*The Book of Songs*, p. 164) notes: "'The Fire ebbs' is explained as meaning 'Scorpio is sinking below the horizon at the moment of its first visibility at dusk.'"

[44] That is to say, they have trouble with clothes, crops, and thieves.

[45] Following the Wu text in reading 富 for 福.

HSI K'ANG

A Refutation of Juan K'an's Essay—Residence is Devoid of Good and Bad Fortune: You Must Rather Preserve Your Life

(Nan Chai wu chi-hsiung she-sheng lun)

::

The spirits of Heaven and Earth are far away and distant, and good and bad fortune are difficult to understand. Even though men of mediocre abilities might exhaust their resources, none would understand the principles involved, and it is easy by this to become confused about the Way. Therefore the Master [Confucius] stopped answering when questioned about the end; he was cautious about spirits and prodigies and about them did not speak.[1] And this is why the ancients displayed their benevolence to others but kept how it works to themselves.[2] They knew these things could not be shared with the masses. It is not that they intentionally concealed them; these are things they would not understand.

I have no interest in discussing such matters. But you, with your opinionated mind and shallow views, are certain and have no doubts. To be so definite as this is enough to be considered

---

[1] Following the Wu text in omitting the 來 in 來問終 (Lu Hsün mistakenly leaves it in). Hsi K'ang has in mind two passages in the *Analects*. *Analects* 11:12 (p. 20) reads: "Chi-lu [Tzu-lu] asked how the spirits of the dead and the gods should be served. The Master said, 'You are not able even to serve man. How can you serve the spirits?' 'May I ask about death?' 'You do not understand even life. How can you understand death?'" (Tr. by D. C. Lau, *Confucius: The Analects*, p. 107.) The other passage is *Analects* 7:21 (p. 13): "The topics the Master did not speak of were prodigies, force, disorder and gods." (Tr. by D. C. Lau, *Confucius: The Analects*, p. 88.)

[2] Reminiscent of the language at the start of *Hsi-tz'u* A.5 in the *I ching* (p. 40): "Display it in benevolence; conceal it in its function." (顯諸仁, 藏諸用)

A Refutation

dogmatic. I have thought over your essay,[3] and there are many points I do not understand. Respectfully I avail myself of your words to produce this refutation.

If for the direction [of your door] you infer what to do from metal and wood, you will never know where it should be.[4] No one has the "good" method.[5] In this world there are no naturally correct ways, and among methods, no solely good techniques. "If you are not the [right] man, the Way cannot be vainly pursued."[6] Even in the rites and music, in governing and punishments, in matters out of the ordinary there are things that are unfamiliar; how much the more [will this be true] with the hidden and unseen? But even if you wish to distinguish and

---

[3] Literally "the essay that has come" (*lai-lun* 來論).

[4] This needs to be explained. Five Elements theory classes surnames in accord with the five musical notes—*chüeh* 角 (E), *chih* 徵 (G), *shang* 商 (D), *yü* 羽 (A), and *kung* 宮 (C)—which then correspond to the five elements (wood, fire, metal, water, and earth, respectively) and the five directions (east, south, west, north, and center, respectively). Thus for each family, there is an "appropriate" direction which its house should face. But the determination of this appropriate direction is done differently by different specialists, and it is this confusion to which Hsi K'ang presumably refers. For example, Wang Ch'ung in his *Lun-heng* ("Chieh-shu" 詰術 chapter: 25.3b) quotes a work entitled *T'u-chai shu* 圖宅術 as saying, "The door of a family with a D surname should not face south; the door of a family with a G surname should not face north," and then he continues: "Thus D is metal and the southern direction is fire; G is fire and the northern direction water. Water overcomes fire, and fire harms metal." On the other hand, Wang Fu 王符 (alive A.D. 76–157) in his *Ch'ien-fu lun* 潛夫論 ("Pu lieh" 卜列 chapter: 6.4a) says that the opinion of common workmen, who say that the exit gate for a D house should be on the west, is wrong because that would put the entrance gate on the east, and if the entrance is on the east, metal will be cutting into wood.

[5] Following Tai Ming-yang's suggestion (p. 274) of emending 食治 to read 良法.

[6] Quoting from the *I ching*, *Hsi-tz'u* B.7 (p. 48). The immediate context is relevant. Legge (*I Ching: Book of Changes*, p. 399) translates: "[The *I Ching*], moreover, makes plain the nature of anxieties and calamities, and the causes of them. Though (its students) have neither master nor guardian, it is as if their parents drew near to them. Beginning with taking note of its explanations, we reason out the principles to which they point. We thus find out that it does supply a constant and standard rule. But if there be not the proper men (to carry this out), the course cannot be pursued without them."

A Refutation

clarify the spiritual and unseen, dispel confusion and root out impediment, establish the beginnings to clarify the causes, examine[7] [the data] to investigate the essentials, and then consider that you have the proof[8]—if you merely bring up [examples] of the ignorant masses,[9] or [someone who] has not studied[10] silkworm eggs, and angrily reject it, saying, because of this, there are no principles of Yin and Yang or good and bad fortune; can we help but compare you to someone who is choking and faults the grains, or someone who is drowning and blames the boat and the oars?

In your essay you say that a "one hundred years" palace cannot make a doomed infant live long, and that building counter to the Bow or Dipper K'uei would not cause a P'eng-tsu to die young. You also say that Hsü Fu's predicting the marquis of T'iao, and Ying Pu's first being tattooed and later becoming a king, were both [cases of] human nature and fate.

My response is this: this means that fate has that which is fixed, and long life is where it is; calamity cannot through intelligence be escaped, and blessing cannot through effort be brought about. Ying Pu was afraid of pain, but ended up suffering the knife and the saw; Ya Fu was afraid of going hungry, but in the end he died of starvation. In all things and all matters, whatever one encounters, there is nothing that is not one's fortune and fate.

If this is so, then in the ages of T'ang and Yü, how was it that fates were all equally long,[11] and with the soldiers at Ch'ang-

---

[7] Filling in the lacuna that occurs here in the text with the *shen* 審 found in the Wen-chin text. *Shen-tuan* 斷 is a set expression meaning to examine something and then pass judgment.

[8] Following the Wu text which has 乃爲有徵. The Huang text has a lacuna at the 有 and has 徵 for the last character.

[9] Referring to Juan K'an's argument of having someone from the masses live in the residence of the three high ministers.

[10] Filling the lacuna here with the 不察 we find in the Ch'eng text.

[11] T'ang 唐 and Yü 虞 were the reign designations of Yao and Shun. People were supposed to have lived long in these ages of virtue.

A Refutation

p'ing, how was it that fates were all equally short?[12] This is what I have doubts about. If things are as you say, then even if you were as scrupulous as Tseng [Tzu] or Yen [Hui], you could not dodge disaster, and [even if] you were as evil as Chieh or Chih[13] you would be sure to enjoy prosperity. If good and bad fortune are fixed from the beginning and cannot be diverted, then why did the ancients say "The family that accumulates goodness will necessarily have a surplus of blessings,"[14] and "If you tread sincerity and think of obedience, you will receive help from Heaven"?[15] It must be that one is requited with blessings only if he has first accumulated goodness, and divine aid comes only when sincerity is first of all manifest. This is just like the crime's inviting its punishment and the achievement's bringing on its reward. If you first accumulate and then receive the reward, this comes from the principle of the event; it is not a matter of mysteriously and naturally running into it. If you say of all of this, "This *is* fortune"—this is to restrict fortune and fate to conduct [good or bad], and firmly fix good and bad fortune to intelligence and strength.[16] I am afraid that is not the understanding of the present writer. This is also something about which I have doubts.

You also say that if we over-eat and develop indigestion, we

---

[12] See *Shih chi* 73 (Vol. 7, pp. 2333-2335). In 260 B.C. the forces of Ch'in, under the leadership of Po Ch'i 白起, attacked the armies of Chao camped at Ch'ang-p'ing 長平. Four hundred thousand troops surrendered to Po Ch'i, and he put them all to death.

[13] For Chieh and Robber Chih see note 128 to Hsi K'ang's "An Answer to Hsiang Hsiu's Refutation of My Essay on Nourishing Life."

[14] Said in the *I ching*, in the *Wen-yen* on *k'un*, the second hexagram (p. 4).

[15] Also from the *I*: from *Hsi-tz'u* A.11 (p. 44). The passage reads (tr. by Legge, *I Ching: Book of Changes*, pp. 375-376): "It is said in the Yi, 'Help is given to him from Heaven. There will be good fortune; advantage in every respect.' The Master said:—'Yu (祐) is the symbol of assisting. He whom Heaven assists is observant (of what is right); he whom men assist is sincere. The individual here indicated treads the path of sincerity and desires to be observant (of what is right), and studies to exalt the worthy. Hence "Help is given to him from Heaven. There will be good fortune, advantage in every respect."'"

[16] That is to say, if I understand Hsi K'ang correctly, if one is virtuous and smart, he will be *destined* for good fortune.

A Refutation

must have the Yellow Pill. If one's fate is such that he should naturally live, what can he fear from eating too much that he must take good medicine? If you say that taking medicine is in agreement with his fortune, how can it be that residence is not in agreement with it? If you say that even though fate has that[17] which must be, it needs medicine to help it [along], how do you know that fortune does not need residence to assist it? If you say that medicine can be discussed but residence cannot, I am afraid there are those in this world who do talk about it.

You have said "That long life and early death cannot be sought is even more certain than the fact that one's rank, high or low, [cannot be sought]," but you have also said, "The one who is proficient at seeking long life and vigor must first know from whence come early death[18] and disease; only then can they be prevented." So, can long life and early death truly be sought for or not? You have said that "P'eng-tsu's seven hundred years and the early death of an infant—these are all [matters] of one's nature and fate and what is naturally so." But you have also said that if you do not know how to prevent disease and bring on long life and do away with early death, you are seeking for the real in the false, and therefore your "nature and fate are not brought to completion."[19] This means that the coming of long life or early death is determined by how one uses his body, and the completion of one's nature and fate is to be found in skillful seeking. This being so, then why not call one whose life is short, stupid, and one whose life is long, wise? If long life and early death come from being stupid or wise, then this "fate that is naturally so," and the theory that it cannot be sought—why do you pay them any mind? All of these various statements are simply the contradictions of a "sophisticated" essay.

In your essay you say: "Concentrate your breath and make it

---

[17] Emending *yu* 猶 to be *yu* 有. I do this on my own based on the earlier parallel expression 命有所定.

[18] Again following the Wu text in reading 夭 in place of 灾.

[19] Only this last bit seems to be a direct quote.

A Refutation

extremely soft, diminish self-interest and lessen your desires, directly follow that which is appropriate to feelings and nature, and act in accord with the correct measures for nourishing life. Seek for them in the things you hold inside and you will get them." You also say, "To be good at nourishing life, harmony is all that matters."[20] True indeed are these words! I would not say they are wrong. I would simply say that the [measures for] completing one's life are not exhausted by these. "To not enter a state that's in danger"[21]—this is the way to avoid harm from chaotic rule; "doubling the gates [at night] and beating the watchman's rattle"[22]—this is the way we prepare against[23] the violence of the wild and unrestrained; that where we live must be high and clear—this is the way we keep at a distance the suffering caused by wind poisons. Of the things that are outside us and able to cause us harm, these [in no way] exhaust their number. How could one do all that needs to be done by simply maintaining this single harmony?[24]

For concentrating his tranquillity and lessening his desires no one was better than Shan Pao. He reached the age of seventy but had the complexion of a child.[25] One could say this was the result of his gentle harmony. And yet one morning he was eaten by a tiger. How could it not be that this happened because he relied on the inside and disregarded the out? If you say that Pao's fortune [was such that] it was fitting that he should become a tiger's

---

[20] Not a direct quote.

[21] The words of Confucius in *Analects* 8:13 (p. 15). D. C. Lau's translation of the lines goes: "Enter not a state that is in peril; stay not in a state that is in danger." (D. C. Lau, *Confucius: The Analects*, p. 94.)

[22] From the *I ching, Hsi-tz'u* B.2 (p. 45).

[23] Reading the Wu variant of 備 instead of 避.

[24] Following the Wu text in reading 和 in place of 利.

[25] All of this cast very much in the language of *Chuang-tzu* 19 (p. 49, lines 29–30) where we hear of Shan Pao. Of course we have met Shan Pao before in Hsi K'ang's "Answer" to Hsiang Hsiu's "Refutation" of his "Essay on Nourishing Life" (see note 163). For Watson's translation of the Shan Pao story see *The Complete Works of Chuang Tzu*, p. 201.

A Refutation

meal,[26] and that even though he was intelligent he could not avoid it, then of what benefit was his "lessening his desires" so that you say by nourishing life [in this way] you can attain it [long life]? [But] if Shan Pao brought on this disaster by being not yet totally good [at everything one needs to do], then the way for aiding life does not stop with a single harmony. If harmony is not yet sufficient for[27] protecting life, then I don't know what can relieve[28] the suffering caused by external things.

In your essay you say: "If the specialist divines a completed house he has proof, but if you have him build a new one, he has no evidence." May I ask, when you divine a completed house and have proof, do you merely divine the walls and the rooms, or do you divine the good and bad fortune of the people who live there? If you are divining about the inhabitants and [in this way] know whether they will succeed or fail—this comes from divining about people; it is not a matter of divining a completed house. If [on the other hand] you divine a completed house and know [as a result] the good and bad fortune, this means that the residence itself has good and evil in it, and those who live there must comply with it. Therefore the diviner looks at the surface and understands the inside. If residence is able to control people and cause them to comply, then a man who is destined for good fortune will [nonetheless] suffer harm in an "evil" house, and [one who is] wicked and perverse, without principle, will [nonetheless] enjoy blessings in a "good" abode.

Do you make the cause of good and bad fortune out to be nothing but residence? Or, alternatively, do you see it [good and bad fortune] as coming from man,[29] and [for this reason] say that

---

[26] Reading the variant of 虎 that we find in the Chang 張 text in place of 廚.
[27] Adding in the 以 that is in the original Wu manuscript.
[28] Following the Wu text in reading 濟 instead of 齊.
[29] There is another possibility. Where our text here has 更令由人也, the Wen-chin text has 更令由故, and the Wu text has 全 instead of 令. Tai Ming-yang (p. 278) prefers this reading (i.e., 更全由故), and understands Hsi K'ang to be saying that "if one says that good and bad fortune come entirely from the old house, then there would be no evidence for the good and bad fortune of a new house."

A Refutation

a new [house] thus has no evidence? [But] if good and bad fortune definitely come from man, then even though you have a completed house, how could you say you have proof? This being the case, can [residence] truly be divined? Is there truly [any influence] from residence or not?

Your essay says: "[Divination of] residence is just like divination by tortoise shell and milfoil. You can *know* good and bad fortune but you cannot *make* good and bad fortune." My response is that these are similar but not the same. In divining with the tortoise shell, good and bad fortune have no pre-existing sign; the response is made when something is encountered, and it is an omen[30] of what is to come. In divining about residence you do not ask about the character of the people who live there, whether worthy or stupid, you look only at what is already so. There is nothing that changes direction;[31] it is a form that is already set. It is just like looking at [in physiognomy] a dragon countenance and knowing that [this person] is destined for nobility,[32] or seeing the vertical pattern between nose and mouth[33] and knowing [that person] will starve.[34]

Thus each [divination by tortoise and divination of a house] has its cause; they are not things wrapped in mystery. If you see they are the same in determining good and bad fortune, and accordingly say that divination of residence and divination by tortoise are no different, this is like seeing a lute and calling it a harp;[35] it is not only that you do not understand the lute.[36] And

---

[30] Following the Wu text in reading 兆 instead of 地.

[31] The text has 有傳者, which makes no sense. There is a variant of 轉 for 傳, and then one must, as Tai Ming-yang suggests (p. 279), add a 無 at the start.

[32] The "dragon countenance" (*lung-yen* 龍顏) is one that Sons of Heaven have. It is described as the "eyebrow bone rising up sharply" (眉骨突起).

[33] The expression is *tsung-li* 縱理, and I have taken it as equivalent to *tsung-li ju-k'ou* 入口, which is an expression in physiognomy referring to the pattern of the skin between the nose and mouth.

[34] Following the Wu text reading of 知當餓; parallelism demands it.

[35] The *k'ung-hou* 箜篌 was an ancient stringed instrument of (usually) twenty-three strings (vs. the seven of the lute). "Harp" is the translation used by van Gulik in his *Lore of the Chinese Lute*. But the *k'ung-hou* was played horizontally like the lute, not vertically like our harp.

A Refutation

even if, as you say,[37] residence and tortoise shell divination are the same, but we are merely able to know [good and bad fortune] and not make them—then good and bad fortune are already set; even though you know them, what good does it do? Whether you divine or not has no place at all [in determining the result]. And yet the ancients, when they were about to do something, "Ask the tortoise and the milfoil if it was auspicious," to determine which course of action they would follow and select. How could this have been in vain? This, once again, is something about which I have doubts. When King Wu was building the [capital of] Chou, they said "It was the king who examined the oracle, and we made our residence in the capital at Hao."[38] And when the Duke of Chou moved the capital, he divined about [settling near] the Chien and the Ch'an [rivers], but in the end it was only with the Lo that he got the good sign.[39] They [the ancients] also said: "Divine the omen for their tomb and securely place them in it."[40] The ancients practiced this in former times like that, but you refute it now like this—I don't know who can be followed for sure.

---

[36] I.e., Juan K'an not only fails to understand divination of residence, he also misunderstands divination by tortoise shell. Hsi K'ang here clearly has in mind the passage that we find in Huan T'an's *Hsin-lun* (p. 6a): "There are those who take the fox to be the racoon and the zither to be the harp. This is a case of not only not understanding the zither and the fox; they also misunderstand the racoon and the harp."

[37] Tai Ming-yang is probably right in suggesting (p. 279) that there is a character missing here. He feels it should be 來, giving 猶如來論. It might also be 所.

[38] From stanza 7 of poem 244 in the *Shih* (p. 62). Karlgren (*The Book of Odes*, p. 199) translates the entire stanza: "The one who examined the oracle was the king; he took his residence in the Hao capital; the tortoise directed it, Wu Wang completed it; Wu Wang was splendid."

[39] See the *Shu*, "Lo kao" 洛誥 (19.1b in *Shang-shu chin-ku-wen chu-shu*). Legge/Waltham (*Shu Ching: Book of History*, p. 169) translate: "On the day *yi-mao*, I [Duke of Chou talking] came in the morning to this capital of Lo. I first divined by the shell concerning the ground about the Li water on the north of the Ho. I then divined concerning the east of the Chien water, and the west of the Ch'an, when the ground near the Lo was indicated."

[40] From the *Hsiao ching*, Chapter 18 (p. 6). The passage says "residence" (宅), not tomb. But in the context of the chapter it must be read as tomb.

A Refutation

Your essay says: "[Let us suppose] the case of the residence of the three high ministers, and let us have someone from the ignorant masses live in it. That he definitely would not become one of the three high ministers can be known," [and] "Someone might say: '[But] the ignorant masses definitely are not able to live a long time in the houses of nobles.' This being so, there is truly no [influence] from residence." My response is that I am not saying an auspicious house can bring you happiness all by itself. I would simply say that the Gentleman, already possessing virtue and talent, will also divine about where to live. Compliant in conduct,[41] with accumulated virtue, he thus enjoys great fortune. It is just like the good farmer, who already embracing good skills, also selects fertile fields, and what is more, adds to that weeding and hoeing, and thus he gets a full granary in return. If you now see that the ignorant masses are unable to obtain blessings from an auspicious house and thus say that in residences there are neither good nor bad, how does that differ from seeing that in farming you may not get a bumper crop, and saying that in fields there are neither rich nor sterile? Although the good field may be excellent, the crops will not by themselves flourish, and although the house be divined as auspicious, the result will not come about on its own. If the principle of mutual need is truly so, then the good and bad fortune of residence can never be doubted.

But, these days, if people believe in signs and omens, then they reject what is proper to the principles of man, and if they maintain divination and physiognomy, they renounce the good and bad fortune of Yin and Yang; if they support knowledge and strength, they forget what is preserved by the Way of Heaven. How does this differ from knowing that the seasonal rains produce things, and accordingly doing nothing and hoping for excellent crops? For this reason, doubtful and strange theories arise, and one-sided opinions abound. When what they rely on

---

[41] Following the Wu text with 順履 instead of 復順.

A Refutation

is not the same, how can they understand one another? If there were someone who combined all things and perfected them, would it not have to be that half [of his concern] would be with residence and grave?

Your essay says: " 'Good times and lucky days' and 'asking the spirits wherein lies the fault'—these are things the great kings of the past did not have, but that decadent kings [of later ages] love to follow." These words are fine indeed! However, they are not entirely true. T'ang prayed in the mulberry grove, and the Duke of Chou held the jade tablet in his hand[42]—I do not know if these are [examples of] "asking wherein lies the fault" or not. "A lucky day was wu; we sacrificed to the ancestor of the horse and prayed"[43]—I do not know if this is [an example] of "good times

---

[42] The story of T'ang's praying in the mulberry grove to relieve a terrible drought is well known and variously recorded. For example, in the *Lü-shih ch'un-ch'iu* ("Shun-min" 順民 chapter: 9.3b) we find: "Formerly, when T'ang had conquered the Hsia and ruled the world, Heaven [caused] a great drought. For five years [other sources say seven] it did not abate. T'ang then went in person to pray in the mulberry grove." T'ang's words are found in *Mo-tzu*, Chapter 16 ("Universal Love": p. 27, lines 56–58). Watson (*Mo Tzu: Basic Writings*, p. 45) translates: "T'ang said: 'I, the little child, Lü, dare to sacrifice a dark beast and make this announcement to the Heavenly Lord above, saying, "Now Heaven has sent a great drought and it has fallen upon me, Lü. But I do not know what fault I have committed against high or low. If there is good, I dare not conceal it; if there is evil, I dare not pardon it. Judgment resides with the mind of God. If the myriad regions have any fault, may it rest upon my person; but if I have any fault, may it not extend to the myriad regions."'" The Duke of Chou's "holding the jade tablet in his hand" refers to his offering of himself to the spirits, to replace the ailing King Wu, who appeared to be dying. The story is recorded in the *Shu* ("Chin-t'eng" 金縢: 13.1b–2b). Legge/Waltham (*Shu Ching: The Book of History*, p. 136) translate: "Having made another altar on the south of these, and facing the north, he [the Duke of Chou] took there his own position. Having put a round symbol of jade, *pi*, on each of the three altars and holding in his hands the long symbol of his own rank, *kuei* [the jade tablet], he addressed the kings T'ai, Chi, and Wen [that is, their spirits in Heaven]. The Grand Historiographer had written on tablets his prayer, which was to this effect: 'Your great descendant [King Wu] is suffering from a severe and violent disease. If you three kings in Heaven have the charge of watching over him, Heaven's great son, let me, Tan, be a substitute for his person."

[43] The opening line of *Shih* 180 (p. 40). For Karlgren's translation of the poem see *The Book of Odes*, p. 124. Wu 戊 is the fifth of the celestial stems and therefore the fifth day in the ten-day cycle. It is understood to be a "firm" day.

A Refutation

and lucky days" or not. These are all things that you learned from your family,[44] things established by former teachers. And to suddenly one morning turn your back on them is certainly [to act] as though T'ang and [the Duke of] Chou had never been great kings! I trust you will examine this closely once again. Moerover, you must know that these are two worthies; how are they at all like you?

Your essay says: "When a thief is about to arrive, the fundamental thing is to quickly run away; when your food will not digest, the first thing in importance is the Yellow Pill." [But] you only seem to know that these are better than waiting around for awhile and looking for a begging barbarian; you do not know to conquer thieves and sickness before they have taken form, when the end result is hidden and not yet gone astray. We put out fire with water. But though you exert yourself in adding more fuel, you do not know that the chimney should have been bent from the start.[45] How much the more is this true [that one must nip things in the bud] of the minute things of the world, those things that words cannot reach and numbers cannot divide.[46]

Therefore the ancients "kept their views to themselves and did

---

[44] Following Tai Ming-yang's (p. 281) interpretation of *chia-shih* 家事.

[45] A straight chimney increases the chance of a fire. Hsi K'ang might have in mind the speech found in Huo Kuang's 霍光 biography in *Han shu* 68 (Vol. 9, p. 2958), where someone sent a letter to the throne on behalf of Hsü Sheng, a letter which began as follows: "Your servant has heard the following story. There was once a guest who went to visit the master of a certain house. When he saw that the kitchen stove had a straight flue and that the firewood was piled beside the stove, he told the master of the house that it would be best to have a bent flue installed and to move the firewood farther away. If not, he said, there was danger of a fire's breaking out. The master of the house was silent and made no reply. Later a fire did in fact break out suddenly in the house." (Tr. by Watson, *Courtier and Commoner in Ancient China*, p. 150.)

[46] Alluding to the words of Jo of the North Sea in Chapter 17 of the *Chuang-tzu* (p. 43, lines 22–24). Watson (*The Complete Works of Chuang Tzu*, p. 178) translates: "If a thing has no form, then numbers cannot express its dimensions, and if it cannot be encompassed, then numbers cannot express its size. We can use words to talk about the coarseness of things and we can use our minds to visualize the fineness of things. But what words cannot describe and the mind cannot succeed in visualizing—this has nothing to do with coarseness or fineness."

A Refutation

not discuss them;"[47] "they understood things in a divine way, and thus they knew the things to come."[48] Thus they could uniquely see things before the ten thousand transformations and gather the results together at the end of the Great Concord.[49] The common people call this "nature" and do not know why it is so. This being the case, how could this ever be reached by common reason?

Now the shapes and images are manifest and clear, and they are limited in number, and yet they still present an obstacle to us. Heaven and Earth are vast and distant, with many things and many places; that which intelligence knows does not compare to the vast number of things it does not.[50] You hold on to these methods for avoiding thieves and aiding digestion,[51] and say that [in this way] the nourishing of life is already complete and perfect principles already exhausted; you exert your mind to see to the limit but stop at this and return; all which your ideas have not reached you say does not exist. You wish on the basis of what you see to fix for certain those [very] things the ancients had difficulty

---

[47] Alluding to Chapter 2 of the *Chuang-tzu* (p. 5, line 56). Watson (*The Complete Works of Chuang Tzu*, p. 44) translates the passage: "As to what is beyond the Six Realms [up, down, and the four directions], the sage admits its existence [my "kept their view to themselves"] but does not theorize."

[48] A combination of two lines of the *I*, the first from *Hsi-tz'u* A.12 (p. 44), and the second from *Hsi-tz'u* A.9 (p. 43). The Chinese for the first is 存乎其人, and continues 神而明之. Legge (*I Ching: Book of Changes*, p. 378) translates this: "The seeing their [referring to the lines and hexagrams of the *I ching*] spirit-like intimations and understanding them depended on their being the proper men." And, similarly, Wilhelm (*The I Ching or Book of Changes*, p. 324) has "The spirituality and clarity depend upon the right man." But in the present context I should think Hsi K'ang understands this to mean, "They understand things in a divine way and keep it to themselves."

[49] That is to say they understand the process of creation from beginning to end. They know what things are before they come into being (before the "ten thousand transformations") and what happens to them at the end when they all return to their common source.

[50] Echoing the words of Chuang-tzu (to be precise, Jo of the North Sea) in Chapter 17 (p. 42, line 18). Watson (*The Complete Works of Chuang Tzu*, p. 177) translates: "Calculate what man knows and it cannot compare to what he does not know."

[51] Following the Wu text with 避賊消穀 (literally "eliminate the grains") instead of 辟穀.

A Refutation

in talking about; is this not like the summer cicada's discussing ice?[52] And you wish to use what you know to settle the [very] things the ancients rejected;[53] is this not like the Jung barbarian's asking about cotton in China; when he saw the hemp seeds he didn't feel it could be made [from these]?[54]

[As for me] I am too timid to settle this for certain. On the one hand, I would not presume to restrict calamity and blessing to what can be divined; on the other, I would not presume to say that one's home is devoid of good and bad fortune.

---

[52] Or "ice and snow" with the Wu text. This is obviously alluding to Chuang-tzu's remark in Chapter 1 (p. 1, lines 10–11). Watson (*The Complete Works of Chuang Tzu*, p. 30) translates: "Little understanding cannot come up to great understanding; the short-lived cannot come up to the long-lived. How do I know this is so? The morning mushroom knows nothing of twilight and dawn; the summer cicada knows nothing of spring and autumn." He also says in Chapter 17 (p. 42, lines 5–6): "You cannot discuss ice with a summer insect—he is bound to a single season. You cannot discuss the Way with a cramped scholar—he is shackled by his doctrines." (Tr. by Watson, *The Complete Works of Chuang Tzu*, p. 176.)

[53] There is a lacuna of three characters in the text. I follow the Wang 汪 text and others at this point in filling this in with 決古人.

[54] In the *Lü-shih ch'un-ch'iu* ("Chih chieh" 知接 chapter: 16.6a) we read: "There was a Jung man who saw some plain, white cotton and asked about it: 'How do you make it so tightly woven?' [Someone] pointed to hemp and demonstrated. But he angrily said, 'How can you make something so tightly woven from something so loose and scattered?'" Also, in the *Huai-nan-tzu* ("Ch'i-su hsün" 齊俗訓: 11.1b) we find: "When Hu people see hemp seeds, they do not know they can be used to make cotton."

JUAN K'AN

An Explanation to Hsi K'ang's Refutation of My Essay—Residence is Devoid of Good and Bad Fortune: You Must Rather Preserve Your Life

(Shih Nan Chai wu chi-hsiung she-sheng lun)

∷

The *Book of Changes* says: "The Yellow River brought forth the chart and the Lo brought forth the writing, and the sages took these as their model."[1] The *Classic of Filial Piety* says: "We build for them [one's ancestors] the ancestral temple so we may sacrifice to their spirits."[2] For establishing them [spiritual matters] as fundamental, there are [passages] such as these. Tzu-kung reported that "[Confucius' views] on human nature and the Way of Heaven, these we were unable to hear."[3] And when Chung-yu [Tzu-lu] asked about spirits, the Master did not answer.[4] For restricting them as less important, there are [passages] such as those. Why is this? This is because of the so-called "In the realm of light there are the rites and music, in the

---

[1] From the *I ching*, *Hsi-tz'u* A.11 (p. 44). The *Ho-t'u* 河圖 ("river chart") and *Lo-shu* 洛書 ("Lo writing") are understood as magical diagrams revealed to the sages of antiquity. Wilhelm, *The I Ching or Book of Changes*, pp. 309–310, has pictures of both. Also see Michael Saso's "What is the *Ho-t'u*?" *History of Religions*, 17:3 & 4 (February–May, 1978), pp. 399–416.

[2] *Hsiao-ching*, Chapter 18 (p. 6).

[3] In *Analects* 5:13 (p. 8). D. C. Lau's translation (*Confucius: The Analects*, p. 78) reads: "Tzu-kung said, 'One can get to hear about the Master's accomplishments, but one cannot get to hear his views on human nature and the Way of Heaven.'"

[4] Referring again to *Analects* 11:12. See note 1 to Hsi K'ang's "Refutation."

Explanation to Refutation

dark regions ghosts and spirits;"[5] and "we plan for man and we plan for the ghosts to complete the efforts of the world."[6]

Therefore Mo Ti wrote his chapter "Explaining Ghosts,"[7] and Tung Wu-hsin set out his theory refuting the Moists.[8] But the words of these two worthies all fall into the category of taking different routes and both being misled. Why is this? To over-emphasize their [the spirits'] existence is stupid, and to over-emphasize their non-existence is absurd. Therefore both of these masters[9] had one-sided views. Now when you, sir, speak of "the spirits," do you mean those? Then I too would not presume to clearly understand.

But when private spirits are established, the public spirits are abandoned; when unorthodox prohibitions are set up, the orthodox prohibitions are lost; when house and gravesite are divined, the proper ways of the family suffer; and when [rules about] front and back [of the house or grave] abound, then weird ideas flourish. When you speak of "the spirits," do you mean these? Then this is something I must strongly contest.

If[10] we have grasped the main analogy we do not worry over minor details. Thus, "when we see [frozen] water in the vase, we know the world has become cold;"[11] and when we examine the

---

[5] A virtual quote of a line in the "Yüeh-chi" chapter of the *Li chi* (see *Li chi hsün-tsuan* 19.5b).

[6] A combination of two lines from the *I ching*, both of which come from Hsi-tz'u B.9 (p. 49).

[7] In which he argues for the existence of ghosts. This is Chapter 31 of the *Mo-tzu*, translated by Burton Watson in *Mo Tzu: Basic Writings*, pp. 94–109.

[8] Wang Ch'ung in his *Lun-heng* ("Fu hsü" 福虛 chapter: 6.4b) records a debate between the Confucian Tung Wu-hsin 董無心 and the Moist, Master Ch'an 纏子. Tung Wu-hsin rejects the existence of spirits, arguing that Yao and Shun were not given long life (and presumably they would have been if there were spirits) and that the two culprits Chieh and Chou (the last rulers of the Hsia and Shang dynasties respectively) did not die early.

[9] The text should read 二子, not 三子, referring of course to Mo-tzu and Tung Wu-hsin.

[10] 茍夫 should be 夫茍, as it is in the Wu text.

[11] Quoting, for the most part, the *Lü-shih ch'un-ch'iu* ("Ch'a chin" 察今 chapter: 15:18b).

Explanation to Refutation

armillary sphere,[12] we understand the movements of the sun and the moon. You have picked apart my example of silkworm eggs, and as a result have disregarded and not examined [the main issue at hand]. This is like someone choking or drowning who does not yet know why, not even discerning that there is a boat and grain.

Now fate is the lot that we receive, and sincerity and obedience are the principles for completing fate. Therefore [Mencius] said: "The Gentleman cultivates his person in order to wait on fate," and "One who understands fate will not stand at the foot of a high and dangerous wall."[13] Why? Because this is what leads to the realization[14] of [either] an early end or completion. It is just like [the fact that] eating is not fated, and yet for [the realization of one's] fate, one must necessarily eat. This[15] is definitely true. So, when I said in my essay that [even] sitting around idly or acting contrary [to moral norms] would not make a P'eng-tsu die young, and you raised the objection of "sincerity and obedi-

---

[12] I use "armillary sphere" for the sake of having something in translation. This is the *hsüan-chi* 璇機 (also 璇璣 and 璿璣), which dictionaries gloss as an ancient astronomical instrument used at the time of Shun. It is mentioned in the *Shu*, in "Shun tien" 舜典, in the passage Legge/Waltham translate: "Shun examined the *pearl-adorned turning sphere* [italics added] with its transverse tube of jade and reduced to a harmonious system the movements of the Seven Directors." (*Shu Ching: Book of History*, p. 12.) Waltham makes the following notes on this: "The examining instrument was probably a kind of armillary sphere representing the revolution of the heavens, with the transverse athwart the sphere for the purpose of celestial observation. Legge thought the Seven Directors designated the seven stars of the Big Dipper. According to the Karlgren translation, however, the Seven Directors meant the five planets plus the sun and moon."

[13] Both are from *Mencius* 7A, though the first is not a direct quote. The first is from 7A.1, and D. C. Lau (*Mencius*, p. 182) translates the line: "It is through awaiting whatever is to befall him with a perfected character that he stands firm on his proper destiny." The second is from 7A.2 and Lau translates: "Though nothing happens that is not due to destiny, one accepts willingly only what is one's proper destiny. That is why he who understands destiny does not stand under a wall on the verge of collapse."

[14] Reading 實 as a mistake for 寶. There is evidence for this since some texts have both characters.

[15] The 是 is added in the Wu text.

Explanation to Refutation

ence,"[16] you were certainly right [to do so]. What I meant to say in my essay was that if sincerity and obedience have *already* been cultivated, then where one lives and where he is buried are of no consequence. And therefore I simply compared it to the lack of benefit that a "long life palace" has for a doomed infant. You[17] do *not* say that a doomed infant could lengthen [his life] by means of [the right] house, and that P'eng-tsu also lived long because of his residence. The statements on long life and early death make it clear—if you are sincere and obedient you will complete your allotted time, if idle and perverse, your nature will be cut off short. And yet in vain you say "There *are* some in the world who can talk about this."[18] If even you will not say it, who can [discuss] it with you?

Eating a lot harms one's nature but good medicine cures the ill. This[19] is in agreement with one's fortune. But when one thing is wrong [i.e., the possibility that residence is part of one's fortune] and another is right [that medicine is part of one's fortune] one cannot be used to prove the other.

Now long life and early death cannot be sought for in residence but can be found in harmony. Therefore, in my essay I do admit the possibility that people will not understand [how to correctly seek long life].[20] This,[21] you have forgotten in your mind and rebuked me for in writing; your suppression [of my words] does not get back to the beginning.[22]

---

[16] Specifically Hsi K'ang said "If good and bad fortune are fixed from the beginning and cannot be diverted, then why did the ancients say ... 'If you tread sincerity and think of obedience, you will receive help from Heaven'?" See the text and note 15.

[17] The 足子 in Tai Ming-yang's text is a mistake for 足下.

[18] In relation to the issue of whether taking medicine might be a part of one's fortune, Hsi K'ang had said, "If you say that medicine can be discussed but residence cannot, I am afraid that there are those in the world who do talk about it."

[19] The 是 is added in the Wu text.

[20] Following the Wu phraseology of 有可不知.

[21] The 是 is added in the Wu text.

[22] Juan K'an is apparently objecting to the charge of contradiction, the contradiction involved in saying that all things come from nature and fate, on the one

Explanation to Refutation

Your "Refutation"[23] says: "In the ages of T'ang and Yü, how was it that fates were all equally long, and with the soldiers at Ch'ang-p'ing, how was it that fates were all equally short?" Now if we are going to talk about fate, we must distinguish between those who have it and those who do not and not feel uneasy about whether there are many or few. If one man has [a certain] fate, then a thousand or ten thousand might all be the same. If [something like] this cannot be related to fate, can it be related to residence? Then how was it that in the ages of T'ang and Yü, residences were all equally lucky? And how was it that with the soldiers at Ch'ang-p'ing, their houses were all equally doomed? This is also something about which I have doubts.

Your "Refutation" [also] says: "The things that are outside of us and able to cause us harm are simply too many to count. Shan Pao relied on the inside and was harmed[24] by a tiger." According to what you say, in this case Pao forgot what he should have feared and feared what he should have forgotten. And therefore Chang I cultivated the outside but met with the calamity of an internal fever.[25] But although these two were different in [valuing] inside and out, they were alike in not having harmony. "If one morning you lose it, to the end of your days you will not get it back."[26] This is also [a case] of "having a tiger on your tail."[27]

Those who are attentive to the unorthodox will be remiss when it comes to the correct; and those who carefully examine

---

hand, and that one needs to know how to correctly seek long life and avoid harm, on the other. His point now seems to be that even though long life is fated, still one must *know* to hold on to harmony for it to be fully realized.

[23] The Wu text is surely right in having 難 here, not 雖.

[24] Following the Wu text in adding a 害 at the end of the sentence.

[25] If the reader has forgotten Shan Pao and Chang I and their situations, look again at Watson's *The Complete Works of Chuang Tzu*, pp. 201–202.

[26] Quoting, with slight variation, a line from the *Lü-shih ch'un-ch'iu*, "Chung-chi" 重己 chapter: 1.6b in SPPY. The text reads "My life is what I own, and its benefits for me are also great.... With respect to its safety and danger, if one morning I lose it, to the end of my days I will not get it back."

[27] Probably alluding to *Han-fei-tzu*, "Yang-ch'üan" 揚權, 2.12b, where Han-fei-tzu says "If the lord loses his spirit he'll have a tiger on his tail" (literally, a tiger following behind).

Explanation to Refutation

houses tend to slight harmony. My[28] putting [harmony] first is also not intended the way you are taking it.[29] As for your widening the scope [of what must be included in nourishing life], this is something for which I have long hoped.

"Great offering; beneficial forecast"[30]—this is a propitious phrase in divination. A "high nose" and "dragon countenance" —these are the features of a noble. These [on the one hand] are arrived at by the numbers,[31] and [on the other] are natural shapes; they cannot be made. If the nose and countenance could be faked, there would be no [such thing as] physiognomy; and if the lucky phrases could be had through design,[32] there would be no divination. So if someone intentionally plans to build a "lucky" house and hopes for blessings in return, it is just like faking the countenance and nose and hoping to become a noble. Thus Tzu-yang's engraving his palm,[33] and Chü-chün's rotating [his mat to match] K'uei,[34] were completely without value in

---

[28] Filling in the lacuna here with the *tsou* 走, "I" or "me," that occurs in the Wu text.

[29] That is to say, following Tai Ming-yang's (p. 288) line of thought, Hsi K'ang is acting as though Juan K'an's position was that the *only* thing one must do is to hold on to this single harmony. He simply sees that as first in importance.

[30] Following Kao Heng's 高亨 (*Chou-i ku-ching chin-chu* 周易古經今注 [Taipei: Lo-t'ien, 1972], p. 1) interpretation of the four words found throughout the *I ching—yüan-heng li-chen* 元亨利貞. But *I ching* experts are by no means agreed on the meaning of these words.

[31] That is to say, by counting the milfoil stalks one gets the number of the hexagram in the *I ching* which has this forecast—*yüan-heng li-chen* (numbers 1, 3, 17, 19, 25, and 49).

[32] Literally "could be made" (可為).

[33] At the beginning of the Later Han, Kung-sun Shu 公孫述 (style Tzu-yang 子陽) set himself up as king of Shu 蜀, and in A.D. 25 declared himself "Son of Heaven." He was moved to do this when a dragon appeared in his prefectural hall, and then a bright light shone at night; these he took as omens of his authority. Accordingly he engraved on his palm "Emperor Kung-sun." He was killed by government troops in A.D. 36. See his biography in *Hou Han shu* 13 (Vol. 2, pp. 533-578; especially pp. 535 and 543).

[34] The phrase is *yün-k'uei* 運魁, and it means he rotated his mat to be in line with the handle of the Big Dipper (*k'uei* is the first star in the handle), a position of good luck. This, Wang Mang 王莽 (style Chü-chün 巨君) did in A.D. 23 (the last year of his reign), when Ch'ang-an was surrounded by troops. The next day he was killed. See his biography in *Han shu* 99 (Vol. 12, pp. 4039-4191).

Explanation to Refutation

[preventing] their defeat and death. Therefore, I feel that a house that is being lived in with no ulterior motive can be divined; how could this confuse the principles of images and numbers?[35] But if you plan a lucky house and then live in it, it cannot be done; that would be the theory that something can be faked or made on purpose.[36] This being so, it is not the house that controls the man, it is in truth the man that verifies the house.[37] There is no [influence] from residence.[38] It seems that you simply have not yet thought through the fundamentals.

When a hunter goes through the woods, he might meet a tiger and he might meet a bird. To run into a bird is good luck, to run into a tiger the reverse. But if it is to be a tiger, a good diviner can do no more than know it. Therefore, to know good and bad fortune is not [the same] as to make good and bad fortune. Therefore it [the *Book of Changes*] declares: "It matters not whether distant or near, obscure or deep—you will consequently know what is to come."[39] It does not say "You can consequently *make* what is to come."

Thus they [the ancients] *also* divined about things, probably[40] because exhausting all of the principles is the way to complete fortune and fate. But to turn to their divining the reigns and the number of years, that was of no benefit to the prosperity of the

---

[35] "Images" refers to divination by means of tortoise shell, and "numbers" to divination with the milfoil stalks.

[36] Agreeing with Tai Ming-yang (p. 289) that the 何 at the head of the sentence is best omitted, and it is left out in the original Wu manuscript.

[37] Reading 耶 as 也.

[38] Answering Hsi K'ang's question—"Is there truly [any influence] from residence or not?"—with Hsi K'ang's words—其無宅也.

[39] Quoting the *I ching*, *Hsi-tz'u* A.9 (p. 43). The entire passage is translated by Legge (*I ching: Book of Changes*, p. 369): "Therefore, when a superior man is about to take action of a more private or of a public character, he asks (the Yi), making his inquiry in words. It receives his order, and the answer comes as the echo's response. Be the subject remote or near, mysterious or deep, he forthwith knows of what kind will be the coming result."

[40] The 蓋 should come before the 畫.

Explanation to Refutation

Chou.⁴¹ And even if in the good and bad fortune of lands there are "bird" and "tiger" types, if a particular region is evil, then wherever you go [in it] will be bad. It cannot be that there is a difference between east and west, or that the back and the front [of a house], [for different families] should not be the same, or that a "C" surname will have no harm, while a "D" will suffer disaster.⁴² If it is blessed and virtuous then good fortune will come, [doomed for] punishment and calamity then evil will arrive.⁴³ Therefore the *Book of Poetry* says: "We build a house, with a wall of a hundred boards; to the west and south are its doors."⁴⁴ When the ancients built a residence, "the ancestral hall came first, and the stable and storeroom came next; the living quarters were last."⁴⁵ They followed human principles in carrying out their tasks. If we discuss it on the basis of this, then we will know they did not believe in the "punishments and rewards" of Jupiter.⁴⁶ If you practice the ancient ways without opposition you will also agree with my essay. If I have in no way gone astray,⁴⁷ do you not know whom to follow?⁴⁸

---

⁴¹ In a speech to the viscount of Ch'u recorded in the *Tso chuan* (Duke Hsüan, third year [606 B.C.]: p. 182), Wang Sun-man 王孫滿 says: "King Ch'ing [= Ch'eng, of the Chou, r. 1115–1078 B.C.] fixed the tripod in Këah-juh, and divined that the dynasty should extend over 30 reigns, over 700 years. Though the virtue of Chou is decayed, the decree of Heaven is not yet changed." (Tr. by Legge, *The Chinese Classics*, Vol. V, Pt. 1, p. 293.)

⁴² On the C and D surnames see note 4 to Hsi K'ang's previous "Refutation".

⁴³ Translation is tentative. The paired opposites are *fu-te* 福德 and *hsing-huo* 刑禍.

⁴⁴ From stanza 2 of *Shih* 189 (p. 42). For Karlgren's translation see *The Book of Odes*, p. 130.

⁴⁵ Quoting the *Li chi*, "Ch'ü-li hsia" 曲禮下 (p. 2.3b in *Li chi hsün-tsuan*), where this is said, however, of the gentleman when he builds his house.

⁴⁶ For "punishments and rewards" see note 2 to Juan K'an's first essay. A source quoted by Wang Ch'ung in his *Lun-heng* ("Nan-sui" 難歲: 24.13a) says that people believe it is bad luck to move one's residence from south to north when Jupiter is in the celestial position *chia-tzu* 甲子, and it is also bad luck at this time to begin building a house.

⁴⁷ Filling in the lacuna here with the 答 found in the Wen-chin text.

⁴⁸ Coming back to Hsi K'ang's remark—"The ancients practiced this [divination of residence] in former times like that, but you refute it now like this—I do not know whom we can follow for sure."

Explanation to Refutation

In your "Refutation" you say: "I am not saying an auspicious house can bring you happiness all by itself. It is like the good farmer, who, already embracing good skills, also selects fertile fields, and, what is more adds to this weeding and hoeing, and thus he gets in return a full granary." These words are right on the mark! Indeed, if one can cultivate these three things, then the business of farming is complete. But if you, on the other hand, devote yourself entirely to unorthodox ways [of farming], and seek it in what is in vain—this is the man from Sung's so-called "I will help the shoots to grow";[49] it is the way to destroy farming.

If grave and residence are illustrated by this, to what should they be compared? Should it be the technique of planting? Or is it the hoeing and weeding? If all three have their analogues, please do me the service of telling me later. But if there is no proof, then we all the more see that it's wrong. When for divination and physiognomy there is evidence like that, but for grave and residence no proof like this, it [divination of gravesite and residence] cannot be considered the other half.[50]

According to the records, the Duke of Chou asked them [the spirits] to spare the life [of King Wu], but Confucius would not allow Tzu-lu to pray.[51] Now both of these men were sages and

---

[49] Alluding to the story in *Mencius* 2A:2 (p. 11) of the farmer from Sung who wished to hurry along his plants, so he pulled them up. For D. C. Lau's translation of the passage in question see D. C. Lau, *Mencius*, p. 78.

[50] All of this mimics the words of Hsi K'ang who had said, "The ancients practiced this... etc." (as in note 48 above), and also "If there were someone who could combine all things and perfect them, would it not have to be that half [of his concern] would be with residence and grave?"

[51] For the Duke of Chou's request on behalf of King Wu see note 42 to Hsi K'ang's "Refutation". That Confucius would not allow Tzu-lu to pray for him when he was sick is reported in *Analects* 7:35 (p. 13). D. C. Lau (*Confucius: The Analects*, p. 91) translates: "The Master was seriously ill. Tzu-lu asked permission to offer a prayer. The Master said, 'Was such a thing ever done?' Tzu-lu said, 'Yes, it was. The prayer offered was as follows: pray thus to the gods above and below.' The Master said, 'In that case, I have long been offering my prayers.'"

Explanation to Refutation

both of them were sick, so why did they not act[52] the same? Thus we know that the feelings[53] of one who serves are nothing more than these. This is simply[54] [an example] of the so-called "the rites are the outward expression of our feelings."[55] Therefore, because he was in the position of minister and younger brother, the Duke of Chou asked them to spare his [King Wu's] life, but because it was for himself, Confucius did not pray. Is your approval[56] of designing one's residence done [merely] for the sake of propriety, or do you actually believe in it? If it is merely for the sake of propriety, your situation is different from the ancients,'[57] but if you actually believe in it, then you have not yet heard of the manifest truths. In this way you have not yet reached what[58] I have already abandoned, and you will lose what you desire.

Turning to the "good times and lucky days"—this is simply the way the former kings warned people not to be idle and urged them to do their work. But the "times and days" of popular belief comply with uncanny fears and run counter to the principles of events. Although the names for the times are the same, their use is exactly the opposite. When I compare those two[59] worthies with you, I see all the more where we agree [i.e., Juan K'an with T'ang and the Duke of Chou]; I don't understand how we differ.[60]

---

[52] Following the Wu text with 事 instead of 是非.
[53] Following the Wu text in reading 情 here instead of 心.
[54] The 耳 is added in the Wu text.
[55] Probably alluding to the *Han-fei-tzu* ("Chieh-Lao" 解老 6.1b). W. K. Liao, *The Complete Works of Han Fei Tzu*, p. 171, translates the relevant passage: "'Propriety' refers to the mode in which one's feelings are expressed. It is concerned with the cultural embellishment of all righteous acts, such as the mutual relations of ruler and minister, father and son." Juan K'an's point, which will soon become clear, is that the Duke of Chou was simply acting out of concern for propriety, not out of genuine belief.
[56] The 是 is added in the Wu text.
[57] I.e., he is doing this for himself.
[58] Following the Wu text in omitting the 以.
[59] Agreeing with Lu Hsün (p. 107) that the 三 should be 二.
[60] Remember that Hsi K'ang, in objecting to Juan K'an's claim that the great

Explanation to Refutation

Your "Refutation" says: "That which intelligence knows does not compare to the vast number of things it does not." This, in general, is the constant obstacle of the common people of the world. But that which intelligence does not know cannot be falsely sought, and that which it can know—how should it be learned? Therefore the Gentleman of antiquity cultivated his person[61] and selected his techniques, "perfected his nature and preserved it,"[62] devoting himself to this and nothing more. Now according to what you say, do [these matters] lie in the realm of the known? [If so] they can be discerned. Or are they things that are not known? Then they are being falsely sought. Of the two, one must apply to this.

"Little understanding does not come up to great understanding,"[63] and thus you oppose me in claiming there *is* [good and bad fortune]. But one who treats the non-existent as existing is also a summer cicada![64] You fault the limitation of my experience to what is limited. But I also fear you are wandering in a strange land and will have the problem of forgetting how to return.

---

kings of the past did not have "good times and lucky days" and the practice of "asking the spirits wherein lies the fault," had raised the examples of T'ang and the Duke of Chou praying to the spirits, and thus concluded, "to suddenly one morning turn your back on them [former teachers] is certainly [to act] as though T'ang and [the Duke of] Chou had never been great kings! I trust you will examine this closely once again. Moreover, you must know that these are two worthies; how are they at all like you?"

[61] Filling in the lacuna with 身.
[62] Quoting from the *I ching*, *Hsi-tz'u* A.5 (p. 41).
[63] See note 52 to Hsi K'ang's "Refutation".
[64] An allusion to *Chuang-tzu*, Chapter 2 (p. 4, lines 22-23). Watson (*The Complete Works of Chuang Tzu*, p. 39) translates: "But to fail to abide by this mind and still insist upon your rights and wrongs—this is like saying that you set off for Yüeh today and got there yesterday. This is to claim that what does not exist exists. If you claim that what does not exist exists, then even the holy sage Yü could not understand you, much less a person like me." Juan K'an counters Hsi K'ang's allusion to the "summer cicada" anecdote in Chapter 1 of the *Chuang-tzu* with an allusion of his own to the same source.

HSI K'ANG

An Answer to Juan K'an's Explanation to My Refutation of His Essay—Residence is Devoid of Good and Bad Fortune: You Must Rather Preserve Your life

(Ta Shih Nan Chai wu chi-hsiung she-sheng lun)

∴

The former kings handed down their instructions to initiate the regulation[1] of mediocre men. What they established with their words, neither virtuous nor stupid has opposed; and what they followed in their affairs, neither past nor present has changed. This is the reason we have transmitted their teachings. But if it is the profound and mysterious, the spiritual and sublime, or the unspeakable transformation, if you are not the most excellent [kind of being], who is able to share in it?[2] Therefore, one who is skilled at seeking, sees things when they are small and develops them by inference from analogy; he does not take himself as the standard.

According to what you say, if one over-emphasizes their [the spirits'] existence, he is stupid, and if one overemphasizes their non-existence he is absurd. So if someone [believes in] their existence *a little*, will he then not be stupid? And if someone [believes] they are *completely* non-existent, will he then avoid it [the charge of absurdity]? But if by believing in them a little, one is no longer stupid, we would never know where to draw the line for "a little." And if one avoids it by believing they are com-

---

[1] Reading the Wu variant of 制 for 端.
[2] A paraphrase of a line in the *I ching*: *Hsi-tz'u* A.9 (p. 43).

Answer to the Explanation

pletely non-existent, then there is no way we can call overemphasizing their non-existence absurd.

You also say, "When private spirits are established, then public spirits are abandoned." This being the case, then you merely[3] hate the fact that the private injure the public, and the unorthodox harms the correct; it is not that there are no spirits. In the direction of Mo-tzu you establish your feelings [of belief] in public spirits while presenting us [at the same time] with the theory that we must not overemphasize their existence; but you have Mr. Tung trusting to the road of orthodox prohibitions, while you [at the same time] maintain the claim that we must not overemphasize their non-existence. Can the refined tendencies of these two worthies be combined into one without erring in both?

The distinction I am making is that we want to find out if they really exist or not so we can clarify what is natural and not go against it. Of the theories that are held [on this], some are skilled and some are clumsy, and of the teachings that are debated, some are polished and others unrefined. If I look for the main thrust of your elegant essay, [if seems] that you mean to say that the Yellow River [chart] and the Lo [writing] are not genuine; [and that the ancients] wished to avail themselves of the aid of ghosts and spirits,[4] so they built for them the ancestral temple to make sacred their fundamental importance; [and that Confucius] did not answer Tzu-lu[5] in order to caution[6] him about the relative unimportance [of these matters]. If this is so, then is it not true that you believe in the non-existence of ghosts and spirits, in agreement with Mr. Tung? And yet when you once again look

---

[3] The *wei* 唯 is added in the Wu text and seems necessary.
[4] "Even though they knew they did not really exist"—if I understand Hsi K'ang correctly.
[5] The text says Tzu-kung, but I agree with Tai Ming-yang (p. 294) that it should be Tzu-lu.
[6] Reading 敕 instead of 求.

Answer to the Explanation

back at the words of the ancients, you become afraid of the harmful points of this position, and your form and your feelings are opposed. [So] you make the argument that we must follow the public [spirits] and reject the private, wishing to fill in the gap in both doctrines and [thus] be neither stupid nor absurd, and you ridicule both Tung and Mo, saying one can hold the middle ground between them. I am afraid that though your words and arguments are skillful, it is difficult to fit these together. Moreover, this is not what one would expect in a carefully worked out essay.

Therefore, I say that the ancients combined the virtues of Heaven and Earth, and their actions and reactions were all [part of] nature, and of things that stand in succeeding generations, there are none that do not have proof. How could it be that they [the ancients] concealed [the true reason] for setting up the ancestral temple to deceive[7] later descendants, and fictitiously made use of ghosts and spirits to lie to the people of the future? You will say I am no different from Mo-tzu. And I do not deny we are the same in believing in the existence of ghosts. But I do not partially maintain one side. I clarify that which must be, and plan for human and ghostly alike, and bring to completion both light and dark.[8] This is both the way in which I seek results and the point at which we [Mo Tzu and Hsi K'ang] differ.

Your essay says: "They [the Duke of Chou and Confucius] were both sick and yet they did not act the same [with respect to] prayer. Therefore, because he was in the position of minister and younger brother, the Duke of Chou asked them [the spirits] to spare his [King Wu's] life, but because it was for himself, Confucius did not pray. This is the so-called 'the rites are the outward expression of our feelings.'"

---

[7] Reading 期 as a mistake for 欺.
[8] All of this picking up the words of Juan K'an's "Explanation," where he had quoted the *Li chi* and the *Book of Changes*: "In the realm of light there are the rites and music, in the dark regions ghosts and spirits," and "we plan for man and we plan for the ghosts to complete the efforts of the world."

Answer to the Explanation

I refute this as follows. If it is proper for someone in the position of minister and younger brother to practice giving [ritual] form to his feelings, I have never heard of Shun or Yü making requests on behalf of *their* lords and fathers. And if someone does not allow this when it is for himself, I have never heard of King Wu's order to stop the prayer. Was T'ang's praying in the mulberry grove also for the sake of his father and lord? To draw our inference from this, because it was appropriate [in their case] to see prayer as beneficial, T'ang and the Duke of Chou used it; but because there was no reason to pray [in his case], Confucius did not ask. This is "taking different roads but ending up the same,"[9] and "the meaning of acting in accord with the times."[10]

You also say: "'Good times and lucky days' are the way the former kings warned people not to be idle and urged them to do their work." In your first essay you said "'good times and lucky days'—these are things the great kings of the past did not have," and therefore I asked you about the business of "[A lucky day] was wu."[11] Now you have not answered whether this "[A lucky day] was wu" is indeed right or wrong, but rather say "This is the way[12] they warned and urged." These, once again, are words that allow two things at once. Even if "... was wu" was completely a matter of warning and urging, if we search for the theory and go by the name, should we say they did or did not have lucky days?

You also say: "The times and days of popular belief comply with uncanny fears and run counter to the principles of events." Now according to *these* words, what you hate is their uncanny [nature] and opposition [to principle] and therefore you reject

---

[9] Using words (although in reverse order) found in the *I ching*, Hsi-tz'u B.3 (p. 46).

[10] Also from the *I*: from the *t'uan* on hexagram 17 (p. 12).

[11] See Hsi K'ang's "Refutation" and note 43. He was quoting the *Book of Poetry*, poem 180—"A lucky day was wu; we sacrificed to the ancestor of the horse and prayed."

[12] Reading 所以 with the Wu text.

Answer to the Explanation

them: it is not that the great kings [of the past] did completely without lucky days. But that good times and lucky days were used in the ages of glory, and succeeding eras follow with things weird and deluded, is just like [the fact that] the former kings created classical music, and later, decadent ages carry on with tunes licentious and perverse. For you now to be indignant about uncanny fears and as a result want to do away with the days— how is this any different from hating [the music] of Cheng and Wei and consequently destroying the *Shao* and the *Wu*?[13] You have not thought about their origins; but seeing them in this decadent form you detest them and wish to have them removed. Is this not [a case of] coming up against choking or drowning and directing your anger against [something else]?

You have already approved of [regular] divination. Now the Creative and the Receptive have their six children,[14] and in the Branches and Stems there are both firm and yielding.[15] These are controlled by Yin and Yang and fluctuate with the Five Elements. Therefore good and bad fortune can be obtained, and this is where the days and times come from. Therefore the ancients followed them. How can someone approve of the stream and hate its source? I never knew this was possible.

When you come to the Yellow River [chart] and the Lo [writ-

---

[13] If the reader has forgotten the Cheng and the Wei and the *Shao* and the *Wu*—all discussed in "Music Has in it Neither Grief nor Joy"—the tunes of Cheng and Wei were condemned as licentious by Confucius; the *Shao* was the music of Shun and the *Wu* the music of King Wu.

[14] The "Creative" (*ch'ien* 乾) and "Receptive" (*k'un* 坤) are the first two trigrams in the *Book of Changes*, and their "six children" are the remaining six trigrams to make up the basic eight. They are: (1) *chen* 震 (the Arousing), (2) *k'an* 坎 (the Abysmal), (3) *ken* 艮 (Keeping Still), (4) *sun* 巽 (the Gentle), (5) *li* 離 (the Clinging), and (6) *tui* 兌 (the Joyous). (All names according to Wilhelm, *The I Ching or Book of Changes*, pp. 1–1i.)

[15] The "Branches and Stems" (*chih-kan* 支幹) are the "Twelve Earthly Branches" and "Ten Celestial Stems," which combine (one from each set) to give China's sixty-day calendrical cycle. The stems *chia* 甲, *ping* 丙, *wu* 戊, *keng* 庚, and *jen* 壬, and the branches *yin* 寅, *ch'en* 辰, *wu* 午, *shen* 申, *hsü* 戌, and *tzu* 子, are Yang, and hence "firm," while the stems *i* 乙, *ting* 丁, *chi* 己, *hsin* 辛, and *kuei* 癸, and the branches *mao* 卯, *ssu* 巳, *wei* 未, *yu* 酉, *hai* 亥, and *ch'ou* 丑, are Yin, and hence "yielding."

Answer to the Explanation

ing] and the ancestral temple, you say they [the ancients] concealed [the truth] and were not sincere; with the Lei sacrifice to God and the Ma sacrifice to the land,[16] and prayer and supplication—these you say were contrived and have no basis in reality; with the times and days and firm and yielding—these you say were done on the pretext of urging people [to work]. This means that the sages on purpose created things that were empty and false to deceive the world. Even if we were talking about the honesty of a common man I would be ashamed of this. And now we are discussing the ancients! Can there be any other conclusion but that this simply cannot be?

In all of these various matters, it seems as though you have fallen into slander and lies. Is it not likely that your attack on gravesites and homes also does the same?

In your previous essay you said: "Such things as Hsü Fu's predicting that [Ya Fu] would become marquis of T'iao, and Ying Pu's first being tatooed and later becoming a king ... [and the fact that] with sheep that are all in one pen, when a guest arrives some will die—these are all[17] [the result of] the natural state of their natures and fates." Now in your present essay you say: "The high nose and dragon countenance are the features of a noble; they cannot be sought with false intent." This means that fortune and fate are completely fixed in and of themselves. That which is fated to succeed, men cannot destroy; and that which is doomed to fail, intelligence cannot save. If you trap someone who is destined[18] to live in a multitude of dangers, although he might be frightened, he will come to no harm; and if you restrict someone who is slated for honor to the duties of a menial servant, although he might be insulted by the lowly status, he will necessarily end up respected.[19] Po Chi's first being in difficult straits

---

[16] This is one interpretation of the *lei* 類 and the *ma* 禡. They were both offered at the start of a military campaign.
[17] The 皆 is added in the Wu text.
[18] The character should be 當, not 常.
[19] Following the Wu variant of 尊 for 貴.

Answer to the Explanation

but later on prospering[20]—none[21] of these could have been made or could have been sought, they just mysteriously and naturally happened.

If your "all is fortune" theory were definitely like this, then you could keep right on going[22] and the present essay would not stand in your way. But when I happened to object [to this] with [the passage about] "sincerity and obedience," *then* you said "sincerity and obedience are the principles for completing fate." If things are necessarily as you say, then fate will be completed by sincerity and obedience, and it will also be thwarted by their absence. If the completion or destruction of fate is sufficiently explained by sincerity and obedience [their presence or absence], then this is precisely the point I made in my earlier refutation—that long life and early death come from intelligence [on the one hand] and stupidity [on the other]. How could this be a matter of one's "nature and fate and what is naturally so"? [But] if sincerity and obedience do indeed complete fortune and fate, then may I ask which evil ways did Ya Fu follow so that he ended up starving, and what virtues did Ying Pu cultivate so that he ended becoming a king? Which good deeds did the living sheep pile up in order to remain alive, and what crimes did the dead ones commit such that they encountered this disaster?

Having held [the position of] fortune and fate, you further have regrets about sincerity and obedience and wish to have the glamour of using both theories and maintaining them side by side. I am afraid this is like [having] a lance and a shield[23]; the two

---

[20] Po Chi's 薄姬 mother belonged to the royal family of the state of Wei 魏, and at the end of the Ch'in dynasty (209 B.C.), when Kao-tsu defeated the forces of Wei, Po Chi was moved into his weaving rooms. Later Kao-tsu saw her and had her taken to his palace. She became the mother of Han Wen-ti (Liu Heng 劉恆). See *Han shu* 97A (Vol. 12, p. 3941).

[21] The 皆 in the text suggests, as Tai Ming-yang points out (p. 297), that a string of examples preceded, examples which are now lost.

[22] Or possibly—"then it would be consistent throught"—一途得通.

[23] The words are *mao-tun* 矛楯. Hsi K'ang here means it literally, though *mao-tun* comes to mean by extension "contradiction."

Answer to the Explanation

cannot stand together. This is not a place where sophistic words can succeed with both.

In your essay you say: "If we are to discuss fortune and fate, we must distinguish between those who have it and those who do not and not feel uneasy about whether there are many or few. If one man has [a certain fate], then Ch'ang-p'ing could all be the same." You also say [quoting Mencius]: "One who understands fate will not stand at the foot of a high and dangerous wall." I would say that one who knows his fate must [know] there is nothing that is not in accord with it, such that he would fear the high, dangerous wall. If he knows that his fate has its set place, what will he fear from standing under it? But if the wall is truly able to do harm, not choosing between fates that are short or long, then whether one knows his fate or not, if he stands under it there is calamity, if he avoids it there is no harm. Thus how do you know that Po Ch'i was not the dangerous wall [that fell on the soldiers] at Ch'ang-p'ing so that you say "If there are a thousand or ten thousand, it is all fate; we should not feel uneasy about many or few"?[24] If you say that even though Ch'ang-p'ing was the same as the dangerous wall, it was their [the soldiers'] fortune and fate to run into it, then when one's fate is due to arrive, the appointed time is inevitably set, and why give us the warning about not standing there? This being the case, is there truly [such a thing as] fortune or not?[25] This is further something about which I have doubts.

You also say: "If Ch'ang-p'ing cannot be related to fate, can it be related to residence? Then how was it that in the ages of T'ang and Yü residences were all equally lucky?" My original doubts about your previous essay [had to do with the contention] that there is nothing that is not fortune and fate. Therefore I used [the

---

[24] Po Ch'i, remember, was the Ch'in general who put the men to death at Ch'ang-p'ing. See note 12 to Hsi K'ang's earlier "Refutation."

[25] Following the Wu text in adding the 無相也? The pattern is used several times in these essays.

187

Answer to the Explanation

example of] the soldiers[26] at Ch'ang-p'ing not[27] being the same to criticize the inevitability of fortune and fate. [But] if we search widely for causes to clarify the principles of events, why must we use the lucky house as *the* evidence that confirms it? Moreover, in my previous essay I already showed that the lucky house does not work alone. Now in vain you suppress those words: whom do you wish to refute?

You also say: "How was it that with the soldiers at Ch'ang-p'ing their houses were all equally doomed?" If [such] great uniformity is capable of occurring and you become suspicious because there are many, are you not dumber than I?[28] For when you happen to turn to supporting [the case of] fortune, then you say that "a thousand or ten thousand might all be the same." If we examine this logically [literally, "using perfect reason"], the very thing you oppose, can in this be seen. Having concluded that it is worthless to set up a lucky house, and that this is to hope[29] for something and get nothing in return, you wish to save [the argument for] fortune and fate. But because your feelings are difficult to express, you thus speak[30] like this. This could be called "clever fighting."

Your essay says: "Since divination [by tortoise] exhausts all the principles, it is that which completes fortune and fate." This again is something I doubt. In your previous essay you regarded fortune and fate as the essential thing, and then you subsequently added to it sincerity and obedience. This is becoming an endless maze.[31] And now you even further [claim] that divination completes it. So the implements for completing fate are

---

[26] Following the Wu text in adding the 卒 at this point.

[27] Following the Wu text in reading 不 instead of 異, though either variant works.

[28] Following the Wu text. Other texts have simply: "If such great uniformity is cause for suspicion then you are dumber than I."

[29] The 冀 occurs in the Wu manuscript.

[30] The 云 is added in the Chang text.

[31] The expression is *li lou* 離婁, which literally means the shape or pattern of engraved inlay. The root meaning seems to be something winding and tortuous with one thing leading to another.

Answer to the Explanation

[already] three, and we still do not know how many things in the end fortune and fate will need before there will be enough. If one is still short on principles even though he is sincere and obedient, how can these [sincerity and obedience] be called the "principles for completing fate"?[32] If these [fate, and sincerity and obedience] complete one another, then what does divination have to add to fate[33] so that you again speak of its "completing fate"?

May I ask—with respect to divination's completing fate—if Shan Pao had divined, and knew, therefore, that the tiger disaster was about to occur, then he could have hidden himself away in a deep palace, and carefully prepared to protect himself. If the tiger had still gotten to him, that means that divination is worthless; but if he was able [thereby] to be free from concern, that means that his fortune was *thwarted* by divination; how can you say it *completes* fate? If you say that Pao divined and was able to escape because, fundamentally, his fortune was not to be imperiled by a tiger, then the oracles are lies, and we ought to hurry to get rid of them.[34] If you say that everyone has his fate, and we must all follow divination to complete it, then [I must reply that] there are those in the world who to the end of their days do not divine: do they all lose their fortunes and cut short their destined lives? If you say that [whether] one divines is *also* a matter of fortune, then divination is [just] one thing in our fortunes; how can you say it is used to *complete* fortune? This being the case, I do not know if tortoise and milfoil divination, therefore, ought to be considered as being interrelated with fortune and fate, or whether they [divination and fate] complete one another and become one, or whether we should not [rather conclude] that each works on its own.

In your essay you say: "A house that is being lived in with no ulterior motive can be divined, just as one can predict the fate

---

[32] Remember Juan K'an's words: "Fate is the lot we receive, and sincerity and obedience are the principles for completing fate."

[33] Agreeing with Tai Ming-yang that the 卜 here should be 命.

[34] The words 急在攘除 occur in the original Wu text.

Answer to the Explanation

of someone with a dragon countenance. But if someone intentionally plans and builds a "lucky" house and then lives in it, hoping for blessings in return, this is no different from faking the countenance and nose and hoping to become a noble. Thus it is the man that truly verifies the house, it is not the house that controls the man."[35] According to what you say, that we can divine [a house] where someone is living with no ulterior motive must mean that one who is destined for good fortune can proceed with his eyes closed; in moving on, in whatever happens, he lets his fate run its course, and completely in the dark he builds his house but naturally encounters good fortune. If this is true, then how could it only be [true for] the lucky[36] man? All those who have fate can act in total ignorance and still naturally attain it, which is precisely the "fate is naturally so:[37] it cannot be increased or diminished" [position] of your former essay. If, all of a sudden, sincerity and obedience and divination by tortoise shell and milfoil—things that can be intentionally done and made—"complete" this fate that can be neither increased nor diminished, then why do you alone forbid the house that can be made, and say that it cannot be successfully divined,[38] and that it will only be a "pure" [double meaning, "divinable"][39] residence if it is built in total ignorance?

If with our eyes shut we can attain our fortunes, opening our eyes will not add anything to it, and those who are intelligent ought all the more to know[40] this. [But if that is true], when the Duke of Chou was about to build the [king's] residence [at Lo-

---

[35] Not a direct quote.

[36] The 古 should be 吉, as it is in the Chang text and the original Wu text as well.

[37] Following the Wu text in adding 有 in 命有自然.

[38] Following the Wu text which has 今不善相 instead of 不盡相命, and then following Tai Ming-yang's suggestion (p. 301) of emending the 今 to 令.

[39] Agreeing with Tai Ming-yang (p. 301) that on the basis of what follows in another paragraph or two, the *chen* 真 ("genuine") here should be *chen* 貞, "pure." But this *chen* also means "to divine," and I think Hsi K'ang is playing with that double meaning—the "pure" house is also the "divinable" house.

[40] Reading the Wu variant of 識 for 職.

Answer to the Explanation

yang], why did he hesitate at the Chien and the Ch'an, asking the tortoise and the milfoil, and getting the sign for the Lo?[41] If the tortoise shell and the milfoil stalks can truly help in building a residence, then we know that acting blindly is perhaps not the perfectly good principle. If acting blindly is not perfect and final, then how could it be that coming out of the dark is not the [correct] method for seeking it? If you definitely want to say that the tortoise shell and milfoil cannot better[42] one's lot over acting blindly,[43] then you must also think one will not lose his fortune by examining the cracks. Thus, whether one divines or not, and whether he acts [in accord with that divination] or not, in either case he will meet with what he is naturally to attain. And if what one is naturally to attain is complete, then a good diviner ought to know what is going to occur. How can it be that if someone acts without any reason he [the diviner] can know [that person's fate], but if he has an ulterior motive he cannot?

Now you hate this "planned building" and compare it to faking the [noble's] face, and you value [instead] "having no reason" and call this a pure [divinable] house.[44] But the forms of the pure house and the one that was planned are the same. They were both completed by effort, and they are both lucky homes. It is just that [the house built] with no ulterior motive, being the "pure" house, bestows good fortune in blind encounter, whereas with [the one that was] intentionally planned, one's [consequent] happiness is slightly diminished by the use of [prior] knowledge.[45]

---

[41] See note 39 to Hsi K'ang's earlier "Refutation."

[42] Reading the Wu variant of 善 in place of 盡.

[43] Agreeing with Tai Ming-yang (p. 302) that the 住 here should probably be 作.

[44] At this point the text has thirteen characters which are obviously copyist error and need to be omitted—然貞宅之異假顏, 貴夫無故識之. This is partly from what comes before and partly from what follows, and partly incorrect characters.

[45] I.e., you know the good fortune is coming because you have planned the house that way.

Answer to the Explanation

Thus the forms of good and bad fortune truly by nature have their principles, and they can be intentionally[46] attained. And, therefore; in your previous essay [you spoke of] there being evidence when one divines a completed [house]. This being so, then how would we describe the form of such a house? It must be that from far and near[47] it seems just right, and the sides of the hall are measured in regulation. Secure and peaceful, it has a special appearance and can be distinguished from others. They [lucky houses] benefit people with blessings, and therefore we call them lucky; they [unlucky houses] harm people with calamities, and therefore we call them evil.[48] But the facial features of a noble simply mysteriously coincide with good fortune.[49] Thus, although residence [on the one hand] and one's nature and fate [on the other], are each separate things, they are like the farmer and the good field; when they are combined the [desired] result is achieved.

If we suppose the case where some nobles have moved out, and then, delighting in their good fortune, other people go and live there—how could it be that the lucky house selects someone worthy[50] and only then do the inhabitants enjoy good fortune, and it chooses people who are good, and only then are they blessed? If the house has no preference for choosing the worthy, and does not begrudge its luck to those who intentionally plan [to get it], then homes do not refuse people [just as] fields do not reject plows. How could it be that their good or bad fortune, and their doing well or poorly, would not be the same? Those who first enjoyed the good fortune [the nobles] met with it without

---

[46] Reading 有故 with the Wu text instead of 爲故.
[47] Following the Wu text in omitting the 遂 that comes before 遠近.
[48] Hsi K'ang seemed to be describing the appearance of a lucky house, but here moves to a conclusion that would follow from a description of both lucky and unlucky houses.
[49] So houses and noble faces are not the same thing; one is made, the other comes from nature. This point is taken up again below.
[50] Following the Wu variant of 賢 instead of 能 on the basis of what follows.

Answer to the Explanation

seeking; those who later [enjoyed these blessings][51] heard of the good fortune and moved there. They are the same in their living in a lucky house; but in the one case they sought it, and in the other they did not. How can you say it is absurd, that [good fortune] cannot be made? To speak from this perspective, it is not that we verify the residence[52] according to the man; that the residence in truth completes the man is clear.

If you cherish the shape of the face, then Ying Pu's tatooed features did not diminish his high status, and cutting off that high nose would not make a noble any less a noble.[53] From this we can know that the [dragon] countenance and the nose are [simply] the signs of the noble, they are not the things that make him a noble.[54] Therefore, the signs are not the substance of the noble. But the designation "lucky house" and the good fortune itself *are* the reality of the house.[55] If there is no evidence of good fortune, and it is [simply] being called a lucky house,[56] because the evidence is falsely presented, your criticism would be permitted. But if you use signs that are not the substance to refute the lucky house for which there is proof—this is something I do not dare allow.[57] Tzu-yang lacked the substance[58] but still engraved his palm: from this we know the importance of [having the reality] match the name, but that is all. Chü-chün usurped

---

[51] From the parallel it is clear that two characters are missing here: 後 — corresponds to 前吉者.

[52] Agreeing with Lu Hsün (p. 113) and Tai Ming-yang (p. 303) that the 宅 in the sentence should be repeated.

[53] The sentence should end at 公候.

[54] Following the Wu text in omitting the 質 at the end of the line.

[55] Following Lu Hsün's reckoning of the original Wu text: 吉宅字與吉者.

[56] 自 is a mistake for 字, and there must be a 吉 before the 宅.

[57] I hope that is clear. All of this objects to Juan K'an's analogy of the lucky house to the facial features of the noble, Juan K'an arguing that neither can be *made*. Hsi K'ang's point is that the two are not analogous, the physical features of the noble can be removed and he will still be a noble, but the physical features of the lucky house—its design and location— *are* the very things that make it a lucky house.

[58] The substance of the emperor.

Answer to the Explanation

the residence[59] [of the emperor] and rotated his mat [to line up with] K'uei; this was a disaster that resulted from relying on only one thing. These examples cannot be used as criticisms.[60]

To turn to the fate of the noble, this he receives from nature; it can be neither molded nor changed. But residence is an external thing. Whether it is square or round comes from man, and its principle is that it can be made.[61] It is just like the fact that Hsi Shih's purity could not be made, but Hsi Shih's clothes could.[62] Embroidered robes and fragrant flowers are the things that improved her appearance;[63] a lucky house and a good[64] family are the things that complete one's fate. Therefore the world has no methods for making[65] people, but it does have theories[66] about divining where to live. And therefore we know that people and houses cannot be used to illustrate one another. How can we use the people who cannot be made to eliminate the houses that can?

With respect to punishing and rewarding all alike—this comes from their belonging to one and the same family;[67] it is not as you said in your former essay, the result of their divining the [character of] a completed house and getting the good or bad fortune. If you first understand this, we can then discuss the rest.

Your essay says: "When a hunter goes through the woods, he

---

[59] Tai Ming-yang (p. 304) thinks *chai* 宅 ("residence") here should be *kuo* 國, "the country."

[60] Actually, the grammar suggests that the sentence applies only to the last example—"*This* cannot be used..."—but Hsi K'ang surely intends this to apply to both things.

[61] Following the Chang text and others in filling in the lacuna here with 為.

[62] Hsi Shih 西施, the model beauty of antiquity sent by the king of Yüeh to the king of Wu, was mentioned by Hsi K'ang earlier in his "Answer to Hsiang Hsiu's Refutation of My Essay on Nourishing Life."

[63] Filling in the lacuna here with the 儀 of the Wen-chin text. Other texts have *mei* 美, "beauty," which would also be appropriate.

[64] Filling in the lacuna here with the 善 of the Ch'eng text.

[65] Following the Wu text in adding 作 before the 人.

[66] Following the Wu text in putting a 説 after 卜宅.

[67] Translation is tentative. I have followed the Wu the text in adding the 自 before 一家, and take Hsi K'ang to have in mind cases where members of several generations are rewarded or punished because of the actions of one member of the clan.

Answer to the Explanation

might meet a tiger and he might meet a bird. A tiger is bad luck, a bird good. A diviner can cast the stalks and know it, but this is not something he can make." Now according to what you[68] say, the good and evil of lands is like the good fortune of birds and the bad of tigers. So if the hunter first divines, he can choose [his woods] and go after the birds. And if he is choosing where to live, he can avoid evil [places] and pursue the good. Although the lucky land cannot[69] be made, it can be chosen and lived in, just as although one cannot change which it is to be, tiger or bird, one can choose which to pursue. If divination by tortoise and milfoil is that which completes fortune, and the tiger can be divined and the land chosen, why do you believe in one half and not the other?

You also say that "with respect to the good and bad fortune of an area of land, there are those that are like birds and those that are like tigers. It cannot be that a "C" surname will have no harm, while a "D" will suffer disaster." I would cite this as a case of regarding as strange what you do not understand and using it as a criticism. It seems that you have not yet examined the principles of C and D. For even though a particular piece of land[70] might be lucky, it might be strong in nourishing [someone with] a "C" [surname], but weak in nurturing a "D," just as although a good field is generally excellent, there are crops for which it is best suited.

How can I explain this? In surnames there are the five tones, and among the five elements there are those that produce one another.[71] Therefore, people with the same surname do not marry because they hate to not reproduce. If with people it is truly like this, then lands must also be the same. Therefore the ancients, on the one hand, took Yin and Yang as their standards,

---

[68] Reading 知 as a mistake for 如.
[69] Following the Chang text in adding a 可 before the 為.
[70] Following the Wu text in reading 地 instead of 理.
[71] Wood produces fire, fire produces earth, earth generates metal, metal produces water, and water produces wood. See Fung Yu-lan, *A History of Chinese Philosophy*, Vol. II, p. 20, where he quotes Tung Chung-shu.

Answer to the Explanation

and, on the other, harmonized with Firm and Yielding.[72] They correctly understood the principles of human nature, and brought it about that the three powers [Heaven, Earth, and Man] benefitted one another and came together in the Great Concord. It was in this way they exhausted the principles and thoroughly [understood] what was appropriate for things.

Now "identical sounds will respond to one another, and identical ethers will seek one another out."[73] These are allotments of nature. If the notes are not in harmony, then nearby strings will not vibrate, but if the sounds are the same, then even though far away, [the strings] will respond. Although this phenomenon is clear, still no one seems to understand it. If the five notes each has its match, and the five[74] ethers produce one another, then people's homes are like the categories of bird and tiger.[75] How could you see that C and D are not the same, and say[76] that lands are devoid of good and bad fortune?

In your essay [you quote me as saying]: "There are some in the world who can talk about this." [And then you say] "If even you will not say it, who can [discuss] it with you?"[77] I respond as follows. In your previous essay you already said there are those who can divine a completed house. This means they are certainly able to talk about it. And therefore I said "In this world there must be those who are able...." Now you fail to look up what

---

[72] For "firm" and "yielding" days see note 15 above.

[73] Quoting the *Wen-yen* on the first hexagram of the *I ching*, where nine occurs in the fifth place (p. 2).

[74] Taking the advice of both Lu Hsün (p. 115) and Tai Ming-yang (p. 306) in reading 五 instead of 土. Each of the five elements has its "ether" (*ch'i* 氣).

[75] That is to say, if I understand the argument correctly, there are five types of land matching the five surnames and five elements. And one ought to live in an area that "produces" his category. Thus living in one place would be like meeting a bird while hunting, while living in another would be like running into a tiger. It is relevant to keep in mind that not only do the five elements produce one another, but that there is also a sequence in which one overcomes another (e.g., metal overcomes wood, water overcomes fire, etc.).

[76] Following the Wu text in omitting the 之 after the 謂.

[77] The reference is to the possible claim that a lucky house could lengthen the life of a doomed infant, and that this too was the cause of P'eng-tsu's many years.

Answer to the Explanation

you [yourself] said in your previous essay, but reply by upbraiding my criticism of it by [mentioning those] who are able to speak. You must also know that graves and homes do have good and bad fortune.

You also say "that medicine can cure disease because it is one [with your fate] is true; but that the good or bad fortune of your house is one [with your fate], is false."[78] Having said that a completed house can be divined, can you now turn around and say this is false?

The evidence for medicine's curing disease is readily[79] seen, and therefore this gentleman [Juan K'an] believes it, but the payoff for the good or bad fortune of one's house is faraway and remote [in time], and therefore the gentleman has doubts. If you take closeby or distant [as the gauge for something's] being true[80] or false, then I am afraid the places you've looked for things are few indeed. When I see ditches and channels, I do not doubt the vastness of rivers and oceans; and when I see hills and mounds, then I know how high Mt. T'ai must be. But you—when you support drugs you reject houses, and when you see the closeby you deny the distant. This is the reason why people who live by the sea to the end of their lives deny there are mountain trees,[81] and mountain dwellers until their hair turns white[82] refuse to believe in big fish.

Your essay says: "'That which intelligence knows does not compare to the vast number of things it does not.' This, in general, is the constant obstacle of the common people of the

---

[78] Not a direct quote.

[79] Agreeing with Lu Hsün (p. 115) and Tai Ming-yang (p. 307) that 又 should be 文.

[80] The Wu text correctly has 實 after 虛.

[81] Agreeing with Tai Ming-yang (p. 307) that there should be a 木 after the 山. See note 82.

[82] Following the Wu text in reading 白首 instead of 曰. The lines take the form of a set saying, and indeed something similar is found in several other sources. For example, the *Yen shih chia-hsün* 顏氏家訓 ("Kuei-hsin" 歸心, chapter: 5.15b) has "People who live in the mountains do not believe there are fish big as trees, and people who live by the sea do not believe there are trees big as fish."

Answer to the Explanation

world. But that which intelligence does not know cannot be falsely sought."[83]

I refute this as follows. That which intelligence does not know, fortune definitely does not know either. Now why is it that what we unconsciously allow is greater than what we know? It must arise from the fact that originally we say something does not exist, but then we are forced by the evidence to admit its existence. The evidence for things whose existence we are forced to admit will not be included in the number [of things we know]. But if we combine all of these things that have come to be verified, we would simply have to say they are greater in number than that which we know.[84]

If you know that this is so, and there truly are principles you do not yet thoroughly understand,[85] and you do not look for the hidden by means of the seen, search for the causes[86] and investigate the clues, going from 1 and 7 to 2 and 8,[87] then you have neglected[88] the principle of searching for the cause. [The principle involved in searching for the cause][89] is like that which the skilled hunter uses to catch birds. Even though he follows their tracks, there are occasions when he does not succeed. But when has anyone ever caught a bird by not tracking it down? If, because good and bad fortune are not fixed beforehand, you say

---

[83] The Wu text correctly has 求 here instead of 論.

[84] This is a very difficult section. I believe Hsi K'ang to be restricting "what we know" to things actually seen and therefore known in that way. He is therefore concerned to account for our knowledge of things unseen, things we "unconsciously ("blindly," literally, *an* 闇) allow." And he concludes that the number of such things is greater than the number of things we know from actual observation.

[85] Following Tai Ming-yang's advice (p. 307) and emending 還 to be 達.

[86] Reading the Wu text variant of 端 in place of 論.

[87] The text has 由 —— 而得卯未. The Ch'eng text fills in the lacunae with *tzu-wu* 子午, numbers 1 and 7 of the "Twelve Earthly Branches," and since *wei* 未 is number 8, it makes sense to see (as Tai Ming-yang argues, p. 308) *mao* 卯 (branch #4) as a mistake for *ch'ou* 丑 (branch #2).

[88] Following the Wu text with 失 instead of 夫.

[89] This phrase is not repeated in the text. I think it should be and was probably left out by a copyist because of the duplication.

Answer to the Explanation

they cannot be sought, how is this any different from [the hunter], because he has no appointed meeting with bird[90] or beast, not [even] venturing to lift a foot,[91] and remaining seated with no reason [to move]? To speak from this perspective, how can you call "explaining the mysterious and tracing out the hidden"[92] false?

---

[90] Filling in the lacuna here with the 禽 found in the Wen-chin text.

[91] Following the Wu text in reading 舉足 in place of 飢舉氣一足.

[92] Following the Wu text in reading 賾 instead of 頤. The phrase "explaining the mysterious and tracing out the hidden," is from the *I ching*, *Hsi-tz'u* A.11 (p. 44). The full line reads "The sages explained the mysterious and traced out the hidden, probed the deep and exhausted the distant, in order to fix the good and bad fortune of the world."

A Selected Bibliography of Studies of Hsi K'ang and the Thought of the Times

::

Balazs, Etienne. "Nihilistic Revolt or Mystical Escapism: Currents of Thought in China During the Third Century A.D." in H. M. Wright, tr., *Chinese Civilization and Bureaucracy*. New Haven and London: Yale University Press, 1964, pp. 226–254.

Chou Shao-hsien 周紹賢. *Wei Chin ch'ing-t'an shu-lun* 魏晉清談述論. Taipei: Commercial Press, 1966.

Fan Shou-k'ang 范壽康. *Wei Chin chih ch'ing-t'an* 魏晉之清談. Shanghai: Commercial Press, 1936.

Fukunaga Mitsuji 福永光司. "Kei Kō ni okeru jiga no mondai: Kei Kō no seikatsu to shisō" 嵇康における自我の問題(嵇康の生活と思想). *Tōhō gakuhō* 東方学報, 32 (1962), pp. 1–68.

―――. "Kei Kō to bukkyō: Rikuchō shisōshi to Kei Kō" 嵇康と佛教 (六朝思想史と嵇康). *Tōyōshi kenkyū* 東洋史研究, 20:4 (1962), pp. 92–119.

Funatsu Tomihiko 船津富彦. "Kei Kō bungaku ni tōei seru shinsen" 嵇康文學に投影せる神仙. *Tōhō shūkyō* 東方宗教, 31 (1968), pp. 44–67.

Gulik, R. H. van. *Hsi K'ang and His Poetical Essay on the Lute*. Tokyo and Rutland, Vt.: Charles E. Tuttle Co., 1968.

Henricks, Robert G. "Hsi K'ang and Argumentation in the Wei." *The Journal of Chinese Philosophy*, 8:2 (June, 1981), pp. 169–221.

Ho Ch'i-min 何啓民. *Chu-lin ch'i-hsien yen-chiu* 竹林七賢研究. Taipei: Commercial Press, 1966.

―――. *Wei Chin ssu-hsiang yü t'an-feng* 魏晉思想與談風. Taipei: Commercial Press, 1967.

Holzman, Donald. "La poésie de Ji Kang." *Journal Asiatique*, part I. in CCLXVIII: 1 & 2 (1980), pp. 107–177; part II. in CCLXVIII: 3 & 4 (1980), pp. 323–378.

―――. *La Vie et la Pensée de Hi K'ang*. Leiden: E. J. Brill, 1957.

―――. *Poetry and Politics: The Life and Works of Juan Chi (A.D. 210–263)*. Cambridge: Cambridge University Press, 1976.

Hou Wai-lu 侯外廬, Chi Hsüan-ping 紀玄冰, Tu Shou-su 杜守素, and Ch'iu Han-sheng 邱漢生. *Chung-kuo ssu-hsiang t'ung-shih* 中國思想通史. Peking: Jen-min 人民, 1957. Vol. 2.

Selected Bibliography

Hsiao Teng-fu 蕭登福. *Hsi K'ang yen-chiu* 嵇康研究. Taipei: Kuo-li cheng-chih ta-hsüeh 國立政治大學, 1976.

Huang Chen-min 黃振民. "Hsi K'ang yen-chiu" 嵇康研究. *Ta-lu tsa-chih* 大陸雜誌. part I. in 18:1 (Jan. 15, 1959), pp. 24–28; part II. in 18:2 (Jan. 31, 1959), pp. 53–58.

Liu Ta-chieh 劉大杰. *Wei Chin ssu-hsiang lun* 魏晉思想論. Shanghai: Chung-hua 中華, 1939.

Lu Hsün 魯迅. "Wei Chin feng-tu chi wen-chang yü yao chi chiu chih kuan-hsi" 魏晉風度及文章與藥及酒之關係. *Erh-i chi* 而已集. Vol. 17 in *Lu Hsün san-shih nien chi* 三十年集. Hong Kong: Hsin-i 新藝, 1965.

Maspero, Henri. "Essai sur le Taoïsme aux prémiers siècles de l'ère Chrétienne." In *Le Taoïsme et les réligions chinoises* (Paris: Gallimard, 1971), pp. 341–466.

——. "Les procédés de 'nourrir le principe vital' dans la religion Taoïste ancienne." In *Le Taoïsme et les réligions chinoises*, pp. 479–589.

Mather, Richard. "The Controversy over Conformity and Naturalness During the Six Dynasties." *History of Religions*, 9:2 & 3 (Nov., 1969/Feb., 1970), pp. 160–180.

——. Tr. *Shih-shuo Hsin-yü: A New Account of Tales of the World*. Minneapolis: University of Minnesota Press, 1976.

Mou Tsung-san 牟宗三. *Ts'ai-hsing yü hsüan-li* 才性與玄理. Taipei: Jen-sheng 人生, 1963.

——.*Wei Chin hsüan-hsüeh* 魏晉玄學. Taichung: Ssu-li Tung-hai ta-hsüeh 私立東海大學, 1962.

Nishi Junzo 西順蔵. "Kei Kō no ron no shisō" 嵇康の論の思想. *Shūkan tōyōgaku* 集刊東洋学, 10 (1963), pp. 1–17.

——. "Kei Kō no shakushiron no hitotsu no kaishaku" 嵇康の釈私論の一つの解釈. Tokyo: *Fukui Hakase Shoju kinen tōyō shisō ronshū* 福井博士頌寿記念東洋思想論集, 1960, pp. 462–478.

Rushton, Peter. "An Interpretation of Hsi K'ang's Eighteen Poems Presented to Hsi Hsi on His Entry Into the Army." *Journal of the American Oriental Society*, 99:2 (April–June, 1979), pp. 175–190.

T'ang Ch'ang-ju 唐長孺. *Wei Chin nan-pei-ch'ao shih lun-ts'ung* 魏晉南北朝史論叢. Peking: San-lien 三聯, 1955.

T'ang I-chieh 湯一介. "Hsi K'ang ho Juan Chi ti che-hsüeh ssu-hsiang" 嵇康和阮籍的哲學思想. *Hsin chien-she* 新建設, 9 (1962), pp. 25–30.

T'ang Yung-t'ung 湯用彤. *Wei Chin hsüan-hsüeh lun kao* 魏晉玄學論稿. Peking: Jen-min 人民, 1957.

Index–Glossary

::

agate, 67; stamens, 13, 56, 56n
Airs, 76, 78, 102, 105n
airs of the South, 83, 85, 88
An Ch'i 安期, 60, 60n
Analects, 5, 29n, 32n, 33n, 35n, 40n, 41n, 42n, 48n, 49n, 52n, 55n, 66n, 72n, 73n, 74n, 78n, 84n, 100n, 105n, 110n, 111n, 126, 127n, 128n, 136n, 140n, 143n, 149n, 155n, 160n, 169n, 177n
analogy, 14, 79, 80, 170, 193n
ancients, the, 5, 6, 31, 32, 39, 73, 80–82, 86, 100, 103, 141, 154, 155, 158, 163, 166–68, 172n, 175–76, 176n, 177n, 178, 181–82, 184–85, 195
angelica, 52, 64

bamboo tuning tubes, 83, 87
beach wormwood, 53
beat (in music), 73, 93
beautiful and ugly, 45–46, 46n, 80
begging barbarian, 149, 149n, 166
Beginning Nine, 54, 54n
being, 4–5
bells and drums, 65, 74, 74n, 93
benevolence, 6, 113, 126, 128n, 155, 155n
benevolence and righteousness, 6, 66, 139–40, 142–43
Big Dipper, 146n, 149n, 171n, 174n
body, 11–14, 24–26, 30, 31n, 38–39, 45, 45n, 47, 47n, 53–54, 115, 117, 134; effects of drugs on, 57, 57n; effects of wine and grains on, 56; effects produced by different musical instruments, 92–94; nourished by profound things, 54; related to mind, 91
boll-worm, 57, 58n
Book of Changes, 169, 175, 182n, 184n, see *I ching*
Book of Documents, see *Shu*
Book of Poetry, 33n, 58n, 66n, 72n, 73n, 74n, 75, 75n, 76n, 84n, 97n, 101n, 102n, 103n, 105n, 131n, 136n, 138n, 147, 154n, 163n, 165n, 176, 176n, 183
Bow (constellation), 149, 149n, 157
bramble roots, 59
Branches and Stems, 184, 184n
breath(s), 14, 24, 28n, 68, 91, 107, 147, 159; being stingy with, 50; effect of drugs on, 57, 57n; of the four seasons, 89; of wisdom and courage, 127, 131, 132, 134; pure, 11, 23n; special, 11, 22, 35; steady, 26; stimulated by music, 81; natural allotments of, 131;
breath and vapor, 13, 56
Buddhists, 4, 149n

C and D, musical notes, 73; surnames 176, 176n, 195–96
camphor, 28, 28n
Chan-kuo ts'e, 114n
Chancellor P'i 宰嚭, 116, 116n
Chang Hua 張華, 25n, see *Po-wu chih*
Chang I 張毅, 68, 69n, 173, 173n
Chang Miao 張邈, 135, 135n, 139n
Chao, state of, 69n, 83n, 158n
Chao Chih 趙至, 9n
cheng (musical instrument), 92, 92n, 93, 93n
Cheng, music of, 84, 84n, 105, 105n, 106
Cheng and Wei, music of, 64n, 100, 100n, 184, 184n
Chi, river, 69, 69n
Chi Cha 季札, 72, 73n, 76, 78, 78n, 79–80
Chia I 賈誼, 129, 129n, 132–33

203

Index

chiao-she 交賒, see closeby and distant, also distant and near
chicken's heads, 52, 52n
Chieh and Chih, 62, 62n, 158, 158n. See also Robber Chih
Chieh and Chou, 170n
chien 兼, 14, 144, see comprehensive
Chien, river, 163, 163n, 191
chih 智, see intelligence
chih-li 至理, 21–22, 62n, 144, see ultimate order of things, highest truths, and Perfect Reason
Chih's, 82, 82n
Chin, state of, 25, 83n, 88, 89, 89n, 90, 92
Chin shu, 6n, 61n, 109
ching 精, 28n, see essence
Ching K'o 荊軻, 23n, 112n, 130n
Cho's, 82, 82n
Chu-fu Yen 主父偃, 64, 64n
chu-lin ch'i-hsien 竹林七賢, 8
Chuan Hsü, 79n, 84
Chuang-tzu, 3, 5, 7, 11, 13, 43n, 147n, 167n, 168n; views on nourishing life, 10
Chuang-tzu, 10n, 11n, 21, 28n, 30n, 36n, 41n, 45n, 46n, 47n, 49n, 50n, 60n, 61n, 62n, 63n, 64n, 65n, 66n, 67n, 68n, 69n, 75n, 80n, 86n, 93n, 95n, 136n, 153n, 160n, 166n, 167n, 179n
Chü-chün 巨君 (Wang Mang 王莽), 174, 174n, 193
Chung Hui 鍾會, 3n, 4n, 9, 72n
Chung-tzu Ch'i 鍾子期, 77, 77n, 79, 80, 82–83
cinnabar, 12, 57n; Three Fields of, 56n; refined, 58, 58n
Classic of Filial Piety, 169, see *Hsiao ching*
closeby and distant, 197
common lot, 82, 111, 111n
common man, 115, 185
common men, realm of, 27
common names, 115n

common opinion, 61
common people, 13, 25, 52, 117, 149, 154, 167, 179, 197
common reason, 21, 167
common saying, 24
comprehensive, 14–15, 29, 69, 144
concern, 107–108, 112, 115, 118
Confucius, 4–5, 33, 33n, 35, 35n, 36n, 40, 40n, 41n, 48, 48n, 49, 49n, 50n, 55n, 61, 66n, 68n, 72, 76, 78, 78n, 79–80, 100, 100n, 102, 103n, 111n, 126, 143n, 150, 150n, 151n, 152, 155, 169, 177, 177n, 178, 181–83, 184n. See also *Analects*
cravings and delights, 28
cravings and desires, 32, 38, 61–62
Creative and Receptive, 153, 153n, 184, 184n
Creator, the, 31
Ch'an, river, 163, 163n, 191
Ch'ang Jung 昌容, 59, 59n
ch'ang-lo t'ing chu 長樂亭主, 7
Ch'ang-p'ing, soldiers at, 157, 158n, 173, 187, 187n, 188
Ch'en Pu-chan 陳不占, 83, 83n
Ch'en P'ing 陳平, 114, 114n
ch'i 氣, 28n, 89n, see breath(s)
Ch'i, state of, 69, 69n, 83n, 84n; songs of, 92, 94, 98–99
Ch'ih Fu 赤斧, 58, 58n
Ch'ih-sung tzu 赤松子, 58, 58n, 59
Ch'in, state of, 69, 69n, 83n, 112n, 158n; music of, 92
Ch'in Shih-huang-ti, 23n, 30n, 60n, 64n, 112n
ch'ing 情, see feelings
ch'ing-t'an 清談, 3–4, 4n
Ch'iung Shu 邛疏, 59, 59n
Ch'u, state of, 83n, 86, 89, 89n, 90; songs of, 88, 88n, 92, 94, 98–99
Ch'u Tz'u, 56n
Ch'ü Yüan 屈原, 56n, 67n
ch'ü-chung 區種, 24n, 25n, see plot-planting

Index

day lily, 25, 25n
delight and anger, 26, 31, 31n, 66–67, 75, 81, 95, 135
desires, 28–29, 32n, 37n, 38–39, 40n, 45, 48, 61–62, 74, 92, 94, 103, 140, 147, 160–61
destiny, 51–52, 55n, 149n, 171n
dietary regulations, 11, 13
Dipper K'uei, 149, 149n, 157, 174, 194
disease(s), 27, 55, 62n, 145, 149n, 159, 197; of lust, 147, 147n; one hundred, 13, 26, 56
distant and near, 28, 47, 47n, 48
divination, 60, 145, 148, 174, 176n, 184, 188; by tortoise shell and milfoil, 153, 162–63, 175n, 189–91, 195; of old houses contrasted with that of new, 153, 161, 161n; of residence and grave, 177; of residence contrasted with divination by tortoise shell and milfoil, 162–63, 163n
divination and physiognomy, 14, 164, 177
drugs, 12–13, 23–24, 28, 51, 51n, 52, 54, 60n, 197
Duke Ching of Ch'i, 90, 90n, 152n
Duke Hsien of Chin, 112n
Duke Huan of Ch'i, 27n, 60, 60n, 109, 109n
Duke Huan of Chin, 27n
Duke Hui of Chin, 112n
Duke Ling of Cheng, 127n
Duke Ling of Wei, 78n
Duke of Chou, the, 33, 35, 35n, 61, 108, 120–25, 163, 163n, 165, 165n, 166, 177, 177n, 178, 178n, 179n, 182–83, 190
Duke of Shao, 125, 125n
Duke P'ing of Chin, 78, 78n
Duke Wen of Chin, 111, 111n, 112n

early death and disease, 145, 159
Eastern Mountain, 152
eight emotions, 75, 136
eight kinds of sound, 84, 102–103, 105
Elegant, 76, 78, 84, 84n, 100, 102, 105n, 106
emptiness, 4
essence, 28n, 75, 118; begrudging, 50; of grief and joy, 74; of mountain thistle, 58, 58n; of things we eat, 25, 58; scattered as an obstacle to nourishing life, 66; things that poison it, 151
essence and spirit, 13, 23, 26, 56

fame and position, 29, 33n, 39, 43, 67
fame and profit, 66, 138
Fan Sheng-chih 氾勝之, 24n, 25n
Fan Yü-ch'i 樊於期, 130, 130n, 134
Fang Hui 方回, 59, 59n
fate, 26, 26n, 73n, 111, 145, 150–51, 151n, 157, 171, 173, 186–90, 194, 197
feelings, 24, 28, 32, 34, 47, 67n, 71–106, 107–119, 124, 138, 141, 147, 178n, 181–82; as unreliable, 11, 62–63; affected by different kinds of music, 92–95; concealing/revealing them related to morality, 107–119; of right and wrong, 46, 110; practices of nourishing life go against, 37; released by music, 71, 72n, 81; rites and laws go against, 140; rites as outward form of, 178, 183
feelings and nature, 148–160
feng 風, 73n, 76n, 88n, see Airs
feng-shui 風水, 145
ferocity and tranquillity (in music), 93
Fire-star, 154, 154n
Firm and Yielding, 90, 153, 184, 184n, 185, 196, 196n
five colors, 34, 73, 80
five directions, 156n
Five Elements, 4n, 34, 73, 134, 156n,

Index

184, 195, 196n
Five Emperors, 79, 79n
five ethers, 196
five feelings, 36
five flavors, 34, 34n, 95, 106n
five grains, 14, 26, 31, 52, 57, 59, 67; ill effects from eating, 55; introduced by Shen Nung, 33, 53; worms thrive on, 56n
five notes, 196
five regions, 88
five strings, 30
five surnames, 196n
five tones, 73, 80, 89, 89n, 94, 156n, 195
five viscera, 14, 57
flute, 91, 91n, 104n
foreknowledge, 38
forethought, 44
form, 12, 31, 49–50, 58–59, 86, 91, 117, 147, 182–83; and body, 23; and spirit, 24; attacked by emotions, 26; effects of different musical instruments on, 92; of King Wen, 78; related to spirit, 24
former kings, the, 32, 84, 104–105, 105n, 178, 180, 183
fortune and fate, 157–58, 175, 185–89
Fu Hsi, 79n

garden daisies, 54, 54n
gentian, 137, 137n
Gentleman, the, 12, 24, 41n, 42–43, 45, 54, 107, 109, 112, 114, 116–17, 126, 153, 164, 171, 176n, 179, 197
geomancy, 145
ghosts and spirits, 84, 170, 181–82, 182n
glory and honor, 40, 43–44, 63–64
glory and disgrace, 43, 50, 61
gold and cinnabar, 57n
gold elixir, 57n
good and bad (descriptive of music), 73, 76, 76n, 80, 94

good and bad fortune, 4–5, 14, 86, 91, 145, 154n, 155, 157–58, 161, 161n, 168, 172n, 179, 184, 192, 197–98; associated with celestial bodies, 146n; being open and being private as the gates to, 110; in music and song, 78; knowing it contrasted with making it, 153, 162–63, 175; of regions and lands, 176, 195–96; of Yin and Yang, 164; principles of, 46
good times and lucky days, 151, 165–66, 178, 179n, 183, 183n, 184–85
Great Accord, 29, 29n
Great Broth, 105, 105n
Great Concord, 167, 196
Great Harmony, 63, 96, 102, 105
Great Man, 93n
Great Peace, 102
Great Simplicity, 139
Great Thoroughfare, 50n
Great Unity, 93, 93n
Great Way, 102, 108, 118, 139
Great Way, 108
Great Yang, 66
grief and joy, 26, 31, 71–106, 135; principles of, 84; released by music, 81
guiding and nourishing, 11, 23, 23n, 35–36, 48

Han, state of, 69n
Han-fei-tzu, 27n, 82n, 173n, 178n
Han shu, 74n, 82n, 89n, 129n, 130n, 166n, 174n, 186n
harmony, 35, 35n, 42, 45, 65, 67n, 73, 74, 81, 89, 94, 100, 100n, 102–103, 106, 135, 172, 196; as important in nourishing life, 29, 29n, 39, 150, 150n, 160–161, 173, 173n, 174, 174n; as the essential quality of music, 71, 85n, 95–97; emotions spontaneously released by, 95, 98
harp, 162, 162n, 163n

206

Index

Heaven, 36, 52, 66n, 69n, 70n, 101, 123n, 149n, 150, 151n, 158, 158n, 165n, 172n, 176n
Heaven and Earth, 32, 32n, 36n, 53, 56n, 65, 67n, 73, 84, 101n, 153, 153n, 167, 182; principle of, 27; spirits of, 34, 155
Heaven, Earth, and Man, 196
heaven-given years, 11, 11n
high and clear, 152, 152n, 160
highest things, 22, 28
highest truths, 21, 62
ho 和, *see* harmony
Ho-t'u 河圖, 169n, *see* Yellow River (chart)
Ho Yen 何晏, 72
honor and glory, 142
honor and rank, 123
horse fly, 137, 137n
Hou Chi, 33, 33n
Hou Han shu, 117n, 174n
Hsi-shih 西施, 34, 34n, 45, 194, 194n
Hsia (music of Yü), 84
Hsiang Hsiu 向秀, 7n, 8, 21, 30n, 31n, 32n, 34n, 35n, 37, 39n, 40n, 42n, 47n, 53n, 55n, 61n, 63, 65n, 160n
hsiang-ming 相命, *see* fortune and fate
Hsiao ching, 33n, 42n, 100n, 163n, 169n
Hsiao T'ung 蕭統, 22
hsiao-ya 小雅, 73n, 76n, *see* Elegant
hsien 仙, 10, *see* immortals
Hsien-ch'ih (music of the Yellow Emperor), 84
Hsien-men 羨門, 30, 30n
hsin 心, *see* mind
Hsin lun 新論, 51n, *see* Huan T'an
hsing 形, *see* form
hsing 性, *see* human nature, also nature (human)
hsing-ming 性命, *see* human nature and fate, also nature (human) and fate

hsing-te 刑德, 146n, *see* punishments and rewards
Hsü Fu 許負, 151, 152n, 157, 185
Hsü Yu 許由, 43n, 61, 61n
hsüan-hsüeh 玄學, 3, 4n
Hsün-tzu, 64n
Hsün-tzu, 32n, 100n, 111n
Hu barbarians, 87, 168n
Hua Ch'en 華臣, 128, 128n
Huai-nan-tzu, 31n, 47n, 60n, 89n, 168n
Huan T'an 桓譚, 51n, 60, 60n, 163n
Huang-ti, 79n. *See also* Yellow Emperor
human nature, 37, 131, 139–40, 148, 169, 169n; principles of, 196. *See also* nature (human)
human nature and fate, 146, 157. *See also* nature (human) and fate
Huo Kuang 霍光, 129, 129n, 130n, 133, 166n

I ching, 32n, 35n, 39n, 43n, 54n, 66n, 69n, 70n, 76n, 90n, 101n, 102n, 138n, 151n, 153n, 155n, 156n, 158n, 160n, 167n, 169n, 170n, 174n, 175n, 179n, 180n, 183n, 196n, 199n
I Yin 伊尹, 108, 108n
immortal(s), 4, 10–11, 22, 57n, 60n
Indian rice, 55, 55n
intelligence, 31–32, 38–39, 39n, 53n, 67, 91, 127–28, 145, 167, 179, 186, 197–98; action as a result of *versus* natural action, 45; role played in determining good and bad fortune, 157–59, 185
intervals (in music), 93

jade, 171n; and silk, 74; flowers of, 13, 56, 56n; liquid, 58, 58n; of Pien Ho, 82n, 83n, 112n; tablet, 165, 165n
Jan Keng (Jan Po-niu), 33, 33n, 55, 55n

207

Index

Jen-wu chih 人物志, 126, 126n
Juan Chi 阮籍, 6, 6n, 8
Juan Chung 阮種, 60, 61n
Juan Hsien 阮咸, 8
Juan K'an 阮侃, 5, 14, 72, 72n, 144–45, 146n, 149n, 150n, 152n, 157n, 163n, 172n, 174n, 178, 178n, 179n, 189n, 193n
Jung barbarians, 69, 69n, 168
jujubes, 25n
Jupiter, 146n, 176, 176n

Kao Chien-li 高漸離, 23n, 112, 112n
King Ch'eng (of Chou), 120, 122, 123, 125n
King Ho of Han, 129, 129n, 130
King Hui-wen of Chao, 112n
King Kung of Ch'u, 116, 116n
King Wen (of Chou), 35, 35n, 36n, 49n, 52n, 78, 78n, 79, 82n, 122
King Wen of Ch'u, 116n
King Wu (of Chou), 35, 35n, 36n, 49n, 52n, 78, 78n, 79, 82n, 122, 123n, 163, 163n, 165n, 177, 178, 182–83, 184n
Kingdom of the Naked, 63, 63n
Ko-lu 葛盧, 85–88
Kuan and Ts'ai, 120–25
Kuan Chung 管仲, 109, 109n
Kuan-ch'iu Chien 毌丘儉, 8–9, 121
Kuan-tzu, 109, 109n
kung 公, 107, *see* unselfish
Kung-sun Shu, *see* Tzu-yang
Kuo Hsiang 郭象, 21, 30n
K'uei (music director for Shun), 84, 85n, 100n
K'un-lun, 56n
k'ung 空, 4
K'ung-tzu chia-yü, 77n

Lao-tzu, 3–5, 7, 44
Lao-tzu, 29n, 39n, 41n, 44n, 45n, 48n, 50n, 68n, 108n, 112n, 146n, 147n
leek roots, 59, 59n

Lei sacrifice, 185, 185n
li 禮, *see* rites
li 理, 21, *see* principle(s)
Li chi, 23n, 34n, 41n, 64n, 90n, 93n, 97n, 103n, 105n, 135n, 136n, 138n, 170n, 176n, 182n
Li Fu 里鳧, 111, 111n
Li I-ch'i 酈食其, 54n
Li Lou 離婁, 82, 82n, 85
Li Shan 李善, 7n, 24n, 25n, 27n, 74n, 83n
Li Shao-chün 李少君, 60, 60n
Li Ssu 李斯, 64, 64n
Liang, state of, 88
Lieh-hsien chuan, 30n, 58n, 59n, 60n
Lieh-tzu, 31n, 77n, 93n, 143n
Lin Hsiang-ju 藺相如, 83, 83n, 112n
Liu Ken 劉根, 60, 60n
Liu Ling 劉伶, 8
Liu Shao 劉邵, 126, 126n
Liu-ching (music of Chuan Hsü), 84
Liu-hsia Hui 柳下惠, 41, 41n
Lo, river, 163, 163n, 191
Lo (writing), 169, 181, 184
Lo-shu, 169n, *see* Lo (writing)
long life, 10, 27–28, 51n, 56n, 61, 65, 66, 90, 145, 145n, 157, 161, 170n, 173n; elixir, 58n; things that eliminate, 147
long life and early death, 149, 151, 159, 172, 186
long life and vigor, 145, 147, 159
love and hate, 24, 45, 62, 73, 75, 80–81, 135; of ease and hard work, 32, 139; of glory and disgrace, 32
loyalty, 101, 111, 123, 123n, 124
loyalty and sincerity, 103, 122
Lu, state of, 73n, 76, 77, 86, 152
lute, 8–9, 15, 79, 83, 91, 92n, 95–96, 98, 100n, 105n, 162, 162n; five-stringed, 30n; nature of music produced by, 92–94; of Po Ya, 76; played by Tou Kung, 51, 51n
Lü An 呂安, 8–9, 9n, 126, 131n, 132n, 133n. *See also* Master Lü

208

Index

Lü Sun 呂巽, 8
Lü-shih ch'un-ch'iu, 77n, 151n, 165n, 168n, 170n, 173n

Ma sacrifice, 185, 185n
magic fungus, 29, 29n, 57n
mare's tail, 53
Marquis Huan, 27, 27n
Marquis Wen of Wei, 64, 64n
masses, the, 6, 28, 42, 67, 90, 106, 123, 149–50, 155, 157, 164; of rebellious Yin, 121
Master Chüan 涓子, 58, 58n
Master Lü (Lü An), 127–28
Master of the Left, 127, 128n, 129
mayfly, 60, 60n
meat and grains, 34, 53–54
meat and wine, 6, 33, 54n
melody, 73, 93
Mencius, 49n, 111n, 135, 135n, 171, 187
Mencius, 40n, 70n, 152n, 171n, 177n
metal and stone (musical instruments), 72, 72n, 85, 102
mica, 59
Middle Drugs, 26, 26n, 52n
Middle Kingdom (China), 63
mimosa, 25, 25n
Min Tzu-ch'ien 閔子騫, 66, 66n
mind, 11–12, 21, 24, 28, 30–31, 34, 38, 40, 40n, 42–43, 46, 48–50, 50n, 63, 68, 71, 73, 77, 80, 86–88, 98–99, 102, 104, 106, 108, 111–12, 115, 117–18, 136, 139, 152, 155, 167, 179n
ming-chiao 名教, 108n, *see* moral teachings
Mo-mu 嫫母, 34, 34n, 45
Mo-tzu, 170, 170n, 181–82
Mo-tzu, 43n, 165n, 170n
modesty and yielding, 140
moral teachings, 108, 122, 123
morning mushroom, 59, 168n
mountain thistle, 58, 58n
Mt. T'ai, 152, 197

Mu Hsien 繆賢, 112, 112n
music, 71–106; as a means to nourishing life, 14; as that which releases emotion, 71, 81; classical, 64, 64n, 184; described as being either good or bad, 73, 76; double meaning "joy", 65, 65n; effects produced by different musical instruments, 92–94; effects produced by songs of different states, 92–94; harmony as the substance of, 96; of Cheng, 100, 105; of Cheng and Wei, 64n, 100, 100n, 184; original substance of, 136, 136n; of the former kings, 84; of the lute and zither, 92–94; that has no sound, 102, 103n; the Nine Shao, 64n; uses intended by the ancients, 100–106
music and beauty, 26, 36, 46, 66
music master Chüan 師涓, 78, 78n, 79
music master Hsiang 師襄, 78–79
music master K'uang 師曠, 40n, 78n, 83n, 85, 88, 88n, 89n, 90
musical stones, 49, 77, 77n, 84, 85n, 100, 100n
musical sounds, 84

name and reality, 73, 76, 78, 115
natural, 6, 27, 88, 135, 140, 143, 181; meat and grains are, 34; to weigh one's feelings is, 32; wealth and rank as, 32
natural order, the, 21, 36, 37, 61, 62n, 140
naturally-so, 150, 186, 190
nature, 22, 36, 61, 65, 88, 108, 118, 167, 182, 194, 196; certain emotions arise from, 32; principles of, 34
nature (human), 7, 12, 25–26, 26n, 31n, 33, 36, 45, 48, 50–51, 58, 60n, 68n, 140–41, 141n, 142n, 147, 172, 179; actions based on *versus* actions

Index

based on intelligence, 45; harmed by rich flavors, 29; harmed by strong emotions, 24; of Ko-lu, 87; of the average man, 111, 111n; people good or bad by, 110, 111n; released by wine, 81

nature (human) and breath, 34, 46

nature (human) and fate, 11, 23, 35, 62, 150–52, 159, 172n, 185–86, 192; principles of, 26

no-death, 10, 22, 22n

non-being, 4–5

nourishing life, 15, 33, 33n, 35n, 144, 150, 150n, 161, 167, 174; correct measures for, 148, 160; five difficulties in, 65–66; great principle of, 66; Hsi K'ang's views on, 10ff.; music as a means to, 71; techniques in popular Taoism, 11; the business of, 27, 51

Nü Wa, 79n

one-sided, 14, 68; natural endowments as, 127; opinions, 14, 164; songs that are emotionally, 96; views, 170

open, 110

openness, 111, 111n

Ou-yang Chien 歐陽堅, 22

Pao-p'u-tzu, 57n, 58n

peony, 34, 34n, 105, 105n, 106n

people of the world, 11–12, 22n, 23–24, 26, 38, 47, 54

pepperwort, 53, 53n

Perfect Courage, 133

perfect form, 84

Perfect Harmony, 85, 93, 97

Perfect Joy, 63, 65

Perfect Man, 36n, 40n, 41, 105, 108, 127, 139

Perfect Music, 84–85

Perfect Reason, 21, 46, 144, 188

Perfect Taste, 63

Perfect Virtue, 139

Perfect Wisdom, 133

Perfect Words, 66, 66n

physiognomy, 152n, 162, 162n, 174

Pien Ho 卞和, 82; jade of, 82n, 83n, 112n

pipes and strings (musical instruments), 72, 85, 104, 136

pitch pipes, 83, 85, 87–89, 89n, 90

plot-planting, 24, 24n, 25n, 36

Po Ch'ang-ch'ien 伯常騫, 90, 90n

Po Chi 薄姬, 185, 186n

Po Ch'i 白起, 158n, 187, 187n

Po Ch'i 伯奇, 83, 83n

Po I 伯夷, 82n

Po Ti 勃鞮, 111, 112n

Po Ya 伯牙, 76, 77n

Po-wu chih, 25n, 55n, 58n, 60n, 61n

popular Taoism, 10, 12n

Primal Vapors, 127–28, 131

Prince Ch'iao (Wang-tzu Ch'iao 王子喬), 30, 30n

principles, 5, 11, 21, 23, 27, 29, 35, 43–44, 77, 87–88, 90–91, 115, 118, 128, 153, 155, 156n, 158, 192, 194, 198; controlling near and far, 48; for avoiding a thief, 150; for avoiding misfortune, 150; for completing fate, 171, 186, 189, 189n; for producing life, 39, 39n; human, 176; natural, 80; of benevolence and righteousness, 139; of C and D, 195; of delight and anger, 81; of events, 178, 183, 188; of geomancy, 145; of good and bad fortune, 21, 46; of grief and joy, 84; of Heaven and Earth, 27; of human nature, 196; of humanity, 67; of images and numbers, 175; of joy, 99; of life, 12, 24; of man, 14, 164; of music, 96; of mutual need, 164; of nature, 34, 44; of nature and fate, 26; of nourishing life, 21; of one's nature, 54; of searching

Index

for the cause, 198; of unselfishness and self-interest 119, 119n; of Yin and Yang, 157; one that is easily understood, 131; perfect, 167; that is necessarily so, 141; that one must be open, 110; the main, 85; the perfectly good, 191
profit and glory, 49, 140
profit and harm, 50
profound studies, 3–4
profound truth, 61
punishments and rewards, 123, 146, 146n, 158, 176, 176n
pure talk, 3
purple fungus, 13, 57, 57n
P'ei Hui 裴徽, 5
P'ei Sung-chih 裴松之, 7n, 8n, 72n, 135n
P'eng Tsu 彭祖, 60, 60n, 149, 149n, 152, 157, 159, 171–72, 196n
p'i-p'a, 92, 92n, 93, 93n
p'ien 偏, 14, see one-sided
P'ien Ch'üeh 扁鵲, 27, 27n

quartz, 58n

reason, 28, 44, 46, 91, 122, 125, 127, 139. See also common reason and Perfect Reason
red sulphur, 13, 57, 57n
residence, 4, 14, 49, 144–46, 150–52, 159, 162, 172, 172n, 173, 175, 175n, 176n, 178, 187, 190, 192; as built by the ancients, 176; contrasted with natural facial features in bringing good luck, 193–94; divination of old and new, 153; intentional building of, 191–92; of the three high ministers, 149, 157n, 164; or its inhabitants as the cause of good and bad fortune, 161
residence and grave, 165, 177, 177n
restlessness and tranquillity (in music), 92–95
rhythm (in music), 79, 91, 104
rich flavors, 26, 29, 31, 36, 46, 66
right and wrong, 107–108, 110–111, 115, 117–18, 127, 179n
rites, the, 34, 47, 74, 74n, 76, 78, 78n, 103, 103n, 142, 178, 182
rites and music, 104n, 156, 169, 182n
ritual and law, 6, 139–40
Robber Chih, 36n, 62n, 131, 158n

sage(s), 5, 32–33, 35–36, 39, 41n, 47–50, 84–85, 91, 122, 124–25, 125n, 167n, 177, 185, 199; as one who immediately understands, 87–88
San-kuo chih, 7n, 8, 72n, 120n, 135n
self-attained, 30, 41, 44, 99, 99n, 139
self-interest, 29, 109, 113, 115, 117–18, 147, 160
Seven Worthies of the Bamboo Grove, 8, 21
Shan Pao 單豹, 68, 68n, 160, 160n, 161, 173, 173n, 189
Shan T'ao 山濤, 7–9
Shao (music), 72, 72n, 76, 78–79, 84, 184, 184n
shen 神, see spirit, also the spirits
shen 身, see body
Shen Hou 申候, 116, 116n
Shen Nung, 26, 26n, 33, 33n, 51–53, 59n, 79n
Shen Nung pen-ts'ao ching, 25n, 26n, 62n, 57n, 137n, 148n
Shen-hsien chuan, 60n, 61n
sheng-yin 聲音, see music, also sounds and tones
Shih, 33n, see Book of Poetry
Shih chi, 23n, 28n, 30n, 35n, 37n, 54n, 60n, 64n, 69n, 78n, 82n, 83n, 97n, 109n, 112n, 114n, 116n, 120n, 125n, 129n, 130n, 152n, 158n
Shih-shuo hsin-yü, 4n, 5, 6n, 21n, 22n, 59n, 145

211

Index

shou 壽, 145n, *see* long life
Shou-yang, Mt., 82, 82n
Shu, 34n, 85n, 100n, 120n, 123n, 138n, 163n, 165n, 171n
Shu Ch'i 叔齊, 82n
Shun, 35, 35n, 49n, 72, 72n, 76, 79n, 84, 100n, 171n, 183, 184n
silkworms, 43, 51, 51n, 157, 171; superstitions associated with, 148, 148n
silky spice-bush, 28, 28n
sincerity and obedience, 66, 66n, 158, 158n, 171–72, 172n, 186, 188–89, 189n, 190
six bowels, 13, 56
six directions, 101
Six Classics, 140, 142–43, 143n
Six Disciplines, 138, 140
six realms, 167n
six Yang pitches, 89, 89n
six Yin pitches, 89, 89n
skilled, listener, 76–77, 79–80; specialists (in divination), 151, 153, 161
smartweed, 34
solitary wasp, 57, 58n
Son of Heaven, 40, 117, 123, 162n, 174n
song(s), 72, 74–75, 77–78, 95–97, 104; of Ch'i and Ch'u, 92, 94, 98–99
sounds, 76–77, 77n, 79–81, 91, 96, 196; in harmony and sequence, 74–75, 81, 103; of dying, 83n, 88; of Perfect Harmony, 85; lewd and perverse, 26; produced by lute and zither, 94
sounds and tones, 73, 92, 104
sow-thistle, 34
spirit, 11–12, 45, 50–51, 54, 66, 68, 68n, 107, 115, 117; related to form, 24
spirit and breath, 29, 43, 67, 102
spirits, the, 53, 53n, 148, 148n, 149, 151, 165, 177, 179n, 182; of Heaven and Earth, 5, 34, 53, 155; of the ancestors, 169; of the dead, 155; private *versus* public, 170, 181–82; question of their existence, 170, 170n, 180–82
ssu 私, 107, *see* self-interest
Ssu-ma Hsiang-ju 司馬相如, 28n, 37, 37n, 65n
Ssu-ma I 司馬懿, 7, 121
Ssu-ma's, 6n, 8–9
stalactite, 59, 59n
stone mushrooms, 13, 57, 57n
study, 10, 22–23, 138, 140, 140n, 143, 143n
Sui shu, 22n, 144, 154n
summer cicada, 168, 168n, 179, 179n
Sung, state of, 88; the man from, 177, 177n
Superior Drugs, 26, 26n, 52, 52n, 54, 59
superstition(s), 146, 148, 148n, 149, 154
sweet and bitter, 76, 81, 84, 141
sweet flag (calamus), 59, 59n, 137, 137n, 143, 143n

Ta-chang (music of Yao), 84
T'ai-lao sacrifice, 64, 64n
T'ang, 24, 24n, 35, 35n, 36n, 49n, 108, 108n, 166, 178, 179n; praying in the mulberry grove, 165, 165n, 183
T'ang and Yü, ages of, 157, 157n, 173, 187
ta-ya 大雅, 73n, 76n, *see* Elegant
talented and stupid, 45
talents and nature, 126–27
tangerine, 58, 58n, 136
Tao, the, 60n, 93n, 101n, *see* the Way
tao-yang 導養, 23n, *see* guiding and nourishing
tempo, 77, 79, 93
ten thousand things, 31, 41, 44, 73, 75, 95, 143
thorny limebush, 58, 58n

Index

Three August Ones, 79, 79n
Three Fields of Cinnabar, 56n
Three Worms, 56n
Ti barbarians, 55, 69, 69n
ti whistle, 92, 92n, 93, 93n
T'ien Yen-nien 田延年, 129, 130n, 133
t'ien-li 天理, 21, 62n, see natural order
Ti Ya 狄牙, 84, 84n
Ti-k'u, 79n
Ti-wu Lun 第五倫, 117, 117n, 118
titles and responsibilities, 139
titles and rewards, 137
tone, 76, 77, 79
Tou Kung 竇公, 51, 51n
tranquillity, 28, 37n, 45, 63, 160
ts'ai-hsing 才性, 126n, see talents and nature
Ts'ao Chih 曹植, 92n
Ts'ao Lin 曹林, 7n
Ts'ao P'i 曹丕, 60n
Ts'ao Ts'ao 曹操, 7, 7n, 8
Tseng-tzu, 23, 23n, 66, 66n, 158
ts'o 措, 107, see concern
Tso chuan, 34n, 40n, 53n, 73n, 83n, 85n, 86n, 111n, 112n, 116n, 127n, 128n, 152n, 176n
Tung Chung-shu 董仲舒, 142n, 146n, 195n
Tung Wu-hsin 董無心, 170, 170n, 181-82
twelve pitches, 89n, 90n
twelve tones, 89n
Tzu-chia 子家, 127, 128n, 129
Tzu-kung, 169, 169n, 181n
tzu-jan 自然, see nature, also natural, and naturally-so
Tzu-lu, 169, 177, 177n, 181, 181n
tzu-te 自得, see self-attained
Tzu-wen 子文, 41, 41n
Tzu-yang 子陽 (Kung-sun Shu 公孫述), 174, 174n, 193
Tzu-yeh 子野, 78, see music master K'uang

ultimate order of things, 21, 62, 62n
unseen, the, 27-28, 61
unselfishness and self-interest, 109, 114, 119

Vast Stream, 101, 101n
virtue, 32-33, 33n, 40n, 43, 53, 65-66, 70n, 73-74, 76, 79, 91, 103n, 122-23, 126, 157n, 182; and morality, 43, and sincerity, 53; and talent, 164; injured by fame and position, 29; of the Gentleman, 112; the man of, 117
Void Name, 96
vulgar, 40, 44, 140; fame, 115; office-seekers, 40n; pedants, 80; people, 63; world, 47n

Wang Chung-tu 王仲都, 60, 60n
Wang Ch'ung 王充, 111n, 154n, 156n, 170n, 176n
Wang Fu 王符, 156n
Wang Jung 王戎, 8
Wang Ling 王陵, 114, 114n, 130, 130n, 134
Wang Mang, see Chü-chün
Wang Pi 王弼, 4-5, 72n
Wang Tao 王導, 22
water lily, 52n
Way, the, 5, 38, 41, 45n, 65, 101, 106-109, 109n, 115, 127, 155-56, 168n; of Heaven, 14, 137, 164, 169, 169n
wealth and rank, 31-32, 32n, 33, 39-42, 42n, 43-44; dangers associated with, 51; to be avoided, 12-14
Wei, kingdom of, 3, 7
Wei, state of, 186n
Wei-lü 尾閭, 28, 28n
Wen Ch'in 文欽, 8, 121
Wen hsüan, 7n, 9n, 22, 24n, 25n, 27n, 74n, 83n, 149n
wine, 11, 13, 62, 64n, 66, 84, 95-96, 97n, 98, 104, 147n; disastrous effects of, 55-56; pepper and

213

Index

chrysanthemum, 13, 55; poisoned, 46, 114, 114n; rich, 23; spring, 33, 54, 54n; sweet, 33; twice-fermented, 53; uninhibiting effects of, 81; unstrained, 15n, 26
wine and meat, 39
wine and women, 47, 61, 63
wisdom and courage, 4, 126–34
Wo Ch'üan 偓佺, 58, 58n
worms, 13, 56, 56n
worthy and fool, 75
wu 無, 4, 4n, 5
Wu, state of, 73n, 88
Wu (music), 35n, 79, 184, 184n
Wu Keng 武庚, 120, 122
Wu Kuang 務光, 58, 59n
wu-hsing 五行, 89n, *see* Five Elements
wu-ku 五穀, 26n, *see* five grains
wu-sheng 五聲, 89n, *see* five tones

Ya Fu 亞夫, 152, 152n, 157, 185–86
Yang Hsiung 楊雄, 61, 61n, 83n, 111n
Yang-she 羊舌, 86, 90

yang-sheng 養生, 10n, *see* nourishing life
yao 夭, 145n, *see* early death
Yao, 35, 35n, 43n, 48, 48n, 59n, 60, 61n, 79n, 84; and Shun, 157n, 170n
Yellow Emperor, 34, 84
yellow essence, 13, 57, 57n
Yellow Pill, 148, 148n, 159, 166
Yellow River (chart), 169, 181, 184
Yen, state of, 69n, 112n
Yen Hui (Yen Yüan), 33, 33n, 55, 55n, 77, 77n, 158
Yen-tzu ch'un-ch'iu, 90n
Yin and Yang, 4n, 65, 67n, 134, 146, 146n, 164, 184, 184n, 195; good and bad fortune of, 14; principles of, 157; related to musical sounds, 89, 89n
Ying Pu 英布, 152, 152n, 157, 185–86, 193
yu 有, 4, 4n, 5
Yü, 35, 35n, 36n, 49n, 84, 179n, 183
Yüeh, region of, 63, 88, 179n

zither, 91–93, 97n

Library of Congress Cataloging in Publication Data
Chi, K'ang, 223–262.
Philosophy and argumentation in third-century China.
(Princeton Library of Asian translations)
"Translate all nine of Hsi K'ang's essays, plus the four essays of his opponents in various debates"—Pref.
Bibliography: p.
Includes index.
1. Philosophy, Chinese—Addresses, essays, lectures.
I. Henricks, Robert G., 1943–   II. Title. III. Series.
B128.C3852E5 1983   181'.11   82-61367
ISBN 0-691-05378-2

GPSR Authorized Representative: Easy Access System Europe - Mustamäe tee 50, 10621 Tallinn, Estonia, gpsr.requests@easproject.com

www.ingramcontent.com/pod-product-compliance
Lightning Source LLC
Chambersburg PA
CBHW060511300426
44112CB00017B/2628